AIR GUNNER

AIR GUNNER

Mike Henry, DFC

A Goodall paperback
from
Crécy Publishing Limited

Copyright © Mike Henry, 1997

Published as a new edition by Goodall, 1997

First published by G T Foulis & Co Ltd, 1964

ISBN 0 907579 42 6

A Goodall paperback

published by

Crécy Publishing Limited
Southside, Manchester Airport,
Wilmslow, Cheshire. SK9 4LL

Contents

LIST OF ILLUSTRATIONS

INTRODUCTION

IT is an undisputed fact that the piece of advice most freely imparted to the newly enlisted recruit is 'never volunteer for anything.' To the keen and patriotic alike, such an utterance might at first reek of anarchy but servicemen are not in uniform for long before they agree that to stand firm when called upon to step forward is the wisest policy.

However, during war-time, circumstances exist when one was prompted to take one pace forward and throw one's lot in with fate. Some of the reasons for so doing might be domestic, or the desire to make a name for oneself; maybe a spot of recklessness tempered with ignorance of the situation involved. It could have even been brought about by dissatisfaction with one's environment - perhaps a vitriolic sergeant major or the camp's geographic location.

Nevertheless, I am sure that another reason for *not* sticking one's neck out can be set down to the wiles of NCOs who, by their cunning, obtain (and doubtless still do) volunteers for onerous chores. They have, over the years, used such subterfuge as: 'Anybody interested in gardening?' whereupon the keen, one-pace-forward type finds himself faced with a mountain of potatoes to be peeled. Or 'Who is interested in cricket?' Whoever steps forward in reply to this one invariably found himself a self-elected batman.

Then there are the obvious traps for the unwary: 'Go get the keys to the compass base...', 'Run along to the stores and get the chocks for the Link Trainer.' The Royal Navy and Army must have many of their own particular brand of 'leg pulls'. The cautious, therefore, regard even the most genuine call for a volunteer with profound suspicion.

It is here that I must confess to sticking my neck out after serving a year with the Royal Air Force. I volunteered to fly as an air gunner after already established myself as a wireless operator with both feet on the ground - a 'penguin'. As the first chapter shows, there was a reason for my impetuosity - however scant it may appear to be. My colleagues threw the verbal book at me: 'You must be mad...'. 'You won't last five minutes...'. 'You'll soon be wearing a wooden overcoat...'. 'Air gunners are getting the "chop" faster than that...!'. I spurned their taunts; my decision was irrevocable.

As it happened, their sombre forecasts of early doom fell into, and were whisked away by the slipstream of many flights. I pressed on, as the saying went, to add another eight years to my service career. I learnt the meaning of comradeship, excitement, fear, team spirit, tragedy and humour - in and out of adversity.

With the invaluable aid of my flying log book, I have set down the experiences - many of them odd, some lucky - which my act of volunteering crammed into my life. Combined, they form a story which could not have been told were it not for the skill of the pilots with whom I had the pleasure to fly. It is to them, therefore, that I dedicate this book, and their names are recorded in Appendix 'A'. To assist identification, I have added date, rank (at the time), type of aircraft and unit - I did not log their initials.

Many of them died. The majority I have lost touch with. Several have reached Air Rank. Marshal of the Royal Air Force Lord Elworthy, KG, GCB, CBE, DSO, MVO, DFC, AFC, MA; Air Chief Marshal Sir William L. M. MacDonald, GCB, CBE, DFC; Air Vice-Marshal I J Spencer, CB, DFC; Air Vice-Marshal S. W. B. Menaul, CB, CBE, DFC, AFC, to name but four. (Name-dropping is not my intention, merely to highlight the names of some wonderful people.) It should be added that the navigators and gunners - with whom I shared many pleasurable and 'dicey' moments are (even if not mentioned) not forgotten. They and the ground crews, and others who were all part of the great team, all contributed to a memorable period of my life. God bless them all!

ACKNOWLEDGEMENTS

I am indebted to *Flight International*, the *Central Press Agency*, and the Imperial War Museum for some of the illustrations. To the late Anthony Richardson who kindly consented to my reprinting from *Because of These*, his verse of dedication to Wing Commander 'Bunny' Harte, DFC. Also to Messrs B Cooke, J A G Croxson, S Orland, H P Powell, C Shevlin, R Urquhart and A H Wheeler, for assisting my memory. To my publishers for accepting my story and to my new publisher, Crécy, who have produced it in its present format and allowed me the opportunity of correcting and updating the original manuscript.

CHAPTER 1

March 1939/40

Among the balloons; Radio – theory and practice; First flight.

The corporal recruiting clerk looked me straight in the eye and said, 'What do *you* want to be in the Royal Air Force?'

'A flight mechanic,' was my firm reply.

'Any previous experience with aero-engines?'

'I'm afraid not, corporal.'

'Any experience with other types of internal-combustion engines?'

After my repeated negative, his next remark – and the look on his face – confirmed that he had been through all this before and was getting a bit fed up with it.

'I'm sorry', he said, nearly all of you chaps want to be flight mechanics, and as the RAF is not yet equipped with a million aircraft, only those with experience can be accepted.' At this stage he referred to my newly-started dossier.

'I see,' he continued, 'that you have applied to join this service on transfer from the Royal Corps of Signals, TA'.

'That's right, corporal,' I answered, wondering what sort of challenge he was about to throw back at me.

'Well, with that sort of experience behind you, why not train to be a wireless operator? It's a Group 2 trade.'

Although I hadn't a clue then what Group 2 meant, I thought his suggestion a reasonable one.

'All right corporal, I'll settle for that.'

He sighed, nodded tiredly and jotted something down on my application form. I, too, felt relieved to know that, at least, I was acceptable fodder for HM Forces. What I hadn't realised, however, was that Dick Nash (he and I had enlisted together for moral support) had also asked to become a flight mechanic. For similar reasons he was told to run away and consult a wall chart showing trade classifications, rates of pay, etc. Having in mind the interviewer's previous questions, he had obviously applied a little cunning since he opted to mess about with bombs, guns, ammunition, and the like, to train to be an armourer. Dick wasn't aware that I had chosen a different path to doubtful fame.

On 13 March 1939, Dick and I reported to Adastral House in

Kingsway to join others of the same entry. Embarrassingly, we were marched through office-bound pedestrians to Holborn underground station where we entrained for West Drayton. This small out-post of the Royal Air Force, on the western fringes of London, was a reception depot where, in exchange for a solemn oath of allegiance and about a hundred signatures, one received a number (for what it was worth mine was 637244).

Before signing away six years of our lives, we were given the opportunity to reconsider our dash to the colours. However, having gone that far, my mind was made up (despite the barbarous attack, by the camp hairdresser, on the hair covering it). In fact none of our entry wished to opt out although one chap nearly got himself thrown out.

It happened while we sat in a bare and inhospitable room waiting to sign on the dotted. A burly, straight-backed corporal entered by the main door and strode smartly across the room. Without a flicker of an eyelid one of our number, a tousled redhead, bawled out 'Shut that bloody door, mate.' Had the corporal been fitted with disc brakes all round he couldn't have become static so swiftly. Pivoting slowly, he eyed us all and, with a look on his face a Nazi Stormtrooper would covet, he said icily, 'Who said that?'

'I did, sport,' replied 'ginger', in an unmistakable Australian accent.

'Oh!…You did…did you,' said the corporal acidly. 'Well let me inform you that, had you been attested, your feet wouldn't have touched the ground between here and the guardroom. If you want a court martial in the infancy of your service career, carry on the way you are behaving.' With that he wheeled about and went his way.

There was a deathly 'ush all round; some of us stared blankly at the door through which he had disappeared, others gaped at 'ginger', whose eyes had that dreamy couldn't-care-less look. He was mumbling to himself in a detached sort of way, possibly dreaming up some heinous aboriginal curse, Pommie' corporals for the infliction of. I often wondered how far he progressed in the RAF.

Forty-eight hours later, Dick and I parted ways for our initial training. He was posted to a station in Lincolnshire, while I went to Cardington. I have neither seen nor heard from him to this day. So much for our intended companionship.

* * *

RAF Cardington, a couple of miles from Bedford, proved a fascinating place to us in those days. As well as being an ITW (Initial Training Wing) it was the home of a Balloon Training Unit (BTU). In the latter case it was appropriate since Cardington had been, from the early 'twenties to the mid-'thirties, the home of many famous British rigid airships. Among them was the R.100 which was built and later dismantled there. Its ill-fated successor, the R.101, left Cardington in October 1930 for its maiden voyage but a few hours later it crashed with great loss of life at Beauvais in France.

Cardington's two enormous airship sheds (932 feet long, 177 feet high and 273 feet wide) and the 208-foot mooring mast dominated the surrounding flat Bedfordshire countryside. Where a few years earlier, 800 feet of glistening fabric envelope would have silently emerged from the gaping mouth of its shed, we now saw only diminutive barrage balloons, each riding high above its parent winch truck, being driven out by their crews. How could we have guessed the important part they were soon to play.

The BTU had a mysterious casualty one day. We saw it all from the parade ground. It was a fine day marred only by the raucous commands of our squad sergeant. The blue sky was broken by a little scattered cumulus, and reaching up to it all was the usual gaggle of balloons tethered to their restraining winches. Suddenly, one of them fell to earth a flaming, rent fragment of fabric, its descent being urged by a snarling cable, just like an obstinate puppy at the end of a tugged leash.

We read in the Press the following morning that '...a freak flash of lightning from a solitary cloud over Cardington, near Bedford, set fire to and destroyed a barrage balloon...'

As for the BTU airmen, we didn't go much on them nor did we take kindly to the banalities they constantly threw our way. Only natural for recruits to be sensitive to gibes such as '...you want to get a number not the population of China.' Or 'When we joined they didn't give us numbers, we all knew each other.' Nevertheless, we at least felt a little superior in that our uniforms were blue and not the crumpled, grease-covered garb which they got away with.

Between a multitude of chores, parades and lectures, we did find time to wander down to the airfield. The massive sheds had become an irresistible attraction. Outside the north shed stood a derelict Fairey Hendon night bomber. The Hendon was a low-wing monoplane whose two Rolls-Royce Kestrel engines were faired into the very thick leading edge. It had a spatted and strutted fixed undercarriage, and its sixty-foot fuselage had a cat-walk connecting the front gunner's position with the gun position aft of the tailplane. This machine had been stripped of the essentials to flight but its basic structure was real enough. Eagerly we scrambled over its fabric like starry-eyed schoolboys invited onto the footplate of a 4-6-4 locomotive.

I had never been so close to an aircraft before and I felt an instant stab of pride in my uniform – albeit my foreseeable future held merely a job with two feet planted firmly on the ground.

I clearly remember my first look inside one of the airship sheds. Its echoing vastness made me feel as insignificant as a tick on an elephant's back. The girdered vaulting towered above me and it was very difficult to discern objects at the far end of the shed, so enormous were its dimensions (the mechanically operated doors took about forty minutes to open or close). I stood there trying to develop a mental picture of bygone days when mechanics and ground crews would swarm like ants beneath the massive girth of the hydrogen-filled giant above them. But even my wild imagination couldn't grasp such a scene in true perspective.

Tucked away, almost lost, in one corner of the shed were some old biplanes. Like the Hendon outside, they had seen better days and were not likely to fly again. Walking over as nonchalantly as I knew how, I climbed up and lowered myself into the padded cockpit of one of them – I believe it was a Westland Wapiti. Self-consciously I glanced around to see whether my action had been spotted but all seemed quiet. Looking round the machine, my young imagination took command with Walter Mitty thoroughness. Having seen many RAF Air Displays at Hendon and the screen classics *Dawn Patrol* and *Hell's Angels*, there was plenty of material stored for my flights of fancy. I peeped over the side and saw not the cold concrete but green fields far below; I could hear, above the throbbing of the radial engine, the wind singing through the flying and landing wires; even the blended smells of hot oil, petrol and dope were present... My reverie was shattered by an echoing shout 'Come on, out of there. It isn't a toy. You shouldn't be in here anyway.'

'Sorry,' I said, guiltily climbing down, 'didn't touch anything...only looking.'

When I later visited this shed (or was it the other one?) I spent some time looking at various airship components: engines, cabins, propellers and enormous hoop-like structures from dismantled airships – silent testimony to a bygone age.

My first 48-hour leave in the service was drawing near. I looked forward to the bus journey home when I could relate all. Friday afternoon arrived; we packed our small kit; the door opened and our sergeant shouted 'Before proceeding on leave you will report to sick quarters for an FFI,' (free-from-infection). Out of the 150-odd men in our flight, one had contracted scarlet fever. That unfortunate soul happened to be in our hut and those of us who shared the same accommodation spent ten days in isolation – the others went on leave. I've never heard language quite like it.

Apart from having the rough edges knocked off and learning that '…If yer leaves water in yer water-bottles it gets pregnant…' I left Cardington able to receive the morse code at seven words per minute and transmit at a considerably higher speed. I was also the fittest I had ever been because, together with 150 airmen, I took part in an ambitious physical-training display in front of the general public on the last pre-war Empire Air Day.

For five weeks, up to five hours a day, we practised to verbal or whistled commands and to the beat of drums. When it rained we repaired to one of the sheds where, even with our whole Flight inside, there would doubtless be room for the 56,000 population of Bedford.

* * *

The special troop-train, which zigzagged its dreary way along the 110 miles from Bedford to Calne in Wiltshire, took the best part of a day. The journey wasn't enhanced gastronomically, for our sole sustenance comprised dry corned-beef sandwiches and vintage railway tea. The last lap was completed in a draughty three-ton truck.

Yatesbury, and its adjacent airfield (of First World War origin, I believe), is situated on the main London/Bath/Bristol road, about six miles east of the sausage-and-pie town of Calne. The camp itself covers many acres and stretches for about a mile along the north side of the road; it is a lake of wooden huts which sprawl at the foot of a range of almost barren hills.

When I arrived there, so many men were being trained at the camp that it was divided into several wings, each with its own CO and administrative unit. There were, in fact, about 3,000 people on this plot of Wiltshire chalk, a great number of them directly or indirectly engaged in turning out wireless operators for the RAF.

One of my new-found friends, Trent Galbraith, hailed from Vancouver. In fact he had come over at his own expense to join the RAF, as his brother had written to say how much he was enjoying the life. Trent and I had other views when it came to some of the types we encountered – fortunately in the minority. For example. we tried without avail to fathom the motives of those who filched the plugs from all the wash basins. We had constantly to resort to do-it-yourself substitutes of wood, or balls of soggy lavatory paper. I was disgusted to find, one day, that someone had used the trough of one of the showers as a lavatory. On another occasion we had forcibly to scrub one member of our hut, using a nice stiff floor brush for the purpose, because he failed to keep himself clean – this in spite of the adequate facilities and our warnings which he chose to ignore. Nevertheless, there was a wealth of good material among the bulk of the chaps.

Most of the instructors at Yatesbury were civilians (it was, of course, still peace-time); many were ex-Royal Navy, Merchant Navy or GPO telegraphists and radio engineers. They and their service counterparts taught us Ohm's Law, the morse code, thermionic emission, not to natter in class, semaphore, bandpass tuning, mutual induction, mutual respect and lots of other relevant things. Extra-mural activities included 'gravel-crushing', ceremonial functions to the accompaniment of bagpipes and the usual Wednesday afternoon sports. When *der Führer* really got into his stride and started to throw his weight about in Europe, trench-digging in that tough Wiltshire chalk was added to the curriculum.

Social activities were geographically limited. We had, of course, the ubiquitous NAAFI or the 'Wagon and Horses' two miles away at Beckhampton. We often walked over the hills, weather permitting, from the top of which one could, if so inclined, watch the form of some of Fred Darling's race horses. We also had occasional leave of absence when, if of long enough duration, many of us would hitch-hike up to London. In those days my net weekly wage of about 10s. 6d. would not buy a ticket, even at reduced rates, to London *and* keep me in beer and baccy.

Being on a main road we found little difficulty in getting a lift but it became far easier once war had been declared. Some lifts were better than others. I was once picked up outside the main gates and dropped at Hammersmith Bridge, a hundred yards or so

from my home. On another occasion I got a lift in the back of a
manure truck for about two miles, walked six miles, then in the
cabin of a furniture van for a few more miles, walk two miles, a
comfortable back seat of a limousine for twenty-five miles, to
finish the journey by train when the fare fitted my pocket. This took
time over a journey of ninety-odd miles. Nonetheless, we were
always most grateful to the driver for any type of lift.

While on the subject of leave and the means of getting from A
to B. I was told a story (said to be true) of a group of Scots
stationed at Yatesbury a couple of months after I had left. They, like
everybody else on the camp, were told that travel on leave was
limited to nearby towns and London, in view of the prevailing
severe winter weather. It was thought, justifiably, that those living
in the far north or in Ireland might not get home, let alone return to
camp on time. Armed with travel warrants to London, therefore,
these braw lads from the north formulated a plan which worked as
follows. They foregathered at Euston station, formed up in two
ranks and marched up to the barrier with an acting, unpaid corporal
at their head. A smarter body of men was never before seen on a
London station – or since. The party halted with precision; the
corporal explained to the ticket collector that the sergeant in charge
had the collective travel warrant and would be coming along
shortly and that his squad was being posted to Ailsa Crag (an
uninhabited bird sanctuary off the Ayrshire coast). They were let
through to board the train. When they were well on their way the
ticket inspector arrived on the scene. He was told that 'The sergeant
has the travel warrant and he is *somewhere* on the train, probably
snogging with a WAAF in a first-class compartment, you know
what sergeants are...' They exited the station at the end of their
journey using a similar story (obviously the Ailsa Crag bluff was
for ignorant Sassenachs only). They returned at the end of their
leave by the same methods.

In the unlikely event of a stranger wandering around RAF
Yatesbury in the evening, he might well decide to sign the pledge.
From nearly every billet, at that time, came the penetrating, high-
pitched sound of morse, each hut being equipped with a GEC radio.
Most of us were keen to reach the required speed in morse and
would tune in to Reuters or other stations transmitting in plain
language. These broadcasts came over at speeds varying between
twenty and thirty words per minute. Even though, at that stage, we

weren't competent to take really fast speeds, the only way to improve one's existing speed was to chase a faster one.

Morse is a peculiar subject. Some people were never able to get it, others found it comparatively easy with plenty of practice. Good education or high intelligence did not necessarily guarantee its mastery but those with a musical ear found it easier to learn. It even drove some chaps a little round the bend. They would walk round dah-dit-dah'ing to themselves like so many demented internees. It became an obsession, too, with the keen. I found myself translating mentally into morse the wording on advertising hoardings, tube-train ads., newspaper items or pages of the book I happened to be reading. It was helpful practice but apt to reduce one's circle of friends, especially when heard to utter 'Why dah-dit-dah-dah, dit, dit-dit-dit, old man.'

'The day war broke out...' I was at home on French leave. An acting corporal and myself had hitch-hiked to London on the Friday evening. On Sunday morning, when the PM broadcast the fact that battle was about to commence, I was sitting at home in Barnes, feeling a bit sorry for myself, partly because I shouldn't have been there and also because the female members of my family were engaged in a sobbing match. After the air-raid sirens had been aired, I had a phone call from 'Lofty' who said 'I think we ought to be getting back to camp...' and with that understatement of the year I agreed.

We met on the Great West Road near Chiswick, and started to carve the air with our thumbs. When eventually we did get back, late in the evening, we reported to the guardroom like two prize mutts. We should, of course, have hopped over the fence near our billets a mile back along the road which would have saved not only our boot leather but from being charged as AWOL.

The service police pounced and asked us all sorts of embarrassing questions. Lofty and I had agreed to stick to the same story...

'We went out this morning – early.'

'Then why didn't you take your respirators with you, as ordered?'

'We forgot.'

Whereupon, we were separated and interrogated individually. Not unnaturally I was nervous of the possible consequences, I had never broken the law to this extent before. In fact, there hadn't been a war in my life before. The SP who had dedicated himself to my breakdown pressed his questioning. He left the room for a few moments and returned to say 'Your friend has owned up that you both left camp on Friday, so it's no use you pretending otherwise.'

I fell for it hook, line – the stinker.

'All right, we did go out on Friday.' I refrained from adding 'So what!'

I was then moved back to where Lofty was 'caged' and we were formally charged. I felt such a fool to have let him down. But he appreciated the situation and we walked back to our billet. When we were wheeled in front of the CO the following morning, he listened to the fact that we had no excuse to offer for our misdemeanour and passed sentence: fourteen days' confinement to camp and the stoppage of two days' pay.

There were many others caught out for the same offence that week-end. Although the crime was the same, the punishment varied according to the Wing in which the offender lived. Our CO meted out the stiffest penalty but considering the charge, one cannot really grumble.

Twice a day we donned full packs and tottered the mile to the guardroom where a roll call was made. Between lectures we had fatigues heaped upon us; we had trenches to dig, spuds to peel, floors to scrub and windows to clean. However, one was punished only for contravening the law – or KRs (now QRs) and ACIs (King's Regulations and Air Council Instructions) as we so soon found out.

There were, of course, the inevitable wags whose antics in the classrooms sometimes brightened tedium. I saw one 'innocent' being persuaded to hold the two leads (one in each hand) issuing from a megger – 'Just for a moment, I won't turn the handle fast so you'll only get a slight tingle which is good for you...' The promise meant nothing and the poor lad who held the wires left the floor with a piercing howl of anguish. I felt sorry for him as I, too, loathe electric shocks. A megger is an instrument, not of torture, designed for the specific purpose of testing insulation. When its handle is turned at maximum revs it generates 500 volts – enough said.

On another occasion we were back-tuning transmitters to receivers in one of the classrooms when an SOS signal came from one of the sets. Quickly grabbing a pencil and pad I took down the details: '...*Queen Mary* with 1,000 troops, sinking fast, Lat. 53.12N Long. 35.28W...' There was an impressive silence for a few moments. When the penny had dropped, we rushed to the instructor with our electrifying news. He received it, we thought, with downright callousness.

'Nonsense,' he said. 'In fact, impossible. How could you pick up a message from the Atlantic through a dummy aerial? You ought to know better. Remember, your receivers and transmitters are fitted with dummy aerials to prevent irresponsible messages such as this cluttering the frequencies used by other people.'

We finished our wireless course before air-operating was started from the adjacent airfield. Our experience of air-operating (according to the syllabus) was sitting in the fuselage of an old, wingless, engineless and pilotless aircraft which had been fitted out with the R.1082 receiver and T.1083 transmitter. How anyone could equate this with air-operating experience is difficult to say – obviously the brainstorm of a chairborne signals executive.

One day in November 1939, I rummaged through my kit for a needle and cotton and proudly sewed on my newly-won insignia – a fistful of lightning. I was now a qualified 'sparks', able to receive morse at 22 wpm and pound a key at even greater speeds.

Now was the time to move out in order to put into practice what I'd been taught. I went to the orderly room and asked whether it was known whither I was bound.

'To 6 SFTS,' I was told.

'What the hell is that, and where?'

'It's a flying training school stuck on top of the Cotswold 'ills, near Bourton-on-the-Water, Moreton-in-Marsh and Stow-on-the-Wold. It is called Little Rissington.'

'Really? You could have fooled me. What's it like there?'

'All I know,' said my informant, 'is that the SWO is a perfect so-and-so.'

Station Warrant Officers, like their counterparts in the army, always had pretty doubtful reputations (or parentage), especially to those on the 'lower deck'. In this case I was to find out how right the orderly room clerk was. Not only was the SWO a bit of a martinet, but the food in the airmen's mess was atrocious – so much so that most of it was consigned to the swill bins. I spent a lot of time and money in the NAAFI as one had to eat. Nevertheless, I was luckier than most as, when on night duty, I joined with the duty telephonists one of whom was a born scrounger; he supplemented our meagre rations with real butter, eggs, sausages and potatoes.

How wonderful those midnight snacks were.

RAF Little Rissington (later the Central Flying School of the Royal Air Force) is attractively situated among the rolling Cotswold Hills. It is of pre-war construction: bricks, concrete and sturdily-built hangars, a change from the hutted establishments I had so far experienced. My quarters were in a barrack block not far from SHQ where I worked.

The airfield was also close by and, naturally, the flying activities held my rapt attention. However, it took a long time before I got used to the noise of a North American Harvard in fine pitch, especially when they flirted with the roof throughout the night.

I was stationed at Little Rissington for only three months during which time the severe winter of 1939-40 descended upon Europe. One night it rained steadily and froze immediately, transforming everything it covered. Branches of trees snapped under the weight of ice; telephone lines had given up the struggle and had pulled down their supports for miles along every major road. No traffic could ascend the steep hills to the camp. Flying came to a halt: not only was the airfield one vast skating rink, the hangar doors were iced solid. In fields of longer grass, the picture was awesome – a panoply of steel-blue icy stalagmites as far as the eye could see. So bad was the situation that practically the whole station's personnel was sent on leave. This almost proved impossible but a fleet of taxis braved the treacherous roads and, in relays, took us to Kingham station.

My job in the signal section of SHQ mainly centred upon the receipt of Air Ministry broadcasts transmitted every hour on the hour. There were also two teleprinters, both connected by tie line to RAF Abingdon. These carried quite a lot of traffic, mostly accident reports which were quite detailed communications. Our duties also included the instruction of pilots u/t (under training). Teaching them morse at the slow speed of six to eight words per minute was painful to us and more so to them but they were a wonderful crowd of chaps, mostly of the rank of acting Pilot Officer.

On New Year's Eve, 1940, I was just going off duty when the Station Adjutant came in clutching a bottle, bless him. Needless to add, I did not rush off to my warm bed. Seasonal greetings were bandied about the office before the Adj. declared 'I want the duty wireless operator to be on his toes tonight. The Station Commander wants to see a copy of the New Year's Honours List which the Air Ministry is broadcasting shortly, but only the RAF honours will be sent.'

Hurriedly, signal pads and a few pencils – sharpened at both ends – were produced and laid beside the super-heterodyne receiver. Anstey, who had just taken over from me, didn't look too happy about it all even with a glass of sherry by his side. I had finished my glass and licked my lips noisily. It passed unnoticed. I decided to stay and watch, for a short while anyway. At the appointed hour the list began to pour over the air at a moderate speed but unfortunately it was well laced with irritating static. I could see Anstey squirming in his chair. What with the bad reception, he had to contend with several people breathing down his neck. He hadn't been at it long when, with a disgusted grunt, he took off his earphones and said that it was hopeless.

The Adjutant looked at me with raised eyebrows. Resignedly, I sat down, still licking my lips, donned the phones and listened. Eventually, I got acclimatised to the interference and started to write. The secret of coping with bad reception is to take down what one can, hoping that the blanks can be filled in later by guesswork. As soon as one hesitates when losing a letter or group of letters, more are missed.

It seemed as though that list would never end. I was too busy to notice whether the 'Station Master' had been made an OBE or if the CFI (Chief Flying Instructor) had been awarded the AFC. When finished, I stood up expecting not a pat on the back but another glass of sherry, but the bottle was empty.

It was in the signals office at Little Rizz that I took the plunge and, for the first time, broke the cardinal rule 'never volunteer for anything'. I was sitting at one of the teleprinters waiting for an acknowledgement from the WAAF at Abingdon. I had just typed the first of several confidential accident reports and I was shortly to go off duty. Impatiently, I tapped a non-productive key which had the effect of producing raspberry-like noises at the other end hoping to drag 'fanny' away from her knitting. While sitting there and getting nowhere fast, the door burst open and in stalked our signals W/O. Waving a piece of paper over his head, he said 'Any of you wops want to re-muster as aircrew?'

'Doing what, sir? ' I asked.

'They are calling for volunteer air gunners.'

'For God's sake put my name down,' I quickly answered, 'the shemale at the other end of this teleprinter line won't annoy me again if I can help it.'

'You're mad,' said one of my colleagues. 'You want your brains dusted. They are shooting air gunners out of the sky like clay pigeons,' he lamented.

'It can't be all that bad,' I parried, 'in any case, I cannot stand much more of the stuff they call food in the mess. I'll take my chances.'

'Are you sure, Henry?' the W/O added.

'You bet I'm sure, sir.'

There it was, I had stuck my neck out with a capital N and O for a job which, in those early war days, was said to be 'fraught', 'dicey' and possessing about a three-month life expectancy. However, having committed myself, I began to look forward to this new departure in my career. I refused to dwell on the bleak possibilities and instead wondered what it was like to fly and to fire off countless rounds at those Messerschmitts that weren't already blazing their way to the ground – here was our friend Walter Mitty again.

It wasn't long before things began to happen. A signal came through confirming that 637244 AC2 Henry, F. M. had been accepted for air-gunner training and that his body had received the medical category of A3-B (the medics' Plimsoll line for gunners and observers).

I then went to the stores armed with the appropriate forms and drew boots, black calf, flying; helmet, flying; goggles, flying; suit, Sidcot, flying; and many other bits and pieces which form the budding aviator's kit. Then came the chore of touring the camp to get clearances. Signatures had to be obtained to say that I wasn't about to depart with the Officer's Mess silver or the NAAFI spoon and chain. My next port of call was the orderly room to find out where they intended to transplant my body. I was going abroad! My next unit was to be No. 5 Bombing and Gunnery School, RAF Jurby, Isle of Man.

It was there that I made my first ever flight, in a Fairey Battle, on 10 March 1940, three days short of my first year in the Royal Air Force.

CHAPTER 2

March 1940/41:

Flying training – Training fliers – Bombing the enemy –
Enemy bombing – New squadron

As are most long-distance train journeys during war-time, my cross-country trip to Liverpool must have been a tedious one but my memory holds no shudder-making recollections of it. However, I do remember meeting up with several Jurby-bound airmen on a cold and dingy quayside. In spite of the weather and surroundings, I was beginning to enjoy myself. I had always wanted to travel and this was to be my first sea crossing leading to my first flight.

We embarked on the Liverpool/Douglas ferry and, soon afterwards, sailed down the dreary Mersey into the Irish Sea. There was a pretty heavy swell running that day and summer was a long way off. The boredom of the crossing was alleviated by the sight of several young men in sailor suits who spent most of the time leaning over the taffrail. Their faces had that special expression and colour which can only be inculcated by the mention of oysters and chocolate sauce. Not normally a fashion conscious person, I did observe that olive-green clashed rather fiercely with navy-blue. Oddly enough, we RAF types appeared to be immune from the affects of pitch and roll. Maybe we all happened to be good sailors, or was it because we were a thirsty bunch of airmen who had discovered a bar below deck which was open and eager to purvey?

On reaching Douglas, we disembarked and engaged the services of a Manxman and his cart to haul our kit to the station. The train we boarded was out of this world: small compartments were hauled by an equally small locomotive over a narrow-gauge track. We followed the River Dhoo for a while, then through St. John's, along the coast and inland to Sulby Glen, the nearest one could get by train to Jurby. There were still signs of snow in the sheltered gullies and on the higher slopes of the hills.

The Isle of Man is equidistant from England, Scotland and Ireland, and not much further from Wales. In other words, slap in the middle of the Irish Sea. It is ten miles wide by thirty miles long and is washed by the warm waters of the Gulf Stream. Nevertheless, Admiral Sir Francis Beaufort could not have set foot on the island in winter-time because across its more exposed parts there can blow a wind which feels like force 15.

The island has practically everything to offer. Craggy hills topped by a 2,034-foot mountain; wooded glens sprinkled with waterfalls; fish-laden rivers and marshes stocked to the reed-tops with wild birds; sandy beaches and rocky cliffs for the budding mountaineers. But there was a war on and we had little time to admire Man's charms.

It was also the home of cats without tails and sheep with four horns but not, as might be believed, the birthplace of three-legged men. In peace-time a seasonal flourish of aerodynamically-designed racing motorcycles eat up the roads at breakneck speeds. Apart from the forty-seven miles of Lilliputian steam railway, there are horse-drawn tramcars (said to be the last of their kind on this planet), a national (Manx) tartan of blue, purple, gold, green and white designed to dazzle the unwary; a belief in the 'Little People' and tales of Bugganes (giants).

In direct contrast with Little Rissington, the food in the airmen's mess at Jurby couldn't be bettered. It serves to show how good basic rations could be ruined by incompetence behind the hotplate. As a friend of mine once said: 'As cooks they'd make a bunch of bloody good jockeys.' The sharp Atlantic air whetted our appetites and these, thanks to the efforts of the catering officer, the cooks and the station duty officers (who examined cooks' hands and often tasted the food), were adequately sated. My belated thanks to the then CO of RAF Jurby for so much inner-man contentment.

The course syllabus embraced more hours in the classroom than in the air. While we were impatient to get off the ground, it soon became apparent that much groundwork had to be done before any degree of proficiency in the air was possible. We had to be familiar, down to the last pin and pawl, with the tools of our trade. The Fairey Battle's 'ordnance' comprised one Vickers gas-operated, magazine-fed machine-gun. It was comparatively easy to strip and reassemble without being left with an assortment of strange pieces. We had to be able to diagnose and rectify any one of a pretty large permutation of stoppages. Speed was, of course, essential. In action, the safety of the aircraft and crew might well depend on how quickly the gunner can clear a jammed gun or, in Service parlance, 'get his finger out'.

Other subjects relevant included the theory of sighting, deflection shooting and aircraft recognition. The only means the gunner had of assessing the range of an attacking fighter was to establish (a) what type of aircraft it was and (b) its wing span. He could then tell, by the extent to which it filled his ring sight, how far away – or how near – his attacker was. Instruction was also given on the hydraulically-operated Bristol gun turret (as fitted to the Blenheim in which we also made a limited number of air-firing flights).

Our course began on 2 March 1940. Eight days later we got airborne. The big day had arrived. We reported to that tall, skinny building the parachute section to be fitted with harness and issued a chute. Then to the armoury, each to load two magazines with ammo. We had been taught how to do this but it was always a dangerous pastime. Feeding the 100 rounds of ·303 in the drum was simple enough, it was putting tension on the hefty spring inside the magazine (to enable the rounds to be quickly spewed into the breech) which brought on the pangs of apprehension. One slip and your hand received something like a kick from the back end of a horse.

Thus, equipped with a Sidcot (it was still 'brass monkey' weather), parachute harness, thick woollen socks and flying boots, helmet and goggles hitched round our necks, carrying a parachute and two weighty magazines, we tottered round the airfield perimeter to the marquees at the far side of the field. It was here that we reported for our detail and wherein the staff pilots and ground crews rested between flights. As I staggered across the grass, I happened to look to my left and noticed an aircraft making its approach to land; it seemed to be heading straight for my head. There were no runways at Jurby then, so it was difficult to judge exactly where it would touch down. I didn't know what to do. Should I look stupid and lie flat on the 'deck' or run like a startled fawn? Burdened as I was, and feeling like a trussed turkey, I decided to carry on walking, glancing uneasily over my shoulder at the fast-approaching machine. It alighted behind me, about a hundred yards away. Quite deceiving, I thought. The situation brought to mind the well-known World War I recruiting poster which portrayed the pointing finger and piercing eyes of Lord Kitchener. Whichever way it was viewed the General's eyes and finger remained pointed accusingly and directly at the beholder.

I was later to be told by a pilot that one should stand still when an aircraft is about to land. This makes it easier for the 'driver' to aim the nose of his machine at a clear touch-down point.

The Fairey Battle was a low-wing monoplane designed as a medium bomber and was powered by one Rolls-Royce Merlin engine. It did some excellent work with the Advanced Air Striking Force in France (ten squadrons flew out on 2 September 1939) before the Dunkirk episode. It was, however, becoming operationally obsolescent because of its smallish bomb load and single in-line, liquid-cooled engine (the same power unit as the Spitfire) which made it vulnerable to flak and fighters alike. Nevertheless, it was a suitable aircraft for primary gunnery training, even if rather cramped for two gunners in the aft cockpit. With one gunner standing and the other sitting on the fuselage floor, the Vickers K gun came to hand pretty easily. This gas-operated gun was mounted on a rocking pillar which, in turn, was rotated manually on a scarf ring through a lateral arc of about 160°. The gunner, therefore, had a good beam-to-beam field of fire but he could very easily turn the tail assembly into a colander since no interrupter gear was fitted.

As recorded in my flying log book under the column headed 'duty', the following exercises (one per flight) were carried out: FRGG, FRBT, FRUTT, and FRBRST. I completed two of the first, five of the second, four of the third and four of the fourth – amounting to ten hours flying on fifteen flights (twelve in Battles and three in Blenheims).

What do those abbreviations mean? Well, as far as I can recall:

FR   – Free ring.
GG   – Forget (can't be 'ground to ground' from an aircraft).
BT   – Beam target.
UTT   – Under tail target.
BRST   – Beam relative speed target.

For the air-to-ground exercise, about six targets were placed along the fringe of a secluded beach. Air-to-air firing was carried out against a drogue towed by a Hawker Henley. The latter exercise took place over the sea and varied between the straightforward beam shot to more difficult deflection shots from all angles (other than head-on), simulating most forms of attack which we might encounter at a later date.

*   *   *

As I neared the marquee I saw other gunners returning from

their first exercise. They appeared to be in good spirits which was
most heartening. Entering the tent, I sought the man who was to
carry me aloft for the first time. The authorisation book informed
me that I was to fly in Battle No. 2229 on a FRGG exercise, the
pilot being Sergeant Chadwick. We, the second gunner and myself,
were given a short briefing by the pilot.

'Now listen carefully. You must not fire until you get the OK
from me. As we haven't got intercom the only way I can give you
the signal to fire is by sounding the undercarriage horn three times.
This I will do when I get a green from the control tower on the
range. You will be firing off the starboard beam that is the right-
hand side – *only* at the targets on the beach. Keep your gun on
"safe" until you get my signal. Is that clear?'

'Yes, Sergeant, perfectly clear'.

'Good, then let's go. The aircraft is outside. Decide among
yourselves who will fire first because we haven't time for arguments
over the range. Do not engage a magazine until we are in the target
area. And I repeat, keep the gun on "safe" until you hear my signal.'

The undercarriage horn he referred to is a safety device
designed to warn the pilot that his undercarriage is still locked in
the 'up' position. It sounded-off only when normal cruising speed
dropped to the landing speed but could be sounded at will simply
by throttling back until speed dropped off.

The two of us couldn't get into the machine quickly enough.
Clambering up onto the starboard wing we slid into the rear cockpit.
There wasn't an awful lot of room; we stood there wedged side by
side like a couple of helmeted pilchards in a can, raring to go. The
pilot came out and likewise hauled himself onto the wing and
walked up to the front cockpit. Strange hand signals were
exchanged between him and the ground crew; the engine burst into
life with a muted roar. The structure began to vibrate to its
extremities and the tailplane quivered in an alarming fashion. Two
airmen came aft and lay over the tail – one each side of the fuselage
– with their backsides presenting wonderful targets. There was a
sudden surge of power; the tailplane quivered even more and a
stream of dust and loose bits of grass whirled away under it. Why
weren't we moving? Couldn't anyway with those two chaps
hanging on the back. As we found out later, it was cockpit-drill time;
the chocks were still in position and the bodies draped over our rear
quarters prevented the aircraft from tipping over onto its spinnerless

nose. The pilot was checking for magneto drop. I poked my head over the side with the intention of looking forward and received my first lesson in avoiding the slipstream. It felt like a punch on the jaw.

The engine revs dropped and the 'tail weights' ran forward to remove the chocks; we started to roll and taxied slowly to the take-off point. Making sure that no aircraft was approaching to land, the pilot turned the Battle 90° to face into wind. There was a slight pause, then a burst of power from the Merlin. In no time at all we were racing bumpily across the turf. The tail lifted off the ground and, as the machine reached flying speed, the elevators lifted slightly while the rudder moved fractionally but jerkily from side to side – the control surfaces were biting and effective. We had got unstuck and the ground was fast receding beneath us.

Gaining height, I noticed how the landscape changed in dimension. Lumpy hedgerows, trees and hillocks sank down into a flat patchwork pattern hemmed by the northern coastline. To the south the mountains, with their tops enshrouded by cloud, blocked the view in that direction. My first impressions were as mixed as the odour of oil, petrol and glycol within the fuselage. I certainly felt exhilarated.

Although on this exercise we couldn't have exceeded 500 feet, the feeling of being divorced from the world below was complete. The gentle undulating motion of the aircraft, the steady and reassuring note of its Rolls-Royce engine and the small fluffy cumulus clouds whipping by a hundred or so feet above, all contributed to the excitement of the new realm I had entered.

Making a shallow turn towards the north-west coast, we were soon making a dummy run past the targets below. They looked large enough not to miss which added to my confidence, for I was already a 'dead-eye Dick' with a rifle. Clipping on one of the magazines (I had won the toss to fire first), I made sure that it was securely engaged since it was as much a crime to drop a magazine over the side as it was to kick the CO on the shins. The pilot made a tighter turn to port, then another when, clearly above the noise of the engine, I heard the horn. I cocked the gun and moved the safety catch to 'fire' and waited for the targets to show themselves. I got off a few short bursts at some of the targets; a wing-waggle told me to stop firing, then a smart turn to come round on the targets once again. I had to abandon my shoot after firing only forty-two rounds because of repeated stoppages and because my time had run out –

each detail being limited to fit a tight programme. Needless to add, I was a little annoyed. In fact, sitting on the fuselage floor amid the brassy clatter of empty bullet cases, I fumed while my colleague got off his full 200 rounds to the accompanying stench of cordite fumes which wafted back at me. Forty minutes later we felt the modest bump of a good three-point landing.

We left camp bounds one day for a visit to the 'turret range'. This consisted of a cliff-top field, at the brink of which was a 4 foot-square target, and by the hedge about 200 yards inland there stood a trolley upon which was mounted a power-operated turret. The turret was equipped with two belt-fed ·303 Browning machine-guns. When sitting in the turret one was faced with the butt ends of both guns, between and above which were two padded cheek/chin rests, a piece of armour plate – slotted to allow clear vision of ring/bead or reflector sights. The 'safe/fire' mechanisms were on the inner side of both guns. At the outside of each knee was an ammunition container, the cocking toggle being housed in a sheath on the outside of the right-hand container. At navel level were the controls. These took the shape of stub bicycle handlebars which, when rotated twist-grip-wise, elevated and depressed both guns, at the same time lowered and raised the seat. When turned to the left or right the turret rotated in the same direction. Any one or combination of those movements was made possible only when a valve on the handgrip was depressed, allowing hydraulic fluid to circulate through a system of valves, as directed. The trigger mechanism was on the right handlebar. In the event of hydraulic failure or, in the case of the Blenheim when other hydraulics were in use (flaps, undercarriage) the turret was rendered inoperative, there was a small lever by one's left foot (sometimes referred to as the 'dead man's lever') which, when depressed, allowed the turret seat to sink to its fully down position, enabling the gunner to extricate himself.

It was on this range that an amazing incident occurred involving my two best friends, Michael Galewski (from Sunderland) and Tommy Thompson (Newcastle). Mike was seated in the turret waiting his turn to shred the target. Tommy, standing on the lip of the turret trolley with a gun barrel resting on each of his shoulders, was talking to Mike through the turret aperture. Let's face it, this was the height of folly. The NCO in charge of the range was, fortunately for both parties, fiddling about with the motor behind the turret. Mike must have already set his guns to 'fire' and

inadvertently pulled the trigger. There was a burst of fire –
devastating because of its unexpectedness. Tommy, deafened and
with a detergent-white face, ducked shakily down and nipped
smartly away from the lethal aspirations of Mike. The sergeant i/c
(who hadn't seen all, thankfully) gave Mike the rollicking he so
richly deserved, for firing without permission. It was lucky, too,
that none of us had been standing twixt muzzles and target.

Gun stoppages were the bane of our trigger-happy little lives.
We later found that the cause of most of them – usually magazine
trouble – happened while on air-to-air exercises. When firing at a
drogue (a sleeve resembling a wind-sock), it was impossible to
differentiate between the hits (if any) of either gunner, so the tips
of the bullets were dipped in dope of different colours. Thus, holes
in the 'sock' would be edged with colour, making identification
easy. Unfortunately, the dope flaked off inside the magazine and in
the breech of the gun. As is well known, any piece of machinery –
precision or otherwise – takes very unkindly to foreign bodies
messing about in its vitals. This problem would not, of course,
obtain on a squadron.

My first six flights had been, apart from those accursed
stoppages, uneventful. As an aviator I was beginning to feel an 'old
hand'. My seventh trip, however, proved a little more exciting – for
a few moments anyway. Arriving at the marquee, the authorisation
book contained the information that I was to fly with Sergeant
Taylor on FRBRST. I asked where that gentleman was. 'Here I am,'
said a voice from above. Looking round I saw my pilot sliding
down the tent pole. Being still green and/or wet behind the ears
where flying was concerned, this frolic, apart from being a little
amusing, certainly didn't arouse in me any feeling of foreboding.

We took off after the usual preliminaries and climbed up
towards some cumulus cloud. It was my first experience of flying
into, through and above cloud. How magnificent it all was. I'd
never thought about cloud before, other than to lift a jaundiced
eye towards the stuff when it jettisoned rain, sleet or snow. One
just took those things for granted. But to be up there among it, or
them, was something that really made my day. I noticed, as we
exited a bank of snowy-white, dazzling cloud, a swirling vortex
left at its surface by the propeller. I saw, chasing along an
adjacent cloud, the aircraft's shadow which changed in size as it
traversed the contours. I wondered why it was ringed with a

spectrum, a mobile, circular rainbow.

As we plunged into another mass of cloud, it became a little more bumpy and I spotted minute droplets of water scudding over the perspex canopy, to disappear when we broke free into bright sunshine again. It occurred to me then that even a moron might compose verse up there among the clouds. Suddenly, between a chink in the clouds which were building up ahead, there appeared a green and brown wall bang in front of our nose.

The pilot also saw it for he pulled the machine round into what, in RAF slang, is termed a 'split-arse turn'. For the first (and certainly not the last) time I felt the flutter of instinctive fear. There were mountains in them there clouds, one of them, Snaefell, topped 2,034 feet and we couldn't have been higher than 1,500 feet. However, calamity was dextrously avoided and we made our way to the rendezvous with the Henley over the encouragingly flat sea.

The pilots of the Henleys obviously had great respect for our shooting, because they made sure that their drogue operators streamed the 'sock' on at least 500 feet of cable. I hadn't heard of a case where the towing aircraft was shot down but I did hear that some of the drogue-winch operators accepted bribes from those gunners who couldn't hit a cow's backside with a banjo. They undertook to pierce the drogue with a six-inch nail, in the appropriate colour, at ten 'shots' for half-a-crown.

Chatting to one of the drogue operators over a noggin one evening (I was not negotiating a mammoth score for the morrow), he informed me that their 'profession' was not all beer and skittles. He related how one of his ilk had got caught up in yards of snaking wire when the drogue winch ran berserk. Nothing could be done to release the unfortunate chap until the aircraft returned to base, for the Henley carried only one other crew member – the pilot. The aircraft was put down as quickly but gently as possible with the operator, enmeshed like a spider's breakfast, hanging half-way out of the lower hatch. He was lucky not to lose his head.

While I hold little patience with the fellow who flaps like an old maid, my sympathy always goes out to the keen chap who is just not mechanically minded. There is a fair crop of both types in the services. My first encounter with one of the second category was on a rifle range. We had been given the order to load, a matter of seconds to press home the clip of five rounds. The airman on my left, I noticed, was trying desperately hard to hammer home his clip of five with the bullets pointing downwards instead of the obvious horizontal position – in line with and parallel to the barrel.

At Jurby, I happened to fly with a mixture of both categories – with a spell of air-sickness thrown in for good measure. He was a nice enough sort but with a lethal weapon in his ten thumbs he was a menace to himself, to his colleagues in blue and to the general public within range. So erratic was he that his hands bled from numerous abrasions: everything and anything that was sharp or protruded he found. When we flew together he was first on the firing list and stood there in the cockpit fiddling and fumbling having already committed the cardinal sin of dropping a magazine over the side. I lay back waiting and watching. When the horn sounded – just once (the pilot had merely throttled back to make a turn) – he, the great big nit, commenced to blaze away at all and sundry. A violent wing-waggle, which caused him some uneasiness (more than likely in the stomach), stopped him firing, as intended. But not before he had placed a few neat holes in the wooden control tower down on the range. Fortunately, its occupants, who had done him no harm, escaped unscathed.

Gunners were by no means the only ones guilty of irresponsible actions. We heard tell of a navigator, on the bombing course, who had killed a prize piece of beef with an 11 lb. practice smoke bomb, the real target being about three miles out to sea. These laddies were certainly eligible for the MHDOIF (Most Highly Derogatory Order of the Irremovable Finger), a 'paper' award instituted by some wags at the Air Ministry who, during the war, produced a superlative publication called Tee Emm. This magazine was so popular with aircrews that copies were swiped as soon as they appeared in the mess – a hitherto unheard of occurrence where 'official' publications were concerned. The basic theme of Tee Emm was training (hence the phonetic initials for Training Memoranda). It was humorously written and most of its illustrations were by W Hooper. Its dominating character being a Pilot Officer Prune, the epitome of naive incompetence.

Each issue of *Tee Emm* carried a list of recipients for the MHDOIF. Each incident mentioned actually took place; they were published with the intention of instructing others rather than to denigrate the perpetrators (who remained anonymous). I quote two examples from a copy which I swiped from a mess and still possess.

'The MHDOIF has also been awarded to F/Sgt — for Putting

his Trust in Man Rather Than in Nature.

While flying over the sea F/Sgt — , as rear gunner, was asked by the navigator to obtain some drifts on "white caps".

When after a long interval nothing more had been heard from him, the navigator asked the reason for the delay. F/Sgt — pointed out indignantly that he was still waiting, but the "white caps" had not yet been launched from the aircraft.'

'The MHDOIF is also awarded to F/Sgt — for Not Knowing Where His Finger Was.

On returning from a firing exercise with port engine trouble he accidentally fired off his cannon shortly before touching down. Mistaking this for his port engine blowing up he promptly crashed, severely damaging his aircraft.

On the inside back cover of *Tee Emm* was a drawing of a headstone upon which was inscribed the familiar RIP and underneath it the 'lesson for the month' in the form of an epitaph. My copy's inverted advice read: 'He said he'd show his pals something new in aerobatics.'

*   *   *

For the second time I hunted for a needle in a kitbag to sew on my air gunner's brevet. This had only just superseded the brass 'flying bullet' insignia which was worn on the sleeve. My status had been elevated to wireless operator/air gunner (W/Op. AG) but my rank stayed put as AC2. My pittance was increased to about 3s. 6d. per day, *id est*. £1 4s. 6d. per week.

The course was split – its members being posted to scattered OTUs (Operational Training Units) throughout the UK. My posting was to No. 13 OTU, RAF Bicester, situated fourteen miles from Oxford, sixteen from Aylesbury, fifteen from Banbury and about 600 from Berlin. The aircraft in use there were Blenheim Is and IVs (short – and long-nosed versions, respectively) and the Avro Anson popularly referred to as 'Annie' or the 'flying greenhouse'. Both marks of Blenheim had similar turrets and armament although some of the earlier Is had the single Vickers K mounted in the turret. The Anson was used for cross-country exercises and crew training for the pilots, navigational training for the navigators and wireless telegraphy and procedure for us W/Op. AGs.

An OTU comprised a hard core of experienced instructors whose task it was to mould, from raw stock, competent crews suitably equipped to go into action with a squadron. However, before permanent crews were formed, each pilot, navigator and W/Op. AG was pumped full with theory most of which then had to be applied in the air both by day and by night.

We air gunners hadn't been at Bicester 'five minutes' before we were moved north again on a short (27 April to 6 May) detachment to RAF Squires Gate, the residential area south of Blackpool. We were accommodated in small, *gemütlich* hotels on the sea front at Lytham St. Anne's. In our leisure hours we found plentiful entertainment at 'reduced prices for HM Forces'. Admission to the Tower Ballroom/cinema/zoo or the Winter Gardens, for example, set us back no more than sixpence.

One morning, for a bet, I combed the hair on both my heads and rushed across the esplanade to the beach, paused and plunged into the icy sea. I wasn't in for very long as my goose pimples acquired goose pimples but I felt invigorated and I won the wager.

While at Squires Gate I flew eleven times in three days and it speaks well for the Blenheim's Bristol turret and belt-fed Brownings, in that I fired 2,200 rounds without a single stoppage. Six hours flying were also added to the ten already logged. All the flights were over the sea on air-to-air exercises. After some of those flights, the pilot made a very low pass up and down the coast, hopping the two piers between Lytham and Fleetwood. This was great fun. Not so for the anglers on the piers who ducked nervously and shook their fins vehemently. Nor did it amuse the RAF NCOs on the esplanade whose distracted squads paid little heed to their commands.

One has only to get into the air once to realise that 'noises off' cannot be heard above the roar of the engine(s). Later in the war, when on leave, I would smile indulgently when asked by civilians whether the enemy's air-raid sirens and/or guns could be heard. Moreover I discovered, while at Blackpool, that engine noise did not prevent the incursion of alien odours! Despite the 'petroil' stink inside the aircraft and the howling slipstream outside, I distinctly got a goodly noseful of fish when flying, admittedly low, over Fleetwood. Later I was to experience the smell of burning hay or wood when hedge-hopping the countryside. More frightening was the acrid whiff from a nearby shell burst. The former two 'aromas' were detected only from pretty low altitudes while the latter would penetrate at most heights.

Back to Bicester (pronounced Bister) and the lecture rooms.

The subjects we had already broached were extended in scope and some put into practice. Aircraft recognition, for instance, was and rightly so, considered as important as being able to pull the trigger. For those who couldn't tell the difference between a Messerschmitt 109 and a No. 14 bus, there would be little future.

A great pity that some of the trigger-happy Army and Navy chaps didn't make a more thorough study of the subject. They were not, it seemed, able to tell the difference between a Blenheim and a Ju.88, nor could some of them spot the different features of a Me.109 and a Spitfire. With regard to the Army (Brown jobs we called 'em), we lost a couple of aircraft to the shore batteries on the East Anglia coast when the 'phoney war' turned into the real thing in the autumn of 1940. They would, doubtless, clamber on their sandbags to cheer us on our way as we headed east in the twilight but for some inexplicable reason, they tried like hell to prevent us crossing our own coast on return. It was later established that some of these gun crews were Polish. It was therefore understandable for them to be eager to avenge the ravage of their country, but not too eager.

As for the Navy, their escort vessels to the convoys hugging the east coast of England, gave us many a 'hairy' moment and their trigger fingers remained in a state of itchiness throughout the war. In fact, I was told that *Warspite* bagged fourteen Allied aircraft on D-day! However, all three services were guilty, at some time or other, of fallibility. Take the case of the best-aimed stick of bombs on a major British seaport. It fell from the belly of an RAF Whitley whose crew had, in bad weather, flown a 'blue-on-red' course from their east-coast base. Quite probably they unloaded when the ground defences of that great port had let loose. There were many such blunders, particularly after D-day when the rapid advance of our own front lines caused unfortunate, but only human, errors of judgement.

A tremendous pity that the three services had to wait for the major North African campaign in order to prove how imperative it was for each of them to know what the other was about. Petty jealousies and inter-service bickering should have been swept aside from the word go.

In combat the air gunner's primary responsibility was that of protecting his crew and aircraft against the machinations of enemy aircraft. Naturally, in order to do this, he had to be able to shoot straight as well as knowing whether it was 'one of theirs or ours'. If he was also a wireless operator, his terms of reference included giving what assistance he could to the navigator. While he was bound to keep W/T silence when over enemy territory, other than in an emergency, his job was to obtain fixes and homing bearings when the aircraft's position was in doubt or as a cross-check of the navigator's calculations. These chart and calliper boys had a tough time in those early war days when navaids were, by modern standards, primitive and unreliable. What with the blackout and inaccurate meteorological forecasts, it wasn't difficult to stray from track, even to get completely lost. Under such conditions only the P/O Prunes would venture to descend through cloud.

When not staring at a blackboard or messing about in simulators, we were airborne. My first day's flying at Bicester, on 18 May, consisted of three flights in Avro Ansons (my third type) for a total of 4 hours 55 minutes. The third one of those jaunts was at night, my first experience of flirting with the stars. Night flying (only carried out by 'idiots and owls' so it was said) offered a new set of impressions.

In the surrounding darkness there was a warm glow from inside the aircraft from the softly illuminated array of instruments on the pilot's fascia panel, the shielded, flexible lamps over the navigator's charts and the wireless operator's desk, while the valves of the latter's transmitter would slowly incandesce when switched on. Over the air could be heard the staccato of morse from aircraft and ground stations far and wide, an unintelligible cacophony to which one simply got used.

Below, depending on the weather and phase of the moon, not much could be discerned in war-time. Up to medium altitudes one could see the lights of vehicles moving through the blackout countryside even though their headlamps were masked; or a plume of white smoke streaming back over the glowing firebox of a speeding locomotive. With a full moon shedding its ghostly sheen on the ground below, lakes, rivers, railway lines and even greenhouses would suddenly glitter and fade. On nights free from enemy activity there were the twinkling lights of many aerodrome flarepaths interspersed with beacons whose brightly 'dashing code letters punctuated the darkness with monotonous regularity.

Navigation at night, especially in bad weather, required more than the usual assistance from the radio. Ironically, as the weather grew worse so did the reception from the radio; the greater the need the greater the efforts required to obtain assistance. In electrical storms it was, of course, damn near impossible.

Most of our flying from Bicester took place, of necessity, over the south-west and west of England and Wales and over the Channel, Bristol Channel, Atlantic and the Irish Sea. Quite frequently when over the latter stretch of water and at the medium-to-low altitudes, our radio would be screened by the Welsh mountains and to maintain a log under those conditions was frustrating.

Often we had to resort to the trailing aerial. This gadget consisted of about 150 feet of wire, weighted at one end with a dozen or so lead balls, wound round a drum which was attached to the inside fuselage near the floor. The drum was controlled by a handle and an insulated thumb-screw type of brake. The weighted end was housed in a cylinder the end of which protruded slightly from the underside of the aircraft's belly. To stream the aerial one would slowly unwind the screw and let gravity take over, at the same time making sure that the drum was partly braked by the friction of a gloved hand. This prevented the drum from spinning too fast and the aerial breaking free from it when coming to a sudden stop, another sin to be avoided. To wind the thing in one just turned and turned and turned the handle, God knows how many times. This operation was a *must* before landing or low flying.

While on the subject of handles, it is indelibly stamped on my memory the fact that the Anson's undercarriage (in the earlier versions at any rate) was retracted and lowered by means of a handle in the pilot's cockpit. It was usually one of the wireless operator's chores unless there was a passenger or navigator in the second pilot's seat. If I remember a'right, it took over 140 turns of that handle to get the wheels home and even then, like the Fairey Battle, they still protruded untidily from the underside of the aircraft.

Quite frequently something occurred to mar a wireless operator's day. Flying in the vicinity of Bristol one afternoon, with the weather deteriorating, the Anson's two Armstrong Siddeley Cheetah engines were giving of their best while we underflew a pall of filthy, ominous-looking cloud. I had to shut down the radio because of piercing static which made W/T reception impossible. Looking out of the window I gazed abstractly across the port wing from its root up the oil slick to the engine nacelle. On seeing the propeller disc covered in what at first looked like sparks, my eyes bulged like organ stops. I had read about St. Elmo's fire but this was my first experience of it. I was fascinated yet frightened for I had in mind the volatile fuel contained within the wings. Out of the corner of my eye I noticed a flickering light coming from my radio equipment. It was the small 'P' lamp of the transmitter aerial ammeter which flickered like a peace-time ad. in Piccadilly Circus. I checked the transmitter and found that it was switched off. How eerie it all was.

At the end of May we made our first practice ZZ landing at RAF Abingdon, south of Oxford. This exercise was devised to facilitate the approach to an airfield during bad weather, bringing the aircraft to its perimeter by means of a series of homing bearings. The pilot should then be able to make a visual landing. The wireless operator, having tuned his receiver to a special frequency, would ask permission to carry out a ZZ; he then transmitted long dashes broken by a pause and the aircraft's call-sign. The ground station would swing loop aerials and plot the aircraft's position. To interrupt the wireless operator's transmissions, the ground station tapped out a stream of 'dits' and, when commanding attention sent: 'QDM 225 1435' (meaning 'The magnetic heading for you to steer towards me, with no wind, is 225° at 14.35 hours.'). The operator passed this info. to the pilot who, in turn, applied it t'compass. To make this exercise a fair one, for it was more often than not carried out in good visibility, the pilot followed the headings given irrespective of where they might lead him. Invariably, we found ourselves heading straight for a row of hangars or a bunch of trees several hundred yards from the airfield. Such was the efficacy of the system. Needless to add, the remarks from the front cockpit would have made a Billingsgate porter blanch. If such a procedure were to be carried out in an emergency, I would hazard a guess that the odds against making a good, clean approach would be about 6-to-4. Nevertheless, in the absence of radar, electronics and modern 'tit boxes' in those days, it was better than nothing at all and it served to give a little confidence to some.

It was at the beginning of June when I was, at last, introduced to my permanent crew. The pilot was P/O Newland, the navigator's name I forget. The three of us were to complete our training as a team before moving to an operational squadron. Before that day arrived, however, we had to co-ordinate our individual talents during ten more days intensive flying: cross-countries by day and by night, bombing exercises, gunnery practice, formation flying and so on. Practice, practice and more practice.

When the course finished in the middle of June, I had spent seventy-six hours with my feet off the ground, to say nothing of the hours spent in lecture rooms, in simulators, on the range and in the local pubs.

The big day had arrived. We were now ready for our baptism of action with one of the many Blenheim squadrons stationed in East Anglia but which one? For me none of them, for I was summoned to the Flight Commander's office. He said as I entered: 'Ah! Come in Henry, stand easy. I have to tell you that you will not be leaving here for a while as the signals officer has recommended you for screening.'

'Not leaving, sir? But—'

'That's right. We are short of wireless instructors and until more replacements arrive from the squadrons, we have no choice but to adopt this measure. I appreciate how you feel about it but there it is. You shouldn't have got such good marks for your wireless operating,' he added with a smile.

Of course, I hadn't the status to start a verbal battle and could only utter a half-hearted 'Very good, sir.' As it happened, it turned out in my favour because I heard later that P/O Newland's aircraft had been shot down over Germany. He survived to dwell behind the wire of some *Stalag Luft* or other but I do not know what happened to the navigator or my replacement.

Thus, still with the rank of AC2 I joined the instructors of 'C' Flight, No. 13 OTU (formerly No. 104 Squadron – whose motto 'Strike Hard' described how I felt after my cancelled posting). Actually, this unexpected move was flattering but it rankled. Not long afterwards an AMO was issued which laid down that all air gunners were to be elevated to the rank of sergeant forthwith. It came as, to say the least, a surprise. When this bombshell broke loose, I was in the Flight signals section fiddling about with something or other. Our NCO i/c, Sergeant Townsend, came up and tapped me on the shoulder saying: 'Go to the stores and get issued with tapes.'

'Tapes?' I enquired, wondering how the devil I had jumped to the rank of corporal. 'Are you pulling my leg, Sergeant?'

'No, I'm not. You are, with effect from today, Sergeant Henry; go get them and sew 'em on before you are charged with being improperly dressed.

So, out came the needle and cotton once more. That evening, a few of us self-consciously meandered through the portals of the

sergeants' mess. Its inmates' reaction to our presence wasn't very
pleasant. We were snubbed, that much I do remember, but I could
well understand their feelings. Most of the warrant officers and
'chiefies' (flight sergeants), the majority of whom sported 'long-
distance' medals, had taken years to attain their rank and to
witness a crowd of 'pip-squeaks' leaping into their midst by the
snap of an Air Ministry finger was a bit more than they could
stomach. However, they soon cooled off when realising that we
were specialised in our own right and that our life expectancy was,
on average, far shorter than theirs. The atmosphere became a little
less oppressive when Sergeant Townsend came up to us and
offered his congratulations with a sincere handshake. That friendly
gesture I will never forget.

For a short time I kept one of my uniform tunics bare of
chevrons and after dark I would surreptitiously repair to the NAAFI
to join some of my old pals.

At the end of June I had an interesting trip to Farnborough with
the Chief Flying Instructor, S/Ldr Elworthy. As it is today,
Farnborough was a hive of active boffinry, lots of top-secret projects
being hammered out behind locked doors. It was very interesting to
be shown over a Messerschmitt 109 which still carried French Air
Force markings for it had only recently been presented to Britain by
the French Government. Where they got this flush-riveted, sleek
German-built fighter from (and another which they kept for
themselves) I do not recall. Come to think of it, I wasn't told.

The CFI, a tall, dignified New Zealander, was very popular with
all who worked under or with him and I am delighted to record that
he reached the topmost rung of his service career on 1 September
1963, when he became Chief of Air Staff.

Indeed, all the staff pilots with whom I flew and worked at
Bicester were excellent types. There was F/O Rathbone, MP, who
frequently gave me a ride up to town in his MG. I also had the
pleasure of meeting his charming American wife. She, like
countless others, received the dreaded telegram from the Air
Ministry several months after I had left Bicester. Others I
remember well were 'Tubby' Coombes, Roy Ralston, Lynch-
Blosse, Sigurdson, Tully, Sillito and 'Sandy' Powell.

One day all the instructors were assembled in the flight office.

'Tomorrow,' said the CFI, 'this station is to be inspected by the
King so I want everybody to be on their toes. Aircraft not on the

flying programme will be lined up in front of the hangars, first thing. Staff aircrew and selected pupils, will stand by for inspection. Normal working dress and field service caps will be worn. Flight commanders will report to me at 0900 hours for final details.'

We wondered, having already had one postponement, whether this visit would take place. 'Let's hope he arrives this time, does his stuff and lets us get on with our work,' said one of the staff pilots. There was nothing disrespectful behind that sentiment, he merely reflected the general dislike of daily routine being disrupted, on such occasions, by masses of 'bull'.

The following morning, in groups of pilots, navigators and W/Op. AGs, we were lined up in front of several aircraft. After a considerable wait, the King, looking very smart in the uniform of Marshal of the Royal Air Force, and his retinue approached the apron and began his tour of inspection. Arriving at our group he was told by a conducting officer that we were '...newly-trained, un-blooded air gunners awaiting posting to a squadron...' His Majesty stopped to question the gunner on my immediate right, Sergeant Bingham, a blue-eyed, blond, lanky six-footer.

'How long have you been here, Sergeant?' he enquired.

'Only a few days, sir. I have just returned from a squadron after finishing my first tour.'

'Really? You *have* been in action then?'

'Yes, sir, with 110 Squadron.' He didn't add that he had taken part in the first raid of the war on 4 September 1939. However, that was that and we went back to work.

The task I disliked most, after joining the staff at Bicester, was accompanying a staff pilot on formation flying. To be turret-bound in the leading aircraft of a vic of three while two less experienced pupil pilots did their best to tap on my turret cupola with their wingtips, was enough to scare the pants off the toughest Tartar. There I would sit watching every move they made. I suppose really that it was less dangerous than it appeared to the 'joe' in the back seat. Nevertheless, some of the pupils were nervously erratic and they weaved in and out and up and down as though they were sloshed. And when I could almost count the eyelashes of the pilot in a neighbouring aircraft, it was too damn close for this chicken.

On the other hand, it was sometimes pleasant to have two good 'formators' and to have them escort us safely about the sunlit countryside. The three aircraft would undulate gently, usually out of phase like lethargically-controlled puppets. It was a wonderful feeling of serenity and even the dull roar of the Bristol Mercury engines seemed less obtrusive under such conditions.

Recorded in my log for the first week in July are: 'High-altitude formation using oxygen', 'Advanced formation' and 'Low-level formation cross-country'. The first was interesting in a novel way. At 20,000 feet (then considered high altitude) one felt not only divorced from affairs mundane but bloody cold. Advanced formation was just a little less nerve-racking than the elementary stuff, while the third exercise can only be described as exhilarating. Admitted, I had been flown low along the Blackpool beaches a few times and had partaken of the fishy airs of Fleetwood but, compared with hedge-hopping all over the country for a couple of hours, they were dull.

Low flying had its hazards. Birds often got in the way; they could penetrate perspex with the velocity of a shell, stove in a wing leading edge or splatter themselves over the 'pots' of the radial engines. Then there were the high-tension cables; they seemed to appear from nowhere and untimely disaster was only prevented when their supporting pylons were spotted. Flying low over the sea, too, provided its own kind of danger. Gauging one's distance from the wave-tops was, at times, terribly difficult. So deceptive was it, in fact, that many aircraft returned with bent propeller tips, vibrating engines and red-faced pilots. Extreme caution was also necessary when flying low in formation since the slipstream of the aircraft in front could easily flip an aircraft onto its back, thus courting impact with solid ground. However, provided that the pilot was alert and didn't allow bravado to oust common sense, these risks could be minimised.

Also logged were five long-distance formation flights totalling seventeen hours. These, and all the other shorter exercises, soon piled up the flying time. By 17 August, when I finished my stint at Bicester, I had accumulated 185 flying hours. Comparing that total with those of World War I aviators (sometimes a pilot would go into action with no more than ten hours to his credit) I felt well equipped to face my opposite numbers in combat.

At long last I was to break with training and get down to the real thing. Before moving on from Bicester, a few words on social activities there. The town itself was about a mile from camp. It sported a fair number of pubs, some better than others, and, as far as I remember, two cinemas. There was a very pleasant restaurant called Mary's where we ate well at reasonable prices. To think of the times I sat at one of Mary's tables ploughing through a mixed grill, all the while oblivious of the fact that her husband was a pilot in the RAF and that he was soon dramatically to feature in my life. But that's another story.

The rail journey from Bicester to London was a good one and fast. The last train out of town on a Sunday, however, left at 6:10 pm. Being fifty minutes before opening time this somewhat curtailed one's week-end pleasure. There was some elation therefore when it was announced that the railway authorities had agreed to stop the midnight express to Wolverhampton at Bicester (Sunday only). This gave us a few more hours in which to whoop it up in dear old 'smoke'.

I arrived at Paddington one Sunday and asked for the midnight to Bicester. I was directed to a platform, found a seat and noticed that it pulled out just after midnight. Instead of proceeding nor'-nor'-west it took the west-nor'-west route and I landed up in Oxford at twenty-to-two in the morning. The contents of my pocket would certainly not permit the hiring of a taxi, so I walked into town and got a lift as far as Kidlington on the Banbury road. It was here that I had to turn off for the loneliest, straightest and most maddening walk in my peripatetic experience. The maddening bit was caused by walking towards a flashing beacon for the best part of five miles; every minute of it a red winking hell and every inch of that ten-mile trudge carried a curse for one particular railway employee. I arrived back at camp with aching feet and with the milkman.

On another occasion, I was on the right train and it had pulled into Bicester station. An airman behind me in the corridor asked whether he had arrived at 'Bycester'. I confirmed, opened the door and frightened the life out of him by disappearing suddenly and completely. The train, too long for the platform, had to pull up for a second time. Knowing this I *had* looked out of the window and *had* seen the white-edged platform below me. Stepping out I clawed the air for a second and then fell flat on my face in the dirt. The door from which I had stepped was immediately above the lower end of the sloping platform, hence the white line still being visible. Have you ever missed a stair to stagger horrifyingly another nine inches? Well multiply it by about four and you know how I felt.

*   *   *

On 19 August, I was flown to RAF Wattisham to join No. 110 (Hyderabad) Squadron then under the Command of W/Cdr Sinclair. (In 1941 he was awarded the George Cross for going to the assistance of the crew of a Blenheim which had crashed on the airfield with full bomb load.) My operational pilot was to be F/O 'Sandy' Powell whom I knew back at Bicester. I was thus to make a start with an experienced pilot although he, too, had yet to savour the fruits of hostile activity.

Wattisham was built before the war and like the majority of early war-time airfields had no runways. Situated on the border of West and East Suffolk, its nearest centres of civilisation were Stowmarket, five miles nor'-west, and the county town, Ipswich, about twelve miles to the south-east.

Arriving for the first time on an operational station, a completely different 'atmosphere' was sensed for there was the unmistakable air of competence about the place. The whole unit, from the CO to the lowliest 'erk', was geared to work with near precision, for it was liberally lubricated with team spirit, know-how, sense of mission and a healthy inter-squadron rivalry. It comprised an entity of loyal affiliation: there were the airborne and the chairborne, the fitters, the riggers, the cooks, medics and firemen, drivers, fliers, leaders and followers. There were, of course, the black sheep – there always are – but their presence went unnoticed for responsibility was denied them. The whole 'machine' stood at its mark ready to meet any demand made upon it by its controlling function, Group Headquarters.

The sister squadrons, Nos. 110 and 107, were equipped with Blenheim IV medium bombers. Led by 110, these two squadrons held the distinction of leading the first attack of the war on 4 September, its leader, F/Lt Doran, earning for himself the first DFC of the war. It should be added that the first sortie, a reconnaissance, was made on 3 September by another 2 Group Blenheim squadron, No. 139.

In those days, every squadron was identified by a code (in most cases it consisted of two letters). No. 110 Squadron had recently changed from 'AY' to 'VE' (No. 13 OTU's letters being 'EV' later 'SL'), while No. 107 Squadron was 'OM', formerly 'BZ'.

The second war-time CO of No. 107 Squadron, W/Cdr Basil Embry, was shot down before I arrived at Wattisham but he turned up like the proverbial bad penny three months later after escaping from enemy-occupied territory. When he stood outside one of the hangars, dressed in a smart lounge suit and a Panama hat, those who didn't know him might have thought 'Just another little man from the ministry or something...' But his size belied the dynamic character he really was. His dramatic escape was retold in *Wingless Victory* by the then squadron adjutant, Anthony Richardson. I didn't know it then but I was to become a member of 107 Squadron on four occasions and in 1945, I was to serve under Air Vice-Marshal Embry when he was AOC in C, No. 2 Group, Brussels.

Three days after joining the squadron we buzzed round the circuit on an air test lasting fifteen minutes. The following day a battle order was posted and one of the 'A' Flight crews listed was F/O Powell, Sgt Richmond and Sgt Henry – we were 'on'. That night, weather permitting, we were to 'dice' beneath the stars and amid other more tangible 'illuminations'.

The briefing was a new experience and it proved a quietly efficient and nonchalant gathering. I felt excited, apprehensive, eager but a little afraid. I had been told by some cheerful swine that the first and last sortie of a tour were the dangerous ones. There were, thankfully, many exceptions to this observation. Although superstition is normally a woman's prerogative, aircrews had their own special brand. It was, for example, considered an act of suicide to write a farewell letter before charging into the fray. A large number of pilots, navigators and gunners carried lucky charms (I always carried a steel shaving mirror in the left breast pocket of my uniform and wore a green silk scarf). 'Lucky' items of clothing would remain unwashed for months for fear that its owner might be called upon to fly without it.

The briefing was thorough in every detail. The target was given first which brought from the assembly a whistled 'pheeeew', a hushed murmur or a deathly 'ush. Then followed the intelligence reports: known flak concentrations, best place to cross the coast, approach to target, convoy movements across our track etc. The navigation and signals 'kings' had their say as did the 'Met' man (or 'seaweed basher as he was labelled by some). The Station Commander, Group Captain O R Gayford (whose service background included many record-breaking, long distance flights), often finished the proceedings with a few well-chosen words terminating with a variation of 'And the best of luck chaps.'

Our target for that night was the airfield at St Omer, in northern

France (the same area where Basil Embry had been nipped out of the sky). Take-off was to be half an hour after midnight. I had plenty to do before returning to the mess for supper. The recoiling portions of my two Brownings (kept in a special gun-cleaning room in the hangar) had to be given the final pull-through and cleaning. I then repaired to the signals section to collect a crate of accumulators for the three pieces of aircraft radio: the R1082 receiver, T1083 transmitter and the TR9 which provided intercommunication between the crew and R/T for the pilot to ground or other aircraft. To avoid making more than one trip to the distant dispersals, two of us would carry between us the two crates of accs. and carry the vital pieces of 'ordnance' over our shoulders. We also helped each other with the routine checks. The intercom at all three crew stations; the receiver and transmitter; oxygen valves; the IFF set; the rheostated lights in all positions; the trailing aerial; the dinghy; replace the recoils of the guns, engage the ammunition belts, check contents of the ammo. containers, close breech covers, check the electric reflector sight; kick the main wheels and trudge back to the hangars to the signals section once more. We couldn't check the turret hydraulics until airborne. Other than that we had little to do.

The IFF set, by the way, was a top-secret piece of equipment. In a grey box, it was anchored to the fuselage floor just behind the gunner's position. It had an 'on-off' switch and a series of numbered switches. We were briefed to leave it on a certain number unless an emergency threatened when another digit was selected. The set would then automatically transmit on a special frequency, helping those at 'home' to plot the aircraft's position. There was also a detonator incorporated (what the modern rocket wallah would call a 'destruct button') should the aircraft force-land intact in enemy territory.

From the signals section we collected a stack of 'bumph'. This included the 'Q code', a list of frequencies and call-signs, beacon identification list and a really red-hot, more secret-than-that list of 'colours and letters of the period'. The latter was printed on rice paper so that it could be consumed hastily in the event of descending among the hostile natives. The colours were fired from a Very pistol while the letters could be flashed on an Aldis lamp or from the downward recognition lamp on the belly of the aircraft. For instance, from 1000 to 1400 hours, the colours might be red/red or green/white, and the letters GZ (challenge) and BE (answer).

The Very pistol in the Blenheim was stowed up front and to meet the contingency of overflying a convoy (unseen on a really dark night) the appropriate cartridge was always up the spout, if one was wise. The Navy had the unhappy habit of issuing the challenge on their clattering signal lamps at about 1,000 words per minute. They only flashed twice. If no reply was forthcoming before the last blink of their lamp was swallowed by the night, they might fire everything they could lay their hands on. We just *had* to be on the ball to forestall those bridge commands 'Fire, fire, fire.'

Having completed all our chores, we wandered to the mess for our supper (not, we hoped, our last). Here was another source of annoyance for the 'chiefies' and old-sweat 'penguins' for it made some of them hopping mad to see us scoffing an egg and bacon (after a sortie only) when eggs were as scarce as television in Tibet. We also received extra chocolate and sweet rations, fruit juice and chewing gum (the latter was supposed to keep our mouths moist). I don't, however, remember tucking into a pile of carrots, eyesight for the use of.

Everything was ready; after the last aircraft had landed from air test and the empty bomb trolleys had been parked, a blanket of peace descended over the station. All was still as day turned to dusk and to darkness complete. Take-off wasn't late enough for us to grab some sleep so we played bridge in the mess. This was my first experience of the game but I found it absorbing and time-killing. It also kept my mind off thoughts of shells and bullets and searchlights and wings coming off and flames eating at my backside, of parachutes riddled with holes and other gruesome figments of a fertile imagination.

We didn't, as was sometimes supposed, wallow in brandy before departing for enemy shores although we might have found solace or Dutch courage in a few snifters. Perhaps one glass of beer was taken with a meal. Not only had we to prevent our faculties from slipping into a bewildered limbo but the customary calls of nature had to be discouraged at a time when it was least convenient to answer. For the gunner it meant vacating his turret, undoing his parachute harness, unzipping his Sidcot, lifting sundry sweaters, undoing more buttons etc. He then groped for the rubber 'bottle' which was clipped to the side of the fuselage, relieve…relief, then readjust the whole caboodle before climbing back into the turret feeling frozen in a place where he normally has warmth. During that time, no watch had been kept for night fighters.

For the same reason, flasks of hot coffee were rarely uncorked until well on the way back at a lower altitude and within spitting distance of friendly shores. Pilots were even more unfortunate in this respect for the Blenheim was not fitted with 'George' (automatic pilot). On one of my night flights, though, the aircraft began to perform like a circus horse with fleas. Lowering the turret seat I looked forward but could not discern what was happening. I enquired on the intercom. 'What the hell's going on up there?' in a friendly tone, of course. No answer. I gulped, and called again.

'Hello, hello, can you hear me?'

'All right, all right,' from the navigator, 'he's only having a leak.'

About an hour before take-off I wandered with others down to the hangar. We dressed slowly, for to sweat before flying at altitude was asking for frostbite; even in the autumn it was very cold at 20,000 feet. We then boarded the squadron bus, slumped down on the hard, cold seats and were driven off into the darkness. My two pals, Eric and Mac, got off at their respective aircraft, each with a cheerful 'See you at breakfast, Frank.' We always parted with some such expression and didn't consciously set any store on it. But one night Mac didn't utter a word when he left the bus. Eric and I thought it odd and wondered whether he was feeling a bit off colour. That night his aircraft hit the trees near the airfield when his pilot was going round again and had committed the *faux pas* of pulling the flaps up too soon. Mac alone survived the crash but his serious injuries kept him in hospital for a long time.

While on the subject of implied premonition, there was the case of a navigator who, after briefing, persisted in going the rounds telling everybody that he wasn't coming back that night. Naturally, he was told to 'belt up', 'don't be stupid' etc. His crew took him off but they never came back. Had it been the pilot who had made such a statement, then one could only arrive at the conclusion that he intended to commit suicide, maybe to evade his bank manager or his mother-in-law or something. But a navigator…?

While on the subject of navigators, there was the case of one of that happy breed who had been badly shot-up early in the war. After many months in hospital he was discharged and returned to the squadron. He had asked to go back on 'ops.' and was given a crew but as his aircraft approached the Dutch coast he lost his nerve and asked the pilot to return to base. The pilot tried to talk him out of it;

he told him that if he broke down then, it would be tantamount to throwing his flying career to the four winds. The navigator half-heartedly agreed and they pressed on until the searchlights began to flicker on ahead, first one, then two more, another and so on, until the sky was alight. This time he meant it when he asked the pilot to return. The pilot not unsympathetic, tried hard to help him over the first 'style' and said: 'No, old boy.' The navigator then selected the undercarriage 'down'. The pilot reversed the procedure. The flaps were then slammed down, the pilot 'upped' them and so it went on up, down, up, down, until the pilot just had to wheel round and return with his badly shaken navigator. One felt so sorry for such cases.

To 'un-digress'. At each dispersal, three men would leave the 3-tonner and waddle across to their aircraft which stood silently on its hard standing, the ground crew waiting patiently to help them into the machine before going about their various jobs.

'Number 3772' came a voice from outside the truck. This was our aircraft. With my signals satchel, parachute and thermos flasks, I clumped over to the port wing root from where we climbed up onto the wing and into our respective hatches. Sandy and 'Rich' made their way up the port wing and disappeared into the front cockpit. I dug my boots into the steps built into the fuselage side, lowered myself through the aft hatchway and climbed down the short, fixed ladder inside. The ground crew handed me my gear which I stowed in the appropriate places. Nothing must be loose for there was the danger of fouling the unguarded control cables. It was easy, too, for small objects to disappear beyond reach behind the armour plating aft of the radio and turret. Even my receiver coils were attached to pieces of string for fear that, in the darkness, cold fumbling hands would drop them when they might easily roll to an irretrievable position down in the tail.

Having shut and bolted the hatch, I killed some of the gloom by turning on a small glim lamp. Engaging my radio plug in one of the many sockets dangling from the fuselage formers, I flicked the microphone switch on and off. Hearing a lively crackle in the 'phones I knew that the intercom circuit was alive. Looking along the tunnel of the fuselage I could see the pilot and navigator beyond the 'well' (a hollowed-out part of the wing centre section, incorporating the main spar and in which was kept the TR9, the dinghy and other spares). The ever-present smell of petrol, oil and other typical aircraft odours fouled the air.

Sandy soon had himself strapped securely in his seat and gave
the signal to start the engines. The ground crew had already primed
the Mercurys by means of a small pump in the undercarriage
housing of each nacelle; the trolley-battery operator gave the
thumbs up sign. Sandy switched on the ignition and pushed the
starter button of first the port and then the starboard engine. The
propellers turned over in a squeaky, laboured sort of way until each
engine fired. The silence of the Suffolk countryside was shattered as
was the sleep of those in the vicinity. Oily smoke poured back over
the quivering tailplane while the aircraft stood there gently straining
against the chocks. When both engines had been run up and cockpit
drill had been completed, trimming tabs were neutralised, pitch
controls moved to 'fine' and compass set. There was a tap on my
hatch. I moved back and opened up; the undercarriage links (made
conspicuous with a red but oily flag, they locked the undercarriage
to prevent accidental retraction when the aircraft was on the ground.
By the same token, they prevented retraction when airborne) and
pitot-head covers were thrust into my hands. I slammed the hatch,
stowed them and crawled back into the turret.

'All OK in the back?'

'Yes, sir. Intercom OK, links and pitot cover in.'

'What about you, Rich?'

'Fine, can hear you both. Your first course is 064 magnetic.'

'Chocks away' was waved by Sandy and we started to taxi out.
At the end of the flarepath we stopped; a final check: lower 15° of
flap and wait for the 'green' from the duty controller in the caravan.
The Aldis flickered its 'go-ahead'. With engine gills closed we
turned into wind, the throttles were moved to the top of the gate and
we were rolling. Bouncing slightly over the uneven grass surface
we soon lifted off and climbed away into the night. With half a ton
of high explosive in the belly of the aircraft, it wasn't a fast rate of
climb. In my 'back to the engine' position I saw the single row of
flares disappear in the haze. The winking red glow of a flashing
beacon pierced the darkness at regular intervals until it, too, was
swallowed by the night.

Our route took us out over the Suffolk coast well to the north of
Harwich and its attendant balloon barrage. Climbing steadily to our
operational height over the North Sea, we turned onto a southerly
course and headed for the French coast. The Dunkirk episode came
to mind as we neared those very beaches. Swivelling my turret and

looking forward I could see searchlights clawing the sky. As we got
nearer, I saw my first flak (from the receiving end, that is). It was
being hose-piped towards an unseen target well ahead of us. It
ascended seemingly slowly as though it were tinsel being carried
aloft by playful cherubs. But when we got above it, that multi-
coloured stream of tracer whipped by the aircraft at its true and
lethal velocity. Another type of flak, 'flaming onions', was squirted
at us. Like a string of Christmas-tree decorations they ascended,
levelled out at our approximate height and exploded one after
another. The heavy flak one noticed only when it was close enough
to hear and smell, and that was close enough, thank you. On a
moonlit night their black puffs could easily be (and often were)
mistaken for balloons. I think that the most unnerving experience
was to look down and watch, hypnotised, the three-foot muzzle
flashes of a heavy anti-aircraft battery, then to wait to see how
accurate their aim was.

The firing was spasmodic after leaving the coast and as we flew
inland it became quieter below and above. Circling for a while, the
navigator picked out the target and the aircraft was lined up for the
bombing run. The 'Left, left…steady. Leftabit…steady…' of the
practice bombing days now took on grim reality. We were about to
discharge high explosives onto something, someone below. A
fleeting thought of horror was suddenly quelled when 'bombs
gone' coincided with a fresh burst of hostility from below.
Searchlights vied with each other in their groping for victims. A
master searchlight stood out more proudly than the others, its violet
hue stabbing even further into the heavens.

Between scanning the sky for night fighters and looking down
fascinated at the dark, unfriendly scene below, I wondered how
soon it would be before the comparatively frail alloy shell of our
aircraft was pierced by hot steel or thrown into sharp relief by a few
million candlepower. Having seen our bombs explode in the target
area, we wheeled round onto a reciprocal course and headed
homewards. We again ran the gauntlet at the coast but were soon
out of range. The pyrotechnics ceased and the searchlights
flickered out one by one, almost, it seemed, with a frustrated sigh
for allowing a fly to slip through their web.

Still keeping my eyes peeled for signs of air attack, I
occasionally got glimpses of tracer and searchlights astern until
distance dwarfed them and blackness finally engulfed all signs of

enemy activity. There followed a period of elation; a tranquillity I'd never known before but was to experience many, many times. As we approached the Suffolk coast I was feeling positively exuberant. We were practically home and dry but danger still lurked should there be night intruders in the base area.

It hadn't been a very difficult or dangerous sortie but as an overture to our tour of operations, it had had its moments and, over a steaming mug of coffee, these were related in detail to the intelligence officer (IO) at de-briefing (interrogation it was then called).

Four days were to pass before we made our next sortie. On the evenings when flying was cancelled (mostly because of bad weather) we caught a small private bus which rattled its way through twisting lanes to Stowmarket. On such a stand-down we let our hair down. There was little to do in that town other than boost the publicans' profits since, like most provincial towns (even the larger ones), it was 'dead' at about 9 pm. We would consume copious draughts of ale and, if our pockets could stand it, sometimes indulged in a Stowmarket black-market steak.

On the week-ends there was usually a 'village hop' where we would weave round the floor trying our best to decipher some of the local dialect which was whispered into our ears. Nearer to Wattisham was the small village of Barking Tye. On its green, stood a ye olde worlde pub in which I first saw performed the 'muffin man', the party piece of one of our navigators. It was amusing to watch but could be most uncomfortable to attempt. However, with several pints 'on board', who cared. A glass of beer was placed on the head and, without touching it, one rotated with sergeant-major erectness while singing the muffin man song. It might sound easy but when unsteady on one's undercarriage one could get awful wet. Anyway, the local inhabitants got a kick out of it and it was clean.

Quite a few of the lads had motor-cars of some sort or another for they could be bought for a song in those days. The big difficulty, of course, was the fuel situation. Seeing the ground crews filling their petrol lighters from an aircraft tank, the aviators with cars naturally thought that they were entitled to some. This, as you'd doubtless agree, was a sinful assumption. You might even argue that a wee drappie for a lighter is just within the law but to fill a gallon can is, during war-time, a crime, and you'd be right. But one thing you could not be expected to know was that in order to fill a lighter, one turned a small tap on the underside of the wing tank; it produced not the gentle pin-prick-squirt as from a penny refill but almost a raging torrent with a couple of grams in the lighter and a half gallon on the 'deck'.

It brings to mind the time when, prior to the visit of HM King George VI to Bicester, over 100 gallons of petrol were used to remove the grease from a hangar floor.

However, the cars were used sparingly; 100 octane for short local runs to local pubs and rationed 'pool' for longer journeys when, for example, one had a spot of leave.

Our second venture into hostile air space was to Deauville, a little to the south of Le Havre. It went smoothly enough; no worse, no easier than our first sortie. We landed after that trip at 5 am, so by the time I got my head down the sun was already high.

The following day the Squadron Commander flew us down to Hendon (Sandy was in the right-hand seat). Going back a few years when I watched, from nearby Mill Hill, the Hendon air displays by the Royal Air Force, I never dreamed that one day I would be landing there myself in a war-time bomber. It was purely a ferry flight. The 'Wingco' either had an appointment with somebody at the Air House or a spot of leave. We took off again immediately with home so near yet so far. The runway was a little on the short side for a Blenheim but we managed to clear the hangars on our approach to land and to stop before over-shooting into something substantially hard. On take-off we nearly 'bagged' the driver of the 11.35 am out of St Pancras.

At the end of August we were briefed for our third sortie. This time we were Germany-bound. The target was the north-German port of Emden, at the mouth of the River Ems. The approach from the North Sea meant crossing the Frisian Islands. Those heavily defended bastions, covered by a night-fighter patrol, afforded an effective shield for some of Germany's most vulnerable ports: Wilhelmshaven, Bremerhaven, Hamburg, Cuxshaven and Kiel (as well as, of course, Emden). Because of this, most attacks on them were delivered from an inland direction.

I found that after staring at the star-filled sky for a few hours and with the cold night air making one's eyes water, imaginary shapes would begin to lurk nearby. Horizontally-situated stars 'grew' wing spans and the undulating movement of the aircraft would make these apparitions move like the real thing. The harder one stared, the more convinced one would become that something was out there waiting to pounce. I often had my gun sights trained on such a phantom fighter because you couldn't be *too* careful.

When the full harvest moon lifted itself over the horizon one night, I mistook its hazy glow for a distant city blazing from end to end. 'The heavy boys are having a grand slam, tonight' I thought, until that barren satellite made itself known in its less orange-red hue as it climbed higher into the night sky. Flying above cloud on a moonlit night was also dangerous, for an aircraft's silhouette made a wonderful target for the unseen night fighter. If there was no moon, searchlights under the cloud gave the same effect. It was safer, therefore, to fly just above the tops or just beneath the base of cloud (provided that it wasn't too low) so that if attacked it took but a few seconds to dive into it. Of course, the height of the cloud base might be known to the gunners below so you just couldn't win!

Our next, the fourth, trip took place on the night of 7/8 September. We had been briefed to attack the docks at Dunkirk. Recce aircraft had brought back photographic evidence of a build-up of invasion barges there and at all the Channel ports (Antwerp, Ostend, Boulogne and Calais, included). On that night as we flew south over the North Sea, there was an ominous glow on the western horizon. This time it wasn't the moon but came from the direction of London, 100 miles to the west. A Londoner myself, I became anxious for the safety of my parents, relatives and friends but the full realisation of what had happened was not felt until the following morning when the BBC announced that the onslaught against the capital had started. The night-time blitzkrieg had replaced the dog-fights over Kent and the Home Counties; the Battle of Britain had become the Battle of London. When I heard the news, any feelings of guilt I harboured about dropping bombs on others were swiftly replaced by a grim determination to fight back and the ensuing attacks on invasion barges were carried out with an added sense of purpose by all, wherever they lived.

My fifth trip, on 9 September, was to Boulogne. For some reason I forget, I was not flying with Sandy (who had, incidentally, been promoted to F/Lt earlier that month) but with F/O Lynch-Blosse. This was followed by attacks, with my own crew, on Calais (twice), Dunkirk and Boulogne, on 11, 14, 16 and 18 September respectively.

The Channel ports, in late 1940, were among the most heavily defended targets I can remember. Hitler's intention of preserving his invasion fleet was made clear for his minions ferociously threw up everything but the kitchen sink. What made matters worse for us was the altitude at which we had been briefed to attack i.e. between 6,000 and 8,000 feet. At that height, light flak was at its deadliest. It came up like an inverted monsoon of vivid colour; from all directions it poured to culminate at the apex of a cone of searchlights. They were at the time, some of the most terrifying experiences of my life. 'How any aircraft can survive in that lot,' I thought as we made our bombing run, 'is a miracle.' But, as we found out, the age of miracles was not past and we came through unscathed. Many, of course, didn't and were seen to plummet, flaming pyres, earthwards. Those targets made our first two sorties look like a poor man's Guy Fawkes' night in heavy rain.

Towards the end of September, Sandy was posted for test-pilot duties at RAF Boscombe Down. I had already experienced losing one permanent crew (at OTU) and now I was to lose the second. This was the start of a 'bough-to-bough' existence for me but in the long run it may have been my salvation, who knows?

I kept in touch with Sandy for many years. He finished his Service career with the rank of Wing Commander and earned for himself the AFC for his contribution to test flying. After the war he was, for three years, the CFI at the Empire Test Pilots' School at Farnborough where some of the world's best pilots have been trained as test pilots. Sandy's first two books, *Test Flight* and *Men with Wings* were the outcome of his interesting flying career.

There was no niche for me until the end of the first week in October. I spent the last eight days of September flying peaceably around East Anglia with other pilots on the squadron: S/Ldr Young, P/O Yarrow, P/O Parry, Sgt DeLittle until I crewed up with F/Lt Lyon.

Oddly enough it was many months before I was told that F/Lt Lyon was the husband of Mary (of mixed-grill fame at Bicester). Our first op. together began at midnight on 7 October. The target was Boulogne. It was a trip which didn't differ much from the previous ones until we got back to base. It had been my tenth sortie and I was still in one piece. In the usual way we had identified ourselves and had been given a 'green' to land. There was some ground haze but nothing to worry unduly about. We made a long, low, motored approach, the pilot lining up the aircraft with the row of goose-neck flares. When about a mile from the airfield boundary, he switched on the landing lamp (set in the port wing leading edge). Always keen to watch the approach, I noticed that the angle of glide indicators were showing red, we were coming in too low. I looked down and saw the dim outline of trees whipping by beneath the wing; they looked too damn close for comfort and a feeling of impending disaster began to creep through my bones. It was uncanny how one sensed real danger. However, we managed to reach the 'fence' without hitting anything but by that time the aircraft had drifted off course and we were no longer in line with the flarepath.

A burst of power indicated that the pilot had decided to go round again. Phew! I had, by then, managed to get all my fingers and toes crossed. I prayed that he wouldn't pull the flaps up too soon since we had lost several crews and aircraft that way. Not until reaching about 500 feet should the flaps be lifted as the Blenheim (and most other aircraft, too) had the tendency, when doing so, to sink rapidly.

Meanwhile, we were racing low over the airfield, the landing lamp carving a path of light across the grass. We were so low that I could almost have picked up a flare as we crossed the 'path'; there was still no indication of the nose being pulled up to gain height. I repeated my prayer about the flaps in 48-point bold italics. It was still dark and I had no idea in which direction we were heading. Would we hit the hangars or the trees at the far side of the 'field? At the height he maintained it could be either and soon. Still gaping forward, I suddenly saw and felt the port wing drop. This was it. It was; a sudden blinding flash, a few stars, then stillness.

I found myself standing in the fuselage with my feet in the turret cupola which was on the ground. It had become lighter, the reason becoming horrifyingly apparent when looking round I saw flames licking their way down the fuselage. Through the turret perspex I saw bits and pieces burning on the grass outside my 'prison', for I was trapped. The ladder was wedged across my back barring the exit through the camera hatch. There was no way out aft. My immediate thought was, 'The only chance I've got is for somebody to start cutting from the outside, but quick.'

Looking round to my left I noticed a jagged hole in the fuselage side. It was big enough for my head to go through. Through it went and with strength lent by desperation I braced my feet on the facing wall and pushed. A gallon of Guinness wouldn't have bettered my efforts. My shoulders were fortunately protected by a thick leather

Irvin jacket and parachute harness webbing. The metal skin gave and I fell out into the night air then lit by the raging fire.

I saw two men running towards me: the duty medical officer and one of the ambulance crew (they and the fire crew were on the spot very smartly and went about their work without thought for their personal safety) grabbed me by the arms and hurried me to the gaping doors of the ambulance. Any moment the fuel tanks would explode and throw their blazing contents in all directions, as would the oxygen bottles and my ammunition. Before getting into the 'blood wagon' I noticed the pilot staggering from one side of the blazing wreckage and the navigator from the other side. They had miraculously scrambled clear through the smashed-in front section. Both had faces covered with blood but they were alive and on their feet.

The ambulance moved off quickly and as we pulled away we heard the bang and whine of an oxygen bottle getting airborne; my ammunition started to go off in fits and starts. 'Keep your heads down,' said the MO. As we drew further away from the airfield, silence returned broken only by the softly purring Albion engine. I was shepherded into station sick quarters; the pilot and navigator were whisked away to a civil hospital in Ipswich. I learned later that they had both been concussed, not surprisingly, and that the pilot had a broken jaw. I was lucky to get away with a deep cut on the back of my head and a torn thigh which I picked up when getting out of that jagged hole like a human tin-opener. A corporal dressed my wounds and gave me the customary anti-tetanus jab. As I stood up to be led to a nice soft bed, the reaction set in. The room got darker and began to spin but a few moments with my head between my knees brought me back to normal. Once in bed I was given the finest cigarette I had ever smoked and the most delicious mug of hot sweet tea that I can remember. As I sipped and puffed, I thought of the 'line' I'd be able to shoot the following morning. I was so thankful that we had all survived, God knows how, for we had hit the ground at well over 100 mph.

Later, as I lay back going over the whole business, I came to some pretty startling conclusions:

'I must have instinctively ducked before impact, otherwise I would have been decapitated...'

'That gash in my head had happened in the crash...supposing I had been knocked out? ... I'd have fried...'

'Supposing the pilot hadn't turned when he did…we would have hit something head-on…and that meant certain death at 150 mph…'

And so the stark possibilities whirled in my mind. What a night! Sleep was not yet possible. Then the visitors came. The Squadron CO, the engineer officer and the duty pilot. I was asked what had happened. I told them all I saw for there wasn't much more I could say. They had to draw their own conclusions as to the possible cause. After offering their congratulations on my lucky escape, they left. The duty officer added before leaving: 'When I saw your aircraft hit the "deck" I automatically wrote you all off. It was, I'm happy to say, a miracle how you got away with it.'

It was nearly 4 am when I dropped off into a dreamless sleep.

I still possess a snapshot, taken surreptitiously by one of the ground crew the following morning. Although slightly blurred by camera shake, it shows a heap of tangled, charred metal, all that was left of Blenheim No. L.9310. And so ended my one and only sortie with 'Mr Mary'. It was his *only* sortie, too, for a few months later his body was found in the middle of an airfield. Apparently he had been hit by an aircraft. The details were, however, vague and to this day I don't really know how he met his demise.

It wasn't long before I was discharged from sick bay and I made my way to the Flight office. The MO had told me to get flying again just in case I lost my nerve. I sought audience with my Flight Commander, S/Ldr Young.

'Hello, Henry. Congratulations on your escape. How d'you feel?'

'Fine, thank you sir. The MO has recommended that I fly pretty soon. He thinks that I might crack up or something. Would it be possible to have a trip in the "Maggie"?'

I was always eager to fly in different types of aircraft and I knew that the Station Commander had a Miles Magister (a small low-wing monoplane) tucked away in one of the hangars.

'Well, I don't know about that but I'll see what can be done to get you airborne in something. Hang around for a bit, will you.'

'Thanks very much, sir.'

I didn't get a trip in the Maggie and never have, since. Instead, I flew with P/O 'Dolly' Arderne to Horsham St Faith (near Norwich) where we had lunch before doing some air-firing over the Wash and returning to Wattisham.

During those flights and for some time to come, I was to smell burning petrol, oil and paint. On every approach to land, Henry was out of his turret and standing by the hatch ready for a speedy getaway. But I felt no fear of flying as such only the approach to land. That fear eventually wore off.

I only did one operation with Dolly, to Boulogne again four nights after my crash. This, my eleventh sortie, started earlier than the previous trips. We took off at 6.30 pm and were back, safe and sound, just after 9 pm in time for a few snifters in the mess before bed.

At about that time, 110 Squadron was taken over by W/Cdr Sutcliffe. When I was posted early in 1941 to 101 Squadron, West Raynham, I received the following letter from him:

> *Dear Henry*
>
> *I am afraid I did not see you to say good-bye as I had to go to Ipswich to see His Worship The Mayor.*
>
> *I am very sorry to lose you but am afraid it cannot be helped, as we are not allowed to keep spare people or those who are not crewed up. However, I hope you like your new Squadron and also hope that you will keep in touch with us and will eventually return.*
>
> *I would like to thank you very much indeed for all the good work you have done whilst you have been with us.*
>
> *Yours sincerely*
>
> *(Sgnd) W P Sutcliffe, W/Cdr*

He didn't *have* to write such a letter which made it the more pleasurable to receive and keep.

* * *

My score, eleven operations with four pilots, moved up to twelve with my fifth pilot, P/O Bennett. My one wish was to settle down with a regular crew but this was not to be. No. 12 differed from the straight-forward bombing attacks we had already completed, in that it was a 'night intruder' operation. This meant that we stooged around a given area of neighbouring occupied territory to hamper the *Luftwaffe's* flying activities. Our bomb load included some 40 lb. anti-personnel bombs.

The forty-pounder was a nasty little beast. Whereas one could drop safe a 250 or 500 lb. HE bomb from a height of up to 500 feet, the 40 lb. variety would go off if dropped from chest height. There was no real safety device incorporated. During maximum efforts, some bright chairborne spark got the idea of carrying two forty-pounders in each flare rack, under the wing between fuselage and each engine nacelle. All very well to increase our load by 160 lb. but had they seen the number of flares coming adrift during a bumpy take-off, they might have reconsidered that move. It was, after all, risking £20,000-worth of aeroplane and three lives for the sake of four little, horrible bombs. Still, as we were often reminded by cheeky barmaids and shop assistants, there was a war on.

That intruder night of 27 October added the further experience of icing to my fast-growing list. We had flown to the target area on DR (dead-reckoning navigation) because of ten-tenths cloud. We were to make a nuisance of ourselves over the Lille/Douai area of Northern France. In order to frustrate the *Luftwaffe* we had to see the ground, so 'Ben' put the nose down to make a turning descent through that cloud mass. Sitting there dreaming as there was no point in scanning for fighters in that swirling vapour, I suddenly noticed a pinging noise on my turret cupola. It was some minutes before I realised that it was ice breaking adrift from the leading edges of the wings (they had been plastered with anti-icing paste). There was still no sign of levelling out and we had been losing height for what seemed ages. Looking forward I saw the soft, ghostly glow of the exhausts in the all-enveloping cloud. It was just like driving through a London pea-souper. Hearing not a 'dickie bird' from the pilot or navigator, I called up to find out if all was well. There was no reply. I called again. Still no reply. Suddenly we levelled out under the cloud base so obviously we were still under control. 'Ben' had, naturally, wanted to clear those icing conditions soonest and had been engrossed with the altimeter reading. The cloud base was down to about 1,500 feet and it was pelting with rain below it.

As might be imagined, it was most disconcerting to get no reply on the intercom. This happened to me several times. It happened, in fact, on my next trip with Ben. It brought to mind the story of a Whitley that had crash-landed by itself earlier in the war. The rear gunner opened his turret doors, clambered into the fuselage to find no sign of movement. 'They must have got out pretty smartly', he thought. Leaving the aircraft he still saw no sign of life in the immediate vicinity and the story, said to be true, went on: the Whitley had been badly shot up and the pilot had ordered the crew to bale out, then he left himself after seeing an apparently empty aeroplane. He was not to know that 'tail-end-Charlie' was still in his turret, oblivious of the parlous state of his aircraft, not having received the pilot's message. His intercom plug had either been pulled from its socket (a common enough occurrence) or it was out of action. The age of miracles, again.

However, having established that all was in order, I looked down upon the scene below. To my astonishment, there were lights everywhere. 'Don't they know there's a war on,' said Ben. 'It's like bloody Blackpool in peace time.' We had arrived on the scene without warning, that much was clear. We saw an airfield ahead lit up like a Christmas tree. The flarepath was on and the nav. lights of an aircraft could be seen moving along it. In the circuit there were several aircraft, all with nav. lights ablaze, cutting through the rain just below the cloud base. It was a heaven-sent opportunity.

'Can you fly alongside and a little below one of them, Ben?' I asked, excitedly, for here was a situation that even Walter Mitty couldn't dream up.

'OK, will do.'

Just as we were overhauling a large four-engined job (either a Junkers 90 or a Fw. 200 Condor), the navigator who couldn't resist the brightly lit target below, let go some of the bomb load. Almost immediately the lights went out and the aircraft in the circuit nipped into cloud. Other lights came on for three or four streams of red tracer and a couple of searchlights made a bee-line for our position. We, too, climbed hurriedly into the murk and away to try to locate another airfield. Meanwhile, I was mouthing obscenities at the navigator. The only 'printable' remark I made was: 'Why, you "mickey-mouse-happy" clot. What did you go and do that for?'

('Mickey mouse' was, for some obscure reason, the term used for a type of bomb release which permitted bombs to be dropped in a long, medium or short stick, rather than the push-button type for a salvo.)

I had been cheated. I was irked. The dream of every air-gunner had been rudely shattered by an impatient navigator. His bombs could have been dropped with effectiveness, later.

We flew around for over two hours that night, dropping a few bombs here and there but we didn't see another enemy aircraft. However our aim, to disrupt the enemy's night-flying programme (in that area), had been fulfilled.

Back in the operations room, I learned to my chagrin that one of the gunners had reported having shot down a Junkers 90 for which effort his pilot was awarded the DFC.

The only other occasion I remember when we saw an enemy aircraft taking off with its nav. lights ablaze, happened when we were returning from Germany one night. Approaching Gilze Rijen (between Breda and Tilburg in the Netherlands), we saw a large flarepath flicker on. A Junkers 88 (we found out later) took off from it and set course in the direction of Rotterdam (going our way, to England?). My pilot opened the 'taps' to catch him up but before we could close with him, his nav. lights were doused (as was the flarepath) and he was swallowed by the night. Just my luck!

On 1 November, the day before my twentieth birthday, we were, by way of a change, to be on the 'receiving end' for Wattisham suffered an early-morning air attack.

There had been a preliminary air-raid warning (sounded on the guardroom steam-whistle) followed by the all-clear a few minutes later. I was sitting up in bed toying with the idea of leaping out of it when a few seconds later my mind was made up for me. Without warning, a Dornier bomber roared across the roof-tops machine-gunning as it went. The frosted glass of a window opposite shattered as bullets tore through it to 'thunk' into the wall beside me. Before you could say 'a' I was out and under the bed dragging my mattress with me, self-preservation being a particularly strong part of my make-up.

There followed, from the direction the attacker had come, the sound of explosions for the delayed-action bombs were going off. Nearer and nearer came each ground-shaking crash. Soon, I thought, it would be our turn, for the aircraft had gone directly overhead. There was a deafening crash and our room was filled with brick dust and the acrid smell of spent explosive. I found myself shaking like an aspen and on all-fours among a carpet of fragmented glass. Then came the shouts and screams from across the hall in our block and from the other barrack block on the far side of the square.

Sorting myself out, I quickly dragged on my battle dress and shoes and went outside to see whether anything could be done. As I reached the door I was nearly sick when seeing a chap being carried out, minus head. We discovered later that it was our room orderly. He was a wonderful lad, always punctual and ever cheerful as he went about his job of sweeping our room. For the first time that we could remember, he had overslept.

The casualty list was high. Later we saw how the bomb which

had hit our block had been deflected from its course (to our side of
the block) by bouncing badly on the square, the dent in the asphalt
telling the story. It had pierced the wall, exploded inside and had
brought down the flat concrete roof, crushing nearly all beneath it.

When the raider was about half-way back to its base, our air-
raid siren sounded. Not realising that it was the result of a time-lag
on somebody's part, we went underground, but speedily.

The only amusing incident on that terrible morning was the
sight of Tom Hoggard (Doran's gunner) staggering out of the
ablutions holding an egg-size lump on his head. During the attack
he was about to wash, instead he ducked under the doubtful
protection of the wash basin. The bomb explosion blew the door
from its hinges and caught Tom right across the backside, almost
pushing his head through the wall.

I went on leave the following morning. The first three days I
spent with friends in Stowmarket. Before catching my train to
London and the blitz I saw, from a distance, another air attack on
Wattisham. It was really being given the once-over.

At the end of my leave I was thankful to return. I hadn't liked
being cooped up in the cellar at home for most of the night. Perhaps
my first taste of bombing and the sights I saw at Wattisham on that
November morning, accounted for my dread of air attack. One thing
I was sure about, that being shot at in an aircraft was preferable to
cringing in an air-raid shelter. I feel sure that most aircrew felt the
same way, even though the balance of odds might favour the shelter-
dwellers. Psychologically, it felt better to be mobile and to sit
behind two machine-guns, albeit useless against AA shell-fire.
Nevertheless, I held the greatest respect for the civilian population
of Britain's major cities, London in particular. When on leave, I was
always given such a friendly welcome by those who spent a lot of
their time on the platforms of London's underground network. Their
cheerful cockney stoicism never seemed to flag.

'Give the bastards what for,' they would say as I walked by.

'Good luck to yer, son,' and so on, mostly with a broad grin and
a raised thumb and even a pat on the back.

There were many raids on Wattisham while I was there. The
most effective attack, as far as the enemy were concerned was
again carried out at nought feet in daylight. Its consequences were
to make themselves felt for quite a time. Despite the newfangled
rocket device dreamed up by some boffin (and which could have

been effective against low-flying aircraft had it been installed in sufficient numbers and used at the right time), three Dorniers made three runs, with impunity, over the camp. They dropped a new weapon. Known as the 'butterfly bomb', it was a small cylindrical canister (about the size of a $\frac{1}{2}$ lb. cocoa tin). Attached to it was a fusing wire which turned under the influence of two propeller-like vanes as the bomb fell. In spite of its size, it was a deadly anti-personnel contraption. Scores of them were dropped all over RAF Wattisham, many of them on the airfield. Some went off, the majority lay unexploded all over the place for they had been dropped too low for complete fusing.

All flying was cancelled until every one of them had been found and dealt with. So small were they that their position was concealed by the grass. All ranks were mustered and issued with a bundle of sticks. Before making a sweep of the airfield, in line abreast, we were told: 'If you see one, don't touch it. Just mark the spot with a stick and move on. Be very careful if you don't want your feet or your genitals blown off.'

With those encouraging words ringing in our ears we proceeded, with utmost caution, to tread the grass. When the job had been done, armourers went out with a van to collect them. While this was going on I happened to be talking to someone by the control tower. There was an explosion on the 'field; a small puff of black smoke hovered in the still air at the site of the tragedy, for tragedy it was. A sergeant armourer had gently picked up one of the canisters and it had exploded in his hands. He lay there on the grass with his stomach sagging out. Nothing could be done for him and he died a couple of minutes later, the second casualty during the clearing operation.

The Royal Navy bomb disposal people were the only ones with experience of those ghastly little weapons. They were contacted for advice and were horrified to hear that the unexploded bombs had been put 'safely' in the bomb dump. It was made quite clear that the slightest vibration might set one off which, of course, meant the lot and others besides. Even the noise of the engines of a low-flying aircraft could trigger one. The 'web-footed' types came to Wattisham and courageously moved the canisters elsewhere and detonated them by very remote control. From that day I raised my cap to anybody connected with bomb disposal.

The two squadrons had been grounded for the best part of forty-eight hours. The corporal in charge of the rockets was still at his post, unable to push the 'fire' button without the permission of an officer!

It had been nearly a month since I last stuck two fingers up at the enemy ground defences. On 23 November, I flew with 'Ben' (operationally) for the second and last time which was my thirteenth sortie. This time we were to smarten up Dortmund in the Ruhr, or 'Happy Valley' as it was called with some respect by bomber crews. The trip was uneventful as far as we were concerned but I think that it was the night when I saw an aircraft plunge to the ground in flames (it was, according to the BBC, the one aircraft missing that night). There had been a moderate amount of heavy flak and masses of searchlights in the target area (fifty miles in diameter, from Gelsenkirchen to Cologne and from Dortmund to Krefeld).

Before crossing our own coast on return, we had always to request a bearing (QDM) from base because of the aircraft we had lost to the Harwich balloon barrage. One Blenheim had, in fact, been plotted in the Thames estuary heading west and it wasn't heard of again. A magnetic course of 278° or less was the permissible limit for crossing the Suffolk/Norfolk coast.

That night, as our aircraft flew up and down the coast at about 1,500 feet, I had my head down in the turret waiting patiently to pound the morse key. The frequency was busy and radio etiquette demanded that wireless operators should wait their turn before transmitting. There were many who ignored this courtesy and caused undue chaos on the air. Suddenly the aircraft started to yaw and one of the engines sounded like a broken-down sewing machine. Elevating my seat I looked out to see a stream of what looked like red-hot cinders streaming aft from the starboard exhausts. Then the port engine followed suit, and the aircraft was almost falling out of the sky. Ben put the nose down, at least that's what I hoped he had done. I called up on the intercom. No reply. I called again, still no reply. Depressing my seat I looked forward up the fuselage. I could see signs of life. The navigator. torch in hand, was wrestling with something on the right-hand side of the cockpit. I called again.

'It's all right, Frank. We forgot to switch over the fuel tanks, and the engines got a bit starved,' was the calm-as-you-like reply. Before the stranglehold on the carburettors had been released we had dropped to about 350 feet.

When Sandy had been posted I was transferred to 'B' Flight under the command of S/Ldr MacDougall. This gentleman, formerly

an Army officer, was labelled 'the mad major' because, although a
most competent pilot, he had an appetite for pushing the crews to
their limit. Quite often, after a night sortie followed by the time-
consuming interrogation and breakfast, we were despatched into the
air again for formation practice while the 'A' Flight crews had their
heads down on a soft pillow. I quote one instance: We had completed
a four-and-a-half hour flight to the Ruhr (taking off at 4.45 am and
landing at 9.15 am) and by the time we had switched off engines, got
interrogated, cleaned guns and had breakfast, 'twas 11 am. We were
back in the air at 11.30 for an hour's formation practice.

The crews were getting tired and some even verging on
rebellion. So much so that Mac's navigator thought the time had
come tactfully to broach the subject with his pilot. We were
assembled round the massive crewroom table (larger than a full-size
billiard table) and waited for the skin and hair to fly. He entered
quietly and got straight to the point in the most friendly manner.

'I understand that there is some feeling among you that I'm a
hard taskmaster. Before I say my piece, perhaps somebody will
fill in the details.'

Fair enough! One of the more senior pilots spoke up on our
behalf. Mac listened attentively and having heard our views
admitted that we had worked a little harder than the other flight and
squadron. He had, however, thought it necessary because of the
prevailing situation.

'We might be called upon soon to fly operationally in daylight
and our formation flying must be at its best for you all know what
happens to stragglers. However, as you feel strongly about the need
for more rest after night flying, I'll watch that point. But the
practice formation flying must be kept up, we all need it and it is
for all our sakes. Any more questions?'

Terse stuff but a sincere approach to our gripe. There was a
general response of 'No, sir,' and off he went. One had to hand it
to Mac for he was indefatigable. Whether it was due to the effects
of insomnia or Sandhurst blues didn't matter, for he, too, would
fly by night, breakfast, shave and be back in the air with the rest
of us. He was a small man, about the same stamp and just as
determined as Basil Embry.

Between operational trips we buzzed hither and thither on a
variety of training flights. My favourite jaunt was to visit another
station, have lunch and return 'home' the same afternoon. On 5

December I went on such a trip to RAF Ternhill, near Market Drayton in Shropshire. That delightful county we flew over a lot, using Ludlow Castle as a turning point. My pilot on the outward leg was F/Lt 'Don' Gericke but my log records the fact that Sergeant Stone flew me back, so Don must have had a hard date in the area.

Don Gericke was, I heard later, shot down and got himself put in the 'bag'. I was most surprised to meet up with him six years later at Nuremberg. He was a S/Ldr and flew one of the Mosquito aircraft allocated to the 'UK/Fürth International Military Tribunal Courier Flight', in other words he flew out mail (then the fastest mail run in the world, so it was claimed) from England to the Press Camp.

Still a spare gunner on the Squadron I fell for the odd jobs one of which I'll never forget: duty beacon NCO. At dusk I would be driven to a site about five miles from the airfield and dumped there with a caravan and a flashing beacon on its trailer. The beacon, operated by a motor generator, was not unlike the flarepath chance light. Its vertical zigzag, neon-like tubes would blink its message throughout the night, the powerful red light visible for many miles from an aircraft. The identification letters, flashed in morse, could be changed by the insertion of a disc round the edge of which variably-spaced cams made and broke the circuit. Quite simple really until the bloody thing broke down. This happened to me once in the early hours just as our aircraft were due back in the circuit. I had to flash the letters by hand, lifting a heavy contact breaker up and down for what seemed an eternity.

It was not unknown for the beacons to be machine-gunned by high-spirited *Luftwaffe* pilots. Fortunately, I didn't suffer from such an outburst of levity. I did, nonetheless, have an amusing experience when the beacon had been plonked in a narrow country lane, bang outside a small, white stuccoed church. The beacon had started its stammering message, casting its reddish glow on the trees and hedgerows and on the church. I hadn't been there for long when the vicar came out. Wringing his hands he said 'Sergeant, would you please move that light somewhere else? As you perceive, it lights up my church and it might lead to its being bombed.'

Hastily, I reassured him about the bombing but brought on the pains again by mentioning that the beacons were normally *only* machine-gunned. He again pleaded for its removal. I then had to explain without disclosing military secrets, that the lamp was in a set map-referenced position and that the crews of many aircraft, would, later that night, be depending on it when returning from the 'other side'. In any case, I hadn't the authority nor the means of shifting it and that it would only be there for a couple of nights, anyhow.

He thanked me all the same, said good night, and wandered off, his retreating figure turning from black to dah-dit-dah red, until he disappeared from view behind the vicarage bushes. A little later he came out and gave me some apples. How nice.

A few nights later, on 10 December, I found myself on the battle order for my fourteenth op. with my sixth crew. The pilot, Sergeant Harvey Wright, had 'lost' his regular gunner; Sgt Cornwall had been sent to RAF Hospital, Ely, with a suspected punctured eardrum, which meant certain grounding.

The three trips I did with Harvey and Norman (the navigator's surname is lost in the maze of my memory) were full of excitement. The first of them was to Bremen where we were to 'prang' the Focke Wulf aircraft works. Take-off was scheduled for 3 am and the Met report was far from good. Before crossing the Dutch coast on that moonless night, we ran into an extensive front, its ceiling too high for us to climb above and its centre possibly far too turbulent to risk, so we flew under it at about 1,500 feet. We hoped that it would clear near the target.

It was so black as we crossed the coast (not even a searchlight) that we could barely distinguish it. We got the usual pinpoints from two most useful lighthouses, Den Helder in the north and Haamstede to the south.

I suspected night fighters since the absence of flak was often indicative of their presence. Rotating my turret to keep an even sharper lookout, I saw out of the corner of my eye a glow coming from the front of the aircraft. Looking round my mouth went dry for radiating from the front compartment was a blaze of light, accentuated by the extreme darkness around us.

'What the hell have you got on up front? We can be seen for bloody miles,' I shouted.

'Not to worry, Norman is reading the paper.'

'Not to worry!' I answered in my best falsetto. 'If you could see how much light is pouring out up there, you would worry.'

'There's no activity below, Frank, and we are flying low enough to pass for a "friendly" aircraft. If we are attacked we're near enough to cloud to make a quick disappearing act,' said Harvey, conclusively.

'And get knotted,' from Norman as he returned to his paper, undoubtedly the sports page.

'I suppose you're right,' I murmured dubiously, 'and as for you Norman, there's a time and place for everything. No wonder I am always wearing my fingers to the bone getting bearings for you when you sit there like a lounge lizard instead of poring over your charts.'

'Do you know Sevenoaks, Frank?'

'Yes. Why?'

'Well, stuff six of them...' This from the navigator and roars of laughter from them both. I joined in. They were absolutely incorrigible.

'Oh, Frankie,' from Norman, five minutes later.

'Yep?'

'You may stuff the seventh now.'

Harvey was right. We flew across Holland and into Germany unmolested. Not a squeak from the ground. It was eerie. Nearing the target, Harvey thought it wise to climb a bit for the cloud had thinned out a little but its base was lower. At our ETA we were flying at about 8,000 feet but we couldn't see the ground. We circled for a long time hoping to find a 'hole' down through which we could descend, or bomb through it if it was above the target and big enough. We found one break but all that could be seen was a dark patch of ground broken by a stretch of autobahn on which could be seen the lights of traffic. We tried to get down through the hole and under the cloud but it was quickly lost. By that time those below must have got suspicious of our movements because two or three strings of pinkish tracer whipped through the cloud. For thirty minutes or so we stooged round and round without luck.

'We'll have to abandon,' said Harvey. 'Give me a course for the secondary target, please Norman...Ostend isn't it?'

'Yep, coming up.'

I couldn't resist it: 'Shall I tune in to Ostend control and get a bearing for you, Norman?'

'Try 240 magnetic for size and ignore that bum in the back,' came back Norman.

We found Ostend all right and got the usual Channel-port reception. We returned the compliment by straddling shipping in the harbour with four 250-pounders. This was after a cheeky dummy run throughout which I nearly gave birth to half a dozen kittens. We landed at base five-and-a-half hours after take-off, Harvey rounding off the trip with an excellent three-pointer.

What I liked about that crew was their calmness and lack of fuss even if they were possessed of the cheek of the devil. But they were efficient and took no undue risks; I sat in the back seat with every confidence in their abilities and that meant a lot to a gunner in his isolated post. I was to find out how much it meant later in my flying career.

Our next trip (three days before Christmas day) was even more exciting. We took off at 4.45 am to locate and attack the oil refinery at Gelsenkirchen in the Ruhr. I had studied the target map after briefing for I could assist the navigator to look for the outstanding landmarks as I had a clearer view from the aperture in my turret. I had noted, for instance, that there was an 'L' shaped wood and a racecourse near the target. There were many decoys in 'Happy Valley': dummy factories, false fires, camouflaged lakes etc. The only thing they couldn't camouflage was the fast-flowing Rhine. That twisty river was an excellent landmark. Just as well since the other off-putting thing about the Ruhr was the large number of towns practically merging with one another. For example, Gelsenkirchen is ringed with the following towns (within a five-mile radius) Gladbeck, Buer, Bismark, Wanne, Herne, Eickel, Horst, Hessler, Altenessen, Katernberg, Bochold, Wattensheid, Steele, Bochum, Essen and sundry other linking villages. You can therefore imagine the problems involved in the identification of a target in that area notwithstanding the other hindrances of searchlights and flak.

We milled around for what seemed ages trying to find the target. I caught sight of the wood once or twice but by the time the aircraft had been turned they were lost to view. Eventually, Norman sighted the target; Harvey did a hasty line-up and the bombs were dropped. Neatly evading a potent burst of anger from below we turned sharply onto a westerly course for home. Now facing the east I could see a tinge of light on the cloudless horizon. Dawn was approaching fast and we had just over 100 miles (about forty minutes flying time) to go before clearing the enemy coast.

'Better step on it, Harvey,' I said, trying to conceal my anxiety. 'The sun'll be up soon and there isn't a cloud to be seen.'

'Christ yes. Look at the time…I'll put on some more coal.'

After crossing the Rhine and over open country, Harvey put the nose down and we flew at about 1,000 feet, skimming the top of a purplish haze. We had been flying for about thirty minutes when the intercom burst into life with a startling crackle.

'What's our ETA at the coast, Norman?'

'Er...let me see...yes, I make it about 7.35.'

'We should be over Holland, then?'

'Yes...should be.'

Looking down from my perch I could see that the countryside below bore no resemblance to the canal-strewn landscape of Holland. On we flew. ETA came and went. Still no sign of the coast. 'Shall I get a bearing?' I asked, hoping to be of help.

'No, better not, Frank,' replied Harvey, 'we are too vulnerable to give ourselves away. It looks as though we have been accepted as a "friendly" so far. Keep a sharp lookout for landmarks, I think we are well to the south of course.'

Blast the landmarks that was Norman's job. It was quite light by that time and my eyeballs ached from searching the sky. No opposition at all up to then, but 'any moment now' was my constant thought. Eventually we identified Brussels on the starboard side. The wind must have backed and had blown us way off course. We crossed the French coast a little to the east of Calais at about 8.15 am and it wasn't until we were well over the North Sea that we saw some cloud cover. How we had traversed half of Europe in dawn/daylight conditions at 1,000 feet without being intercepted I shall never know. Perhaps sheer audacity coupled with our south-westerly track saved us from being pounced and trounced.

Before landing at base at 9.15 am Harvey flew low three times over my girl-friend's home in Stowmarket. This was just to let her know that I was home safely. When we landed, however, it was discovered that there was a 250 lb. bomb hanging up. I often wonder what the reaction would have been in that peaceful little town had the thing come adrift. Even if it hadn't exploded, 250 pounds of steel would have bent something. The bomb doors of a Blenheim were spring loaded, the weight of the bomb(s) was sufficient to open them, unlike the bomb doors of the bigger bombers which were hydraulically operated.

On 9 January 1941 I did the third and last trip with Harvey and Norman. The target was Gelsenkirchen again. Our previous visit there had taken four-and-a-half flying hours, this time we logged five-and-three-quarter hours. The primary target was abandoned because of bad weather but we must have been over the target area for ages since we had not got lost that night and had bombed the secondary (Rotterdam harbour) on the way out. We were back before midnight as our take-off had been an early one – 5.30 pm.

A few days later Harvey's gunner returned to the squadron. He had a chit to say that his ear'ole was all right. Naturally, he went back to his own crew leaving me spare 'joe' once again. On their next trip they had been kept waiting for a 'green' before take-off so that their engines had overheated and had cut on take-off. The three of them perished amid their own bomb load. Needless to say I was shattered. While I was relieved to have been spared, they were a wonderful crew and I felt their loss tremendously.

Not long before that tragedy, Harvey had bought two small Austin Sevens for a couple of pounds apiece. One had a good engine but a battered and useless body while the other was a nice little car with a clapped out engine. He got to work on them and produced a very nice motor-car out of the bits.

The four of us were leaving camp one evening in that car bound for Colchester when Harvey was stopped by the Service Police.

'Might we look in the car please, Sergeant?'

'Sure, help yourself,' said Harvey.

I sat there sweating because under a blanket between my legs, a two-gallon can of 100 octane petrol was getting 'hot'. One of them spotted it and politely (only in deference to rank) asked me to move. Lifting the blanket he extracted the can with a triumphant smirk on his face – oh how those SPs loved to put the finger on somebody.

'May I pour a little, Sergeant?' he asked, already unscrewing the cap and impatient to pounce. Harvey couldn't very well object.

'I have reason to believe that this is 100 octane, green petrol property of His Majesty's Government,' said the SP ('Had reason to believe...' the silly b knew it was.)

'Yes, you're right,' agreed Harvey, resignedly.

'I would like one of you to accompany me to the guardroom and the driver to follow with the car, please.'

In the guardroom, the can was placed in a bag and, in our presence, sealed. A formal charge was made out against Harvey who had nobly admitted full responsibility. He was later found guilty of the charge and we were thankful that nothing more serious than a severe reprimand resulted from it. Norman's remarks about service policemen would burn a hole right through this paper were they printed.

My last three flights with 110 Squadron were with S/Ldr MacDougall: a quick visit to Harwell and return and some formation practice. A few days later I was posted to No. 101 Squadron, under the command of W/Cdr Singer, at West Raynham in Norfolk. Equipped with Blenheim IVs, the squadron's letters were 'SR'. The sister squadron, No. 18 ('FV'), flew from West Raynham's satellite, Great Massingham, a few miles down the road.

West Raynham is about seven miles from Fakenham and just over thirty from Norwich. The nearest railway station to the camp was about a mile away and formed part of the Midland and Great Northern Line which ran between Norwich and Peterborough via King's Lynn. It provided transportation between 'A' and 'B' but that is all one can say about it. The crews of its infrequent trains seemed to stop at every farmhouse for tea and it was exasperating to feel large chunks of one's leave being chipped away at and between each halt. The 'erks' had dubbed the service the 'swede-bashers' hearse'. The King's Lynn service to London was a little better but not much.

While on the subject of trains, one of the squadron's pilots, returning from leave in the north of England, had boarded a train which, he was informed would stop at Peterborough. This the train failed to do. Standing in the corridor with his case at the ready, all he saw of Peterborough station was a momentary blur. His reaction was immediate – he pulled the communication cord, bringing the express to a screeching halt about a mile further up the line. Grabbing his case, he promptly got off and started to walk back along the line only to be stopped by the guard to whom he admitted having pulled the chain. He gave his name and address and then began to move off towards Peterborough.

''Ere, you can't do that mate. You'll 'ave to get on the train and stay on it as far as the next stop, London.'

'What! After pulling the chain...after being told that it would stop at Peterborough. D'you know I may be on the battle order to fly tonight and if so how am I to get back from London in time?'

'Sorry, mate. Them's my instructions and it's against regulations for passengers to walk along the track.'

And so our friend found himself in London, able to get a train to King's Lynn but without a connection that night on the M and GN. Whether or not he received a bill for £5 I do not know.

Most of the squadron's aircrews were billeted at Weasenham Hall, about two miles from the airfield. It was the home of Major the Hon. Richard Coke (the fifth son to the second Earl of Leicester) and his charming French wife known affectionately to most of us as the 'Pheas'. How she had collected that nickname I do not know. Maybe it was a contraction of the pheasant we shot on their estate with, of course, their permission. Naturally, the 'Pheas' shared our bag and would often do us the culinary honours. She was also invited to those mess parties considered respectable enough. We spent many happy days there as well as at the 'Ostrich', a pub right outside the gates of 'our' stately home.

The only snag in living away from camp, however pleasant the environment, was getting out of bed on a cold winter's morning, missing the squadron bus and having to 'hoof' the two miles to the airfield, more often than not in snow or rain.

On the last day of January I made my first flight from West Raynham, a weather test with F/Lt Hill. He was, by the way, the first pilot to take a Blenheim to Berlin although not briefed to do so. This was no mean feat as that aircraft's duration was insufficient to make that city under normal conditions. Hill, however, was a capable engineer (doubtless one of Trenchard's 'brats') and knew how to nurse his engines and to get from them maximum performance with minimum fuel consumption. Had he not done so he might have finished up in the North Sea with the doubtful advantage of having empty fuel tanks for added buoyancy.

My pilot on 101 Squadron was the 'A' Flight commander, S/Ldr Ronnie Graham and my navigator P/O 'Bunny' Rogers. Ronnie was formerly an Imperial Airways' pilot whilst Bunny had spent many years with the Royal Navy mostly as a navigator on submarines. Thus I was blessed with a very competent crew.

Ronnie was the bluff type, his broad grin invariably stretching from one side of his field service cap to the other, for he wore it straight over his head and pulled down almost to his ears. Bunny, on the other hand, was a slim, six-foot-three, moustachioed Devonian who loved living to the full. His navigation was impeccable.

The Station Commander at that time was Group Captain the Earl of Bandon known to all as 'Paddy' (and to some as the 'Abandoned Earl'). Somebody told me that he was related, in some way, to my pilot but it never occurred to me then to find out in what way.

The first trip with my new crew and squadron was a night intruder over Lille, on 4 February. It was of shorter duration than my previous sortie to the same area with Bennett nor were any enemy aircraft seen practising circuits and bumps. We didn't operate again until the last day of that month but in the interim, got in plenty of practice flying including one of my favourite away-from-home luncheons, to Hooton Park, near Liverpool.

My eighteenth sortie was uneventful. We disposed of our load on the docks and naval barracks at Wilhelmshaven. There was the usual display of pyrotechnics but nothing we hadn't already seen or experienced before. The only incident on that trip can be retold at my own expense. While scanning the night sky and nearing the target, my mind was turning over on a new line of thought. Here was I, crewed up with a flight commander who had the power, among other things, to grant leave. The logical sequel to that mental deduction was to 'strike while the iron was hot' but I nearly burnt my fingers.

'Excuse me, sir. Would it be all right for me to go off on a 48-hour pass on our next stand-down?'

'For Christ's sake, Henry, there's a time and place... We are running up on the target...be quiet.'

'Sorr —'

'Left, left...steady...' from Bunny, before I could terminate my apology.

During and long after interrogation, Ronnie would be heard to say 'There we were, just about to bomb, with the bloody flak searing our arses, when Henry asked for a 48-hour pass...' Roars of laughter greeted his revelation. Ah, well, I got my '48' and my peccadillo had amused them all.

On 13 March 1941, my second anniversary in the RAF, I was once again lifted off the ground on a box-formation flight, bringing my total flying to nearly 295 hours (223 by day and 71 hours 10 minutes with the 'owls and fools').

CHAPTER 3

March 1941/42:

First daylight sortie – Gunnery specialisation –
To Malta – In action with Royal Navy.

In spite of the stately-home atmosphere in which we lived and the nearness of the 'Ostrich', we frequently hankered for the blacked-out lights of the big city. Occasionally, but not often enough, the squadron bone-shaker (later replaced by a comfortable 24-seat Bedford coach) was placed at our disposal on a stand-down evening. The M and GN was sometimes used but the dreary journey consumed most of the few precious hours we had in which to paint Norwich red. For two of us, at any rate, the problem was solved by the squadron *comus*, Sgt Chesterman, better known as Chesty; Standing about five feet three inches in his underwear, he had *the* most saucy, infectious grin. It segmented his face with two arcing furrows, his mouth, almost from ear to ear, and the slits of his nearly closed eyes which blended neatly with well established crow's feet.

He outlined his somewhat nefarious transaction at tea one day.

'Here, know what? I've got us transport to Norwich for tonight,' he said in a furtive whisper.

'How come?' I asked.

'Simple chum. Old shodnasty in the mess is willing to risk his jalopy with me if I return it topped up with juice…and, of course, still in working order,' he added with a chuckle.

'Hold fast, matey,' I felt apprehension prickling my scalp, 'I've already been mixed up with one petrol-snatching team and I don't particularly wish to be promoted to court martial.'

'Safe as houses, cock,' he answered, his smile expanding even further round his face, 'I've laid it on with one of the dispersal crowd who operates well out of sight of the SPs.'

'Even so, it's bloody risky. You know how they are clamping down on 100-octane thievery. In any case, with you driving and with that stuff in the tank of an Austin Seven, the gaskets will blow when we're miles from nowhere or the valves'll be consumed like a mouse eats cheese.'

'Oh rot. Come on, let's get ready to go beat up the town.'

His enthusiasm and loveable chuckle, my vulnerable will power and the promise of an evening in civilisation reduced his irresponsible scheme to innocuity. I was best blue'd and panting on the stately drive long before he had finished grooming his Ronald Colman moustache.

Barely able to see over the steering wheel and through the windscreen, Chesty's driving was like something out of comic opera, even more so on his less-sober return journeys. Homeward bound in the early hours on one such drive, he played havoc with my nerves by deliberately skidding all over the hard, icy snow. On an 'S' bend near Fakenham we bounced from one hard-packed snowy bank to the other at least six times, all the while Chesty, hunched over the wheel, laughed like a drain. A half-wit in a runaway dodgem car would, by comparison, have resembled a Victorian Sunday-school teacher on a tricycle.

While we both had lots of fun with that baby 'dustbin', I was glad to borrow an old Morris Eight convertible one evening and to drive it myself. Its badly fitting and battered hood and the cracked side-screens gave access to every wintery draught in Norfolk. I drove back from Norwich that night in a blizzard. Ordinarily it would not have caused much anxiety but without windscreen wipers and only one serviceable headlamp (its louvered blackout mask as effective as a Venetian blind stuffed with birds' nests) the journey was a nightmare. Fortunately, I was able to follow the rear lights of another car for most of the journey but only by sticking my head out over the side since the windscreen was covered with inches of snow, as soon was my face.

The drive came to an abrupt halt when I ploughed into a six-foot snowdrift two miles from Weasenham. When I eventually reached the sanctuary of the stables (where Chesty and I shared a room) I knew exactly how Captain Scott must have felt some thirty years earlier.

Two of our favourite ports of call in Norwich were the Castle Hotel and the licensed Samson and Hercules dance-hall. In the former we had many parties, in the latter we interspersed our shin-digging with drinks at one of the two bars.

We became very attached to a friendly, red-headed barmaid in the Castle. On her birthday we carried in a large box secured with ribbon. 'Ginger' tittered with delight and promptly set about revealing its contents – a large chamber pot complete with handle. Where another girl would have pouted with dismay or disgust to receive such a present, Ginger hooted with laughter and, giving it the quick once-over with a dish cloth, filled it up with beer for us. From that day onwards we drank from it, loving-cup fashion, until some silly clot dropped it to waste nearly a gallon of best bitter.

*   *   *

On my second anniversary plus one, I joined Ronnie and Bunny on a trip to Dusseldorf. We took off at 8 pm, smote the target while the ground defences threaded thousands of Reichmarks' worth of shells through their expensive illuminations. We flew away unscathed and landed at base three hours after take-off. It had been my nineteenth sortie.

A few days later the squadron was ordered to fly down to St Athan, a few miles to the south-west of Cardiff. We carried a full bomb load as St Athan was a training camp. One silly blighter dropped one of his bombs, a 500-pounder, onto the property of a once placid farmer. It didn't explode as it hadn't been fused. He didn't live that one down for ages. The reason for our move right across the country was that anticipated bad weather in East Anglia would have prevented us from operating. The met boys excelled themselves that day, for we couldn't get off from St Athan, either as the weather clamped down there, too.

After supper in the mess and a visit to the camp cinema, we repaired to some pretty tatty billets. They were cold and dismal. Blankets were in short supply so I was thankful for my foresight in bringing a couple of Everhot bags from the aircraft. They helped a lot that night and were still hot when we landed back at base at noon the following day. Everhot bags, almost flat and about nine inches square, were designed to fit into muffs around the radio equipment to prevent the controls from freezing solid. Many a volume control, normally kept fully turned down until required, was broken when being forced from its frozen position which, of course, rendered the receiver useless.

The bags were activated simply by pouring a teaspoonful of water into a small opening at one corner. The water reacted with a special chemical to generate heat, similar in principle to, but not as violent as, carbide. When flying on really cold nights I kept two Everhot bags in the knee pockets of my Sidcot into which my gloved (three pairs: silks, woollens and leather gauntlets) hands would go.

Next to fog, cu-nims and enemy umbrage, the intense cold was our biggest headache. The Blenheim gunner came off worse because his turret was far from draught-proof, there being a large aperture for the two protruding gun barrels which allowed their vertical movement and a few degrees of horizontal traverse. Consequently, when the turret was fully abeam, the biting cold slipstream fairly whipped in. Goggles were mostly ineffective for they steamed up and iced immediately. Condensation from one's oxygen/microphone mask dripped and froze into a beard of icicles. A bar of chocolate would be too brittle to break let alone eat and one dare not remove gloves for fear of frostbite.

In view of the increasing number of frostbite cases among air gunners either because they had removed their gloves or they had walked about too much before take-off in thick socks and flying boots (sweating feet in temperatures of -50°F was just asking for trouble), electrically-heated suits and long, silk-lined underwear were issued. The suit comprised a fleece-lined leather jacket, trousers to match plus the important accessories boots and gloves; it was the extremities which clamoured for protection.

The jacket formed the take-up point for the current and the gloves and trousers were connected to it by plug/socket, while the boots were plugged into the trouser bottoms. The jacket and gloves could be used independently of trousers and boots. Personally, I found the suit cumbersome as did most of the gunners. The gloves, for example, were loose-fitting and floppy at the finger tips which made the delicate tuning of the radio receiver aggravatingly difficult. Having tuned in to a station, one lost it again when withdrawing one's hand from the condenser dial.

Although it was compulsory for gunners to wear that garb during the winter months, most of us quietly ignored it and reverted to the calf-length flying boots, two or three pairs of woollen socks (silk stockings were also effective), usual underwear, two sweaters including the issued white roll-neck affair, battle dress, Sidcot and three pairs of gloves. I didn't feel the cold too much on my body, only hands and feet and face. As for long underwear, I had never worn it before, didn't intend to start and never have climbed into it. I confess that those excellent garments were handed to my father who was just recovering from pneumonia. (I wonder how many years I'll get when the Air Ministry catches up with my past 'crimes'?).

It is fitting, having dwelt on the cold, to mention another means of reducing its discomforts, oxygen. Normally, oxygen was switched on when reaching 10,000 feet, whatever the climate, more or less to obviate anoxia. In bitter temperatures, however, oxygen played an important part in keeping the extremities warm. It was also said to be good for a hangover but I never found it so. On one night-flight I was stupid enough to forget my oxygen tube. When my turret cupola began to take the form of an igloo I decided that it was time to nip back and take a 'gulp from the bottle'. Closing my mouth over the bayonet socket on the fuselage wall I didn't have time to turn on the oxygen valve for the metal quickly burned into my lips. Too bloody late I recalled having once read that Arctic and Antarctic explorers always removed rings from their fingers and watches from their wrists so that no metal touched their skin. I had two lovely fat blisters to suck for the rest of the trip and some pretty icy feet and hands. I never forgot my OT again.

On 23 March 1941, we took part in a five-hour trip to Hanover. Taking off at 8.15 pm we climbed up into the clear night. It was the coldest flight I remember ever having made. With an anticyclone embracing most of northern Europe, the easterly airstream was perishingly brittle. Countless light-years away but appearing sparklingly near, a myriad stars twinkled in massed profusion from a moonless sky. At 20,000 feet or more over northern Germany that night, the outside temperature was -57°F, and brother that's bloody cold. Every breath of that night air was inhaled grudgingly.

Before arriving over the target the intercom came to life:

'Bunny, you'd better give me a course to steer round those searchlights ahead. I don't like the look of 'em. Is it Osnabruck?'

'No, Osnabruck is starboard of track. There's no sizeable town where they're positioned...wait a sec...yes, they ring Dummer See and Steinhuder Meer.'

At that stage I said to myself 'this I must see,' and, at the expense of an icy blast, rotated my turret to get a better view forward. The shock of cold air was nothing compared with the shock I got when seeing, dead ahead, two groups of massed searchlights. I'd seen plenty before but I could see why Ronnie had taken instant dislike to that bunch, for they were ominously stationary, dozens of beams pointing unflinchingly and vertically to the heavens.

'Know what I think? ' said Bunny. 'They've got a night-fighter screen between the lakes waiting to pounce on any aircraft silhouetted against that wall of light. Better change course to 065 magnetic for a while. We'll go north and come in on the target from the north.'

'Right. Turning on to 065. Henry, keep a sharper than sharp lookout…and no requests for leave, mind.' Ronnie added the last quip with a chuckle.

'Very good, sir.' The chasm between the ranks of sergeant and squadron leader was too wide for me to bridge with a friendly 'get knotted.'

The two large lakes, Dummer See and Steinhuder Meer, were excellent landmarks for aircraft on the west/east track bound for Hanover and Berlin. That the enemy was acutely aware of that fact they amply illustrated with their show of candlepower. But the trap was a bit too obvious for us to 'walk' into. As we skirted those two 'fairy-rings' of light, I saw one or two unidentified aircraft (almost certainly night fighters) silhouetted against them. However, we weren't spotted and pressed on to complete the job in hand. What a glorious relief it was, on the return journey, to descend to relatively warmer altitudes, to drink a cup of hot coffee and later completely to thaw out in bed.

April proved to be a lively month. On the 3rd, Ronnie was detailed, as duty pilot, to supervise the return of the squadron from hostilities. Again, the met report was unfavourable at base that night, so we took off at 6.20 pm and flew to Boscombe Down in Wiltshire where 101 Squadron and other Bomber Command aircraft similarly effected, would put down.

The events of that night put a few years on my life. The weather was fine but a slight ground haze and an air-raid warning turned what should have been a straightforward operation into a bizarre dream. I was stationed with a small van (in radio contact with main control) at the touch-down end of the flarepath. Boscombe's all-grass airfield was equipped with the then modern contact-strip lighting (two parallel rows of electric lights: white, amber and red sections indicating 'safe', 'dodgy' and 'go-round-again', respectively). To the left of that permanent system a glim flarepath had been laid. At its approach end (which coincided with, but at a slight angle to, the contact strip) was the chequered control caravan, a chance light, a landing 'T' and my small van on the tailboard of which I sat until, on two occasions, I was forced to vacate it in a hurry.

Just before midnight the first aircraft entered the circuit and landed. One or two more came in on the contacts until a call from Ronnie in the control tower informed me that a 'red' alert had been received.

'They'll have to come in on the glims. The chance light will be used in emergency only. Contacts being switched off now. Over.'

'Message received and understood.'

The familiar sound of desynchronised engines heralded the approach of enemy aircraft. They flew over very high on their way, I believe, to Bristol. In the circuit, at staggered heights, a gaggle of Wellingtons, Whitleys and Blenheims waited their turn to land.

I heard a constant string of requests to land. The radio was alive as the tired crews in 'Charlie', 'Beer', 'Victor' and 'Orange' vied with each other to get down. A Whitley was the first to make an approach on the glims. As it neared the threshold I could see its red and green nav. lights spanning the darkness and again creating that frightening illusion that the machine was aimed straight at my head. With a roar of motors and flaming exhausts, the black shadow of the 'flying coffin' (as that aircraft was called because of its shape) whistled over the chance light at about fifty feet, and floated down the flarepath like a Tiger Moth in a strong head wind. He couldn't possibly make it and with a burst of power it climbed away for the second attempt. This the pilot again misjudged coming a little closer to the spot 'X' marked by my van. The third attempt I thought would finish between my eyes; I was off that tailboard and away like a scalded cat. He got his wheels on the grass that time and vanished into the darker recesses of the airfield, my nerves flapping like so many ribbons in his slipstream.

The next on the list to further the process of my demoralisation was a Wellington. That laddie, having been given a green to land, knew not his 'up' from his 'down' wind, for he made an approach from the wrong end of the flarepath, taking off again when he realised his error. With a deafening roar he cleared the chance light by a few feet and climbed back into the circuit. 'Next time he'll knock the bloody thing over,' I mumbled to myself. Next time he nearly did, as the red obstruction light on top of it was neatly severed by the Wimpy's port wing as he landed.

This sort of thing, but thankfully not so close, went on until I was relieved, both physically and mentally, at about 2 am when all our surviving Blenheims had landed. Feeling in need of a quadruple brandy (unobtainable), I returned to my quarters to dream of monsters flying about in the night. The following morning I wasn't sorry to see Boscombe Down receding beneath and behind our tailplane.

On the 7th, I completed my twenty-first sortie with my eighth operational pilot, Sergeant Redmond. Our target, the port of Bremerhaven at the mouth of the Weser, was duly 'stung' while its defences clearly illustrated their non-acceptance of our intrusion. Otherwise, it was a comparatively uneventful trip which ended at 1 am.

The following night I was back with my own pilot and P/O Wallenstein; we set course for the same target. The two consecutive sorties differed, however, as chalk from cheese. On the way out Ronnie asked Bunny's replacement to remind him from time-to-time to check that the nose light (a white formation-keeping light) was switched off, as our aircraft had not yet been modified. To prevent this happening, a spring-loaded metal cover was being fitted over its tumbler switch which was mounted near the pilot's left elbow and was thus easily knocked to the 'on' position.

As we approached the target, a factory in the dock area, all thoughts of switches were forgotten. The lads below were really determined not to let us pass unnoticed or, for that matter, pass at all. More and more searchlights flickered on and before you could say 'floccinaucinihilipilification' we were held. The light was so dazzlingly powerful that I would have had no trouble in reading the label on a bottle of Angostura bitters.

'Hold her as she is,' said the navigator, his bomb sight obviously spot on target.

'For Christ's sake hurry up and bomb before we get the chop,' was Ronnie's reply.

'Left a bit…steady…stead-y…bombs gone.'

As soon as the word 'gone' had been uttered the aircraft was put into a steep diving turn to port.

'We'll head out to sea,' said Ronnie, throwing the machine about in a vain attempt to shake off the lights. Heavy flak was carrrrummpping all around us; it was close enough to hear and smell. We soon got clear and out of range, however, and the searchlights collapsed into the ground as they were switched off. It was delightfully peaceful once more. I didn't see the results of the bombing since the glare of light, the gun flashes below and the violent manoeuvring of the aircraft had completely disorientated me.

As we climbed back to a respectable height, Wallenstein efficiently popped the question 'How's that nose light, by the way?'

'Well I'm damned. No wonder they picked us up the bloody

thing must have been on over the target.'

We flew north-west into the Heligoland Bight area (known to Bomber Command crews as the Hornet's Nest), circumnavigated the Frisian Islands and turned onto a south-westerly course for home. Scanning the sky, as was my wont, I spotted the exhausts of an aircraft dead astern. Switching on my 'mike' I passed the tidings to the captain.

'Can't hear you. Something wrong with your microphone?'
'Unidentified aircraft closing astern, sir,' I repeated in my best stentorian manner.

'Sorry, can't hear a thing you're saying.'

The carbon granules in my microphone had frozen solid. I must have done some pretty fast panting over the target. I sat there, finger on trigger, watching like a hawk. A few minutes later the aircraft peeled off and returned the way it had come, obviously a 'bandit' flying a set patrol.

The fun and games had not yet finished. When we arrived over West Raynham, Ronnie called up on the R/T for permission to land. No response from ground control. Round and round we went calling and receiving nothing but silence.

'I'm going in, permission or not. The TR9 must be u/s and I don't want to stop up here all night.'

With that, he dropped the undercarriage (cutting off the power to my turret) and turned onto the approach. As we lost height on the run-in, I noticed another aircraft also on the approach and only a few hundred yards behind. Thinking that he had been given permission to land, I mentioned it to Ronnie. This was confirmed when we were given a 'red' from flying control's Aldis lamp.

'Damnation,' said Ronnie, pulling the aircraft round and back into the circuit. I then noticed that the aircraft behind, instead of going on in to land, had also pulled round and was tailing us. This was rather disturbing unless, of course, he'd thought the red was meant for him.

'Better turn off the nav. lights, sir. The aircraft behind did not go in to land and is following us. It may be a night intruder.' I couldn't be sure; a Blenheim and Junkers 88 are similar and it was practically impossible at night to differentiate between them. That cat-and-mouse activity went on for some time every minute of it adding conviction to the fact that the aircraft pursuing us was doing so with evil intent.

Ronnie had had just about enough of it (so, for that matter, had the navigator and I) and told 'Wally' to 'fire off the colours as I fly over the field. We're going in.'

'Very good.'

In reply to our 'firework' we got a green from below. We sighed with relief when our wheels kissed the grass a few minutes later. At interrogation the blanks were filled in. The pilot of our pursuing aircraft said that when he saw our nav. lights go out (night intruders often used lights to gain the confidence of ground defences and other aircraft in the circuit) he was convinced that we were an 'unfriendly'. He had switched his gun button to 'fire' (the Blenheim was equipped with one fixed machine gun in the port wing leading edge) and would have opened fire had not our Very cartridge colourfully split the darkness.

We found that our machine had been holed in many places which wasn't surprising. The aerial mast was practically severed at its base and leaned drunkenly over the top of the fuselage. Quite a night out!

On the night of the 11th, I found myself with yet another pilot – P/O Jones. At briefing we learned that, for a change, our target lay to the south-west and not in the east. We were going to have a smack at Brest or rather at the two German battle cruisers *Scharnhorst* and *Gneisenau* (S and G or Salmon and Gluckstein, to us) which were, at the time, berthed there under a mass of camouflage netting. The plan of attack was for the Blenheims of 101 Squadron to create a diversion over the target between 3.55 and 4.05 am (each of them to drop 2 x 500 lb. armour-piercing bombs in the process), while Swordfish of the Fleet Air Arm would make a surprise attack at low level. Those slow old biplanes, known as 'stringbags', would, it was hoped, be able to launch their 'tinfish' inside the anti-torpedo nets. As you'll no doubt agree, it was an occupation bordering on suicide. One had to hand it to those FAA Swordfish crews; we thought our job was risky enough at times but they had a very short expectancy of life.

However, the scheme seemed tactically sound and even if we had to spend ten minutes over one of the most heavily defended targets in occupied Europe, it was nice to know that our efforts might distract the enemy sufficiently to enable our FAA friends to slip in unobserved and to make a successful show of it.

Thin cloud obscured the target but there was no doubt that it lay directly beneath us on ETA for gunfire and searchlights turned the cloud layer into a bright, flickering pink carpet. It was like flying above a tropical storm. The gun flashes beneath the cloud gave away the position of that Atlantic port. Had the defences stayed quiet we couldn't have bombed with any degree of accuracy since that wonderful radar navigational aid, H2S, had not yet entered service.

We took our time and the best possible aim dropping each bomb separately with the hope of a lucky hit. The primary objective was to keep the German gunners with their faces to the sky. In any case we didn't expect to do much damage to the S and G even if we were lucky enough to hit either of them since even 1,000 lb. armour-piercing bombs were said to bounce ineffectively off their heavily armoured decks. Nevertheless, reconnaissance photographs taken the following morning showed that one bomb had found its mark and had caused a little damage. The dock area of Brest (already a shambles from previous visits by the heavies) we further 'bent'.

On our return we were briefed to land at St. Eval, near Newquay in Cornwall, there to be interrogated alongside the FAA crews. Putting down a little after 5 am, we gaped at the Swordfish on their dispersals. Pregnantly they stood there each with a torpedo slung beneath its belly. For reasons I forget, they had not got off the ground. Good for them but we might have been told!

After an egg/bacon breakfast, we took off at 8.30 am for base. However, because of bad weather *en route*, we were forced down at Weston Zoyland, near Bridgwater, Somerset. The staff, rarely having the pleasure to receive operational bomber crews, hospitably supplied us with our second breakfast. We finally got off at 11.30 arriving at base in time for lunch – gourmands, the lot of us.

Four days later, flying with my own crew once more, I flew on my first daylight sortie, a shipping reconnaissance at nought feet off Le Havre. The trip was uneventful for we saw no ships only a few spouts of water from badly-placed shore-battery shells. But that trip was the overture, in pianissimo, to a series of low-level daylight attacks on enemy shipping which made everything we had so far experienced seem like a picnic.

At the end of April the squadron was detached to RAF Manston, in Kent. When we arrived over the airfield the sight below was most discouraging. The field was pock-marked with filled-in craters and the hangars and buildings had the appearance of a colossal junk yard. At first sight it seemed impossible for us to land there but we did notice a lot of fighters scattered about the airfield's perimeter. Being in the front line during the Battle of Britain, Manston had suffered badly and it was still being subjected to frequent hit-and-run attacks. Fighter-bombers of the *Luftwaffe* would race across the Channel at wave-top height, bomb and strafe the airfield and away again. During our two-week stay, air-raid warnings practically coincided with attack, giving us little or no time to get our heads down. Admittedly, the warnings were more frequent (up to about fifteen in one day) than committed attacks but who was to know what was about to be served, if anything?

We NCO aircrews were billeted in a 100-foot-long wooden hut near the airfield. It was divided lengthways by one corridor on either side of which were single rooms, while lavatories and 'lavabories' were at the half-way mark. Know something? My mind is a complete blank as to where we partook of nourishment (the solid kind). No matter!

In one of those many daylight attacks on Manston, our hut was narrowly missed by a dirty great bomb but it was peppered with cannon shells. The near miss had moved one of the hut's walls about six inches at floor level. During the attack, one of the squadron sergeants was communing with his soul while squatting on the 'throne' when a cannon shell came through the wall beside him and disappeared through the door. He was last seen doing a three-minute mile towards the nearest shelter, with his trousers tripping his every step.

Also attached to Manston at that time was No. 74 Squadron equipped with Spitfires and commanded by S/Ldr Mungo Park. (The squadron was, shortly afterwards, commanded by W/Cdr 'Sailor' Malan, at RAF Biggin Hill.)

Ronnie Graham was acting commander of 101 Squadron during our stay at Manston, so I didn't fly as often as the other crews. The aircraft were bombed up with four 11-second-delay 250 lb. HEs, thus at instant readiness as were the crews. We sat around in an old wooden hut which passed as a crewroom, with Mae Wests on and parachutes handy (although at nought feet they were of little use) just like fighter pilots waiting to be scrambled. It was mid-spring so there was no call for masses of cumbersome clothing, certainly not at zero altitude. The trips were usually of very short duration which obviated the need for flasks of coffee, chewing gum or stacks of signals bumph.

I always took with me a tin hat but whether it should be worn over my flying helmet or sat upon gave me much food for thought. As my nether vitals would be useless with a hole in my head, I chose to wear it 'topside'. Even so, I didn't relish the thought of painfully becoming a soprano! *Quel dilemme.*

'As well as daily air reconnaissance of the Channel, we have the assistance of a "Jim Crow" at Dover Castle who maintains surveillance of the Straits with Nelson-type spyglass. No enemy ship or convoy should therefore escape our notice, weather permitting. You will be at readiness to take-off immediately and to attack such shipping. Close fighter escort will be provided to and from the target. Flight commanders' navigators will be responsible for providing the necessary headings. You will attack in vics of three and the lower you get the longer you'll remain undetected. Good luck to you all.'

After Ronnie had delivered his short, to-the-point briefing, we sat around in the crewroom playing cards or reading. It was an untidy atmosphere; parachute harness and packs, helmets and navigation satchels littered the floor for the want of locker space. The walls were covered with aircraft recognition charts, illustrated dinghy-drill procedures, security warnings and the inevitable pin-ups. An old gramophone churned out rusty versions of equally old records, its renderings thankfully drowned in the general hubbub. Those of us who couldn't stand too much of the tobacco-laden fug would sit outside or wander off to the aircraft to check equipment.

During that phase of the war, Blenheim squadrons of No. 2 Group incurred heavy losses. Actual strikes sometimes resulted in losses as high as 75 per cent or even 100 per cent. This was because of the method of attack found to be the most effective. It provided ships' gunners with reasonably simple targets. The aircraft's position low on the water, gave the defences the opportunity to correct their aim by means of the splash pattern on the water. Complete surprise was out of the question. Air gunners couldn't contribute their fire on the run-in for they couldn't fire forward. The pilot's single, fixed front gun helped a little but the desirable raking of the decks was impossible. The only evasive action that could be taken was a gentle undulation which, while dangerous at nought feet, gave us little protection – at best a little psychological comfort. Even the best of pilots could be unlucky enough to get one between the eyes in which case it was 'curtains' for the whole crew. The aircraft would hit the water and at over 200 mph it disintegrated immediately. Sometimes an aircraft was seen to burst into flames, leap in the air about 50 to 100 feet and then plunge to its doom in a mass of foam. If the pilot was unhurt and he could lift his stricken machine to about 500 feet, parachutes were of some use otherwise they became redundant equipment.

The whole attack would last no more than thirty seconds plus a minute or two on the run, – in and out – when the heavier calibre guns would have their say. But in that short space of time when hell was let loose, one could die suddenly, receive some nasty jagged holes, acquire a galloping twitch or develop a craving for copious draughts of brandy without soda. Once experiencing that type of sortie, those that followed filled one with foreboding. We virtually lived on borrowed time.

My first with Ronnie (from Manston) was off the French coast near Dunkirk and for the second time our quarry had reached the sanctuary of port. The shore batteries, as usual, spoke up but proved ineffectual.

Two days later, on 3 May, we were quickly briefed to attack a merchant vessel said to be leaving Boulogne harbour. No. 74 squadron were already airborne, circling in two boxes of six (one to each vic of three Blenheims) as we taxied out. Forming up quickly we led the first vic towards the coast. Waltzing with some trees, we cleared the cliffs' edge like barrels shooting Niagara Falls and got down to sea level. The Met forecast had clearly stated 10/10ths cloud over the Channel. Five minutes after leaving our coastline the weather cleared and there stretched to the southern horizon an unbroken expanse of blue sky!

I felt like a million dollars in the 'back seat', for above and to the rear of our three aircraft, six Spitfires formed a comforting arc of protection. This was my first experience of fighter escort and I liked it. Actually, we were one up on the second wave of Blenheims because Mungo Park, a friend of Ronnie's, was flying just above us as personal escort. Looking up I could pick out every detail on the Spit's duck-egg-blue underside; its beautifully smooth elliptical wing broken only by the large starboard intake scoop and sundry small apertures, mostly ejection chutes for spent bullet cases and links.

And thus we sped across the calm sea, an unwavering spearhead with deadly intent. It was a wonderful sight, one I'm never likely to forget. Nor will I forget its culmination.

'Target dead ahead, about seven miles,' broke in Bunny.

'Okay,' answered Ronnie who then transmitted: 'Red section, prepare to attack in loose formation...using plus 9 boost...now.'

The extra boost was applied, independently of throttle, by means of a lever above the throttle quadrant. It was always wired and sealed to prevent its use during normal flying because it reduced the life of the engines as well as increased fuel consumption. However, at that juncture, more speed was an asset; it shortened, in time, the last very dangerous mile or so to the target. The Spits suddenly peeled off and disappeared to the west. This was momentarily disconcerting but they couldn't do much to help us in the attack as their ammunition had to be conserved in the event of enemy fighters appearing on the scene.

Looking forward, I saw the 6,000-ton MV surrounded by a dozen or so harmless-looking small boats. They were as deadly as they looked innocent for they were equipped with rapid-firing multiple pom-poms. They formed up quickly in two lines between which we ran the gauntlet. It was the most frightening thing I had ever experienced; streams of shells churned the water into a thousand fountains. From both beams the deadly pattern crept nearer and nearer to our aircraft while tracer flashed by, horizontally, over and under our tail. I felt like a hero of the silent screen, strapped to a railroad track helplessly watching the approach of an express. 'Won't be long before we buy it, they can't miss us...' I thought. The armour plating behind my turret was, under those circumstances, completely useless.

'Bombs fused and selected,' said Bunny. Looking forward again I saw the MV looming above us...a quick pull on the stick and Ronnie heaved the Blenheim over the masts, at the same time pressing his bomb release button (on the control column). As we leapt the ship like a frisky salmon, I caught a fleeting glimpse of a black swastika on its white and red ground fluttering from the stern, while guns blazed away on the after deck. We were over too quickly for me to retaliate, in any case I had to watch our formating aircraft.

Down again onto the wave-tops to make a very shallow turn to starboard, every second taking us 100 yards away from danger. The pall of smoke from flak and bombs was soon left behind. As we straightened out on our homeward course, the burden of fear released its grip on my stomach to be replaced with elation, closely pursued with a further twinge at the thought of similar, maybe less fortunate, raids to come. I wondered whether the crew of that ship had been as frightened as I and doubtless most of us had been. Two hundred seconds of mutual fear during which there couldn't have been room for anger, only self-preservation.

Meanwhile my faculties were otherwise co-ordinated and I busied myself with a vigilant eye on the sky and sea behind us. Suddenly I stiffened for coming up close behind, very low on the water, were three – four – six fighters. I couldn't ascertain their identity because they were too low to afford a silhouette and their camouflage blended with the dull grey-green of the sea.

'Unidentified fighters dead astern, about 2,000 yards, sir,' said I, having been taught to warn the pilot of all such eventualities. This time my microphone was very much alive, as was Ronnie's.

'Well, man, what are they?'

'Can't see them clearly enough to identify. Have guns trained and ready to fire.'

'Damn it, can't you tell at that range?'

'No sir, markings not visible, no silhouettes, and they aren't closing very much.'

Before the conversation was further protracted into a slanging match (I was irked to think that my excellent aircraft recognition was being questioned), the fighters pulled up to about fifty feet. There was then no mistaking the outline of our Spitfire escort. None of us had seen them approach from their distant stand-off position. It illustrated one of the amazing features of flying: one minute the air could be full of aircraft, the next, one found oneself alone or vice versa. This was often recorded by Battle of Britain pilots who, at one moment would be thrashing about in a dog-fight then, after concentrating on one target, looked round to find the sky deserted. It may sound incomprehensible to non-aviators but it happened.

'Okay, sir. It's our close escort.'

'Good show. Be home in twenty minutes.'

The whole trip lasted exactly one hour although the few minutes over the target seemed like a day. We landed and made for the operations room. The second vic of three Blenheims hadn't been so lucky, we learned. Two of them had burst into flames and plunged to their watery graves before bombing. The sole surviving aircraft was piloted by Sergeant B. Cook whom I joined that evening on a sortie with some of the crews, into Margate. To start with we made short work of a double brandy. We just had to drown the events of that late afternoon for they had badly shaken all of us, more so Cookie and his crew, naturally.

That type of operation was labelled by the post-war Press (many years later) as 'The riskiest job in the Royal Air Force.' How right they were. But I still say that the Fleet Air Arm crews of Swordfish aircraft had an even deadlier task. However, we did obtain a little pride from the fact that the fighter pilots of our escorting squadron referred to us as the 'Death and Glory Squadron' or 'Suicide Squadron'.

We learned the following day, from intelligence, that recce aircraft had confirmed the sinking of the MV. Ronnie was awarded an immediate DFC. (Meeting him in 1942, after I had been commissioned, he went out of his way to say how sorry he was that his recommendation for a 'gong' for both Bunny and me had been turned down by Group. I don't know why he felt so strongly about it, other than the fact that he was such a nice fellow, for after all, we had only been doing our job, as had every soldier on the Dunkirk beaches and every sailor in HMS. *Hood*.)

* * *

Agreed, I don't remember where we messed at Manston but a host of vivid memories remain fresh in my mind. There was, for instance, Wally Palmer, the squadron coach driver. On one occasion when I wasn't on the battle order, he and I wandered to a hillock at the edge of the airfield. From that point we commanded a view of the sea. We watched and waited for the return of our aircraft. When they flew over we saw that only three out of six had so far returned. A wait of another ten minutes or so went un-rewarded – there were no lame stragglers. It was then that I noticed the tears in Wally's eyes. He was, I knew, very attached to the aircrews as we were to him; a lot of ground crews must have shared similar emotions but I had never seen it before (our losses had never been as high before) nor had it occurred to me that there was such a strong bond between us.

Wally's, rather the tax-payers', coach was a useful piece of transport. Instead of the usual run of uncomfortable buses, 15 cwt and 3-tonners, this luxurious Bedford took us into Margate, Ramsgate and once to London while the surviving aircraft underwent inspection and repair. I took Cookie and some of the lads home with me while Wally parked the bus outside his London home. During that thirty-six-hour respite there were many parties. We bade our farewells and returned to our much battered portion of the 'Garden of England'.

Fed up with hanging about in the crewroom one bright, sunny day, those of us with an artistic flair got cracking with coloured chalks to transform the Bedford's dull camouflage. When we had finished with it Wally nearly had kittens. Popeye, Olive Oil, Reilly Ffoul, Donald Duck and Jane and many other contemporary 'characters', adorned its sides. Above the inscription 'Death rides inside' a forbidding skull and crossbones grinned hideously from the back of the bus. An engineering type had found a small metal chimney, complete with cowl, which he fixed to the front bumper; two large paper eyes were stuck to the windscreen. To add effect we stuffed the chimney with oily rags and before driving into Ramsgate that evening, we got them smouldering nicely, leaving in our wake a pungent smokescreen. A couple of days later Wally was driving the empty bus across the airfield when he was overhauled and stopped by the Station Commander.

'I gather that the decorations are not your doing but see that they are removed, immediately.'

When Wally told us the story, he added, 'No sense of humour, some people.'

Later in the war I had the pleasure of meeting Wally again. He had been elevated to the rank of corporal and was 'chauffeur' to a Group Captain whose staff car was a large Buick. Wally must have exerted some charm on his MT seniors for his vehicles were, on the two occasions I knew him, far superior to the run-of-the-mill stuff in the RAF. When we later moved over to France, Wally told me he had one helluva job getting that Buick on a landing craft; something to do with the spongy suspension, I believe.

There was a mania among certain aircrew types to collect and proudly carry back to base anything that was humanly portable and which could be wrenched, twisted, unscrewed, knocked or lifted from its foundation, fitting, support or owner. Over the years, in a variety of messes, I've seen Belisha-beacon globes, garden gates, ashtrays, lavatory seats, lamp-post signs of many shapes and sizes, policemen's helmets (a rare prize), in fact, the lot which had been brought back as trophies. But from Ramsgate one night we smuggled two easy chairs out of the saloon bar of the 'Prince of Wales' (or was it the 'Duke of Kent'?). Naturally, the publican was irate but he knew who had 'em. As intended, we returned them the following evening and stood him as many drinks as he could down. He didn't know that we knew that he'd go easy on the alc' so that he could keep a better eye on his portable property. We noticed that he kept a good watch on his wife, too. Anyway, we parted the best of friends.

The inn keepers and other tradesmen in those front-line towns and coastal resorts were badly hit during the war, both business-wise and bomb-wise. Being in restricted areas they lost all their seasonal trade; also, many of the residents had moved to more peaceful surroundings. The forces, however, spent well especially in the pubs. We also found that cigarettes, chocolate, pork pies and other war-time luxuries were in more plentiful supply in Ramsgate and Margate than elsewhere, inland. This was due to the war-time quota being a recognised percentage of the peacetime quota and seaside resorts had a large peace-time quota.

There was, maybe still is, an underground dance-hall in Ramsgate. It was under the esplanade not far from the tank traps, the barbed wire and mined beaches. Outside its blacked-out door one night, three of us stood swaying at the kerbside waiting for a taxi. We'd had enough. Knowing how choosy the taxi-drivers were in that town, Sergeant Jordan telephoned a taxi company in the name of W/Cdr Jordan. The taxi arrived but, on seeing three bleary-eyed NCOs sheepishly standing there, its driver refused to accept us.

'Wotsh wrong with our money, mate?' asked 'Jordy' menacingly.

'Nothing, but I don't like being called out under false pretences,' answered the miserable driver.

'If we had chold you our rank you woont have come.'

'Yes I would.'

'Oh no you flickering-well woont.'

And so the wrangle went on until, from the black-out, 'What's all this, then?' announced the silent arrival of the law.

'This geezer won't take us to Manston, officer,' said our spokesman, grinning innocently. The policeman had a few words with the driver then opened the door for us to enter. At least one civilian appreciated the fact that if we didn't let off steam once in a while, there just wouldn't be enough straitjackets to go round.

When we got back to the hut, the third of our trio, a wild curly-headed New Zealander, went to his room, left his door wide open and sat on his bed. While he fumblingly removed his tunic and tie, he burst into raucous song, a Maori war chant or something equally penetrating. I couldn't stand it any longer, so I dragged up a large cylindrical fire extinguisher, stood it in the doorway, levelled the nozzle at the noisy bastard and said, 'If you don't stop that flaming row I'll let you have it.' I, too, must have had a skinful that night because the bloke at the other end of the nozzle ate people like me for breakfast.

'Go away,' was all he said, so I pushed the tit. With a bellow of rage he chased me down the corridor but I got to my room and slammed the door and locked it before he could do me serious injury. I could hear him grunting and shuffling about outside, then he went away. I heard something heavy being dragged along the floor; he had returned with another extinguisher. He pushed the plunger and poked the nozzle underneath the door. It produced nothing worse than a puddle on the floor. I lay on my bed and laughed which was simply asking for trouble. It stirred him to more violent action as he thrust the nozzle of the fire extinguisher through the glass panel of the door and hosepiped the horrible liquid all over my room. The only refuge was under the bed. Well, I had started it all.

Looking back on those crazy days, I often wonder how the civilian population tolerated our behaviour. It wasn't always the junior ranks who behaved thus, either. Nor was it confined to the effects of war, for I've heard numerous anecdotes about certain senior officers of the pre-war RAF and very amusing they are too. Mostly though, our high spirits were siphoned off in the confines of the mess. Anyway, we certainly perpetrated nothing worse than the quieter type of students' rag and we came nowhere near to emulating some of the young long-haired morons of today. At least we were spurred by being shot at from time to time.

On 9 May we returned to West Raynham, a sad, depleted squadron. The following day, Sergeant Schonbach flew me to Wattisham for I had been granted a 48-hour pass. It was good to visit my former station again but there were too many strange faces for me to be delayed by reminiscences. I caught the bus to Stowmarket an hour or so after landing.

I was collected on the 12th by Sgt Terry Dodwell and was thrilled to fly in my fourth type, a Wellington, affectionately known as a Wimpy. Sitting in the second pilot's seat I watched Terry go through his 'knobbery' check with a mumbled mnemonic before take-off. Satisfying himself that the fabric-covered beast was capable of lifting us off the deck, he opened the taps with the brakes on. When sufficient boost was registering he released the brake lever. There was a sharp hiss like the sudden application of a lorry's vacuum servos and the Wimpy began to trundle forward, bouncing on the uneven turf as it gathered momentum. Terry, to my alarm, thrust the stick right forward until it almost touched the instrument panel; the nose went down until I thought the props would bite deep into the ground. After a few more gentle bumps we unstuck. With a few deft movements Terry had retracted the wheels, throttled back a little, upped the flaps, and engaged coarse pitch. We set course for West Raynham.

After a while he offered me the controls. I jumped at the chance for I had taken the trouble to find out what the various instruments meant and had voluntarily got in some Link trainer practice at Bicester. Watching the compass, turn and bank indicator and artificial horizon, I held the stick gently but firmly to preserve a steady course. There was nothing to it.

'Try a few turns if you like.'

'Why, thanks.'

Putting on some aileron I found the response sluggish but slowly she answered and came round in a gentle turn. Taking off aileron I found that to hasten the straighten-out I had to apply opposite aileron just for a second.

'Keep the nose up on a turn,' said Terry, without interfering with my efforts. 'You'll find a tendency for the nose to drop unless you ease the stick back a bit.'

'I'm with you.'

So we weaved our erratic course across the invisible borderline between Suffolk and Norfolk, to land forty minutes later at base.

After lunch I went up again in a Wimpy, with P/O Todd, for circuits and bumps. For a change I decided to sample the rear turret. It was a new experience to have nothing in front of my guns but fresh air. It was, at first, an eerie, detached sort of feeling. At take-off and in the air every movement of the aircraft was amplified at the tail end. Though an isolated position, it afforded an excellent field of fire, far better than the Blenheim.

I soon tired of the view and decided to move up front. Opening the turret doors I levered myself through the small aperture and inadvertently leant on the elevator control; the nose of the machine went up until I moved away and sauntered down the fuselage. I

hadn't realised what I'd done until the pilot bawled at me when I
stood behind him. We live and learn. I watched a few landings and
those fascinating nose-down take-offs, then wandered back to the
wireless operator's station. The Wimpy was fitted with Marconi
radio, a great improvement on the old 1082/83 combination. As we
were unfamiliar with that equipment, the W/Op. AGs were sent for
a short course (two days I believe) at RAF Cranwell. The only
recollections of my stay at that Lincolnshire Sandhurst was seeing
a man knocked off his bicycle and killed by the bus in which we
were returning from Lincoln one evening; and, for the first and last
time, trying a dish of tripe which was served in the sergeants' mess.

The squadron was busily engaged in converting to the faithful
but sluggish Wellington when I returned. Many new crews arrived,
including dozens of straight air gunners, since the Wimpy crew
comprised five men. Having got used to the more intimate
threesome of the Blenheim crew, I wasn't keen on the new set-up.
Anyway, a few days later Ronnie and Bunny went on rest at the
completion of our first tour. With twenty-six sorties chalked up, I
flew for the last time with them on 17 May. I met Ronnie only once
more, at Bicester, when he was on his way to India. I heard a few
years later that he had lost his life when the ship in which he was
returning to the UK was torpedoed in the Indian Ocean. Bunny, on
the other hand, I met many times when we were both at Bicester. A
couple of years later I was shattered to hear that after returning
from a daylight low-level in a Mosquito, the great Devonian had
dropped dead of heart failure, right at the ops room door. He had
felt a little off colour on the way out and his pilot, Mike Pollard,
offered to return. 'I'll be all right, I have my medicine with me,'
said Bunny producing and patting a brandy flask. He and, of
course, Ronnie Graham were the cream among crews.

On 24 May I was posted to the Central Gunnery School at RAF
Warmwell, Dorset where, on No. 18 Course, I was one of 45 to
qualify as a gunnery leader. With one exception, F/Lt Douglas of
the Royal Australian Air Force (a pilot with No. 10 Squadron), we
were all air gunners and came from the following squadrons: Nos.
7, 9, 10, 15, 21, 39, 40, 42, 48, 50, 51, 57, 88, 99, 101, 115, 139,
141, 144, 151, 221, 228, 233, 235, 236, 256, 264, 300 (Polish), 600
and 612. This, you'll agree, was a pretty fair representation.

It was an intensive course embracing every aspect of gunnery
applicable to the airborne platform. We acquainted ourselves with

the many different types of British, American and German automatic weapons (as fitted to aircraft), the largest being the 20 mm cannon. Most of us thought we knew it all. Our instructors thought otherwise. We again went through the mill with theory of sighting, harmonisation of guns, deflection shooting and aircraft recognition. But we were further groomed: 'how to lecture' and 'fighting control' had been added to the syllabus.

Our ego was given a face-lift when we were told that, under certain conditions, the gunnery leader, or fighting controller, in the leading aircraft would assume control of the entire formation. This meant that he would take over verbal control when his formation was about to be attacked by enemy fighters. The fighting controller's responsibility, therefore, was to work out which type of formation was best to adopt. In other words, to present maximum fire power against attacking aircraft and to prevent his own formation from being enfiladed. For example, if an attack threatened from the port quarter the fighting controller might transmit as follows:

'Six snappers 3,000 yards red quarter. Prepare to change formation echelon starboard.'

When the controller estimated that the range of the attackers had closed sufficiently, but not quite within their opening-fire range, he would continue:

'Echelon starboard, echelon starboard...go. Prepare to turn port.'

When attack was anticipated, the controller stepped in with 'Turn port, turn port...go.'

Thus the formation would turn into the attack at the crucial moment, presenting the attackers with a maximum deflection shot, at the same time permitting every gunner in the formation to bring his guns to bear. It was quite simple really but its success depended on the element of surprise, correct range estimation and timing.

In every case the operative word of command was 'go'. Nobody moved a muscle until it had been given. The anticipatory commands of manoeuvre were, of course, essential. The pilots were generally enthusiastic about the new technique (provided the gunner knew what he was doing) for they couldn't see to the rear and in any case their attention was otherwise engaged in keeping tight formation, for they also appreciated that the straggler was invariably picked off.

There was a marvellous gadget at Warmwell which gave us practice at deflection shooting. Each gunner took his turn to fire from a turret equipped with, if I remember a'right, one gun and fifty rounds of ammunition. A wooden model of an aircraft ran round the track on rails in front of the gunner. It approached from a simulated quarter attack, then ran across the gunner's 'stern' to give him a maximum deflection shot, it then moved away to starboard and astern, the model disappearing into a shed behind the range. As can be imagined the model, which travelled at speeds of up to 30 mph, gave the gunner some useful practice and, if he was lucky enough to hit it, the holes were patched before it was sent round for the next gunner to fire at. Strange to relate, the lowest scores were registered by gunners who had shot down enemy aircraft and the highest score was made by a small, inoffensive lad who had only just joined a squadron.

The aircraft we used for fighting control practice (usually two, flying line astern and stepped to simulate the leaders of two vics of three) were the Wellington and Hampden, the latter I heard some call the 'flying suitcase'. The attacking aircraft were Spitfires and Defiants. Among the many exercises carried out were range estimation, deflection allowances, fighting control using cine-camera guns and air-firing from both beams onto a drogue.

It was a glorious June day when I managed to scrounge a ride in the Boulton Paul Defiant. The pilot, P/O Matylis, was Polish which at the time held no significance for me. But after his simulated attacks on the Wimpy and Hampden, whose fighting controller was doing his best to cope with the situation, I came to the conclusion that those chaps were dead keen. The sun's rays penetrated the turret perspex from every angle as he threw the Defiant all over the sky. In a vertical attack on the two bombers, whose brown and green camouflage made it difficult for them to be picked out against the countryside below, I hoped that the driver would be able to pull out before making a mess of us both over Dorset soil. It was the only time that I felt sick in the air. This was attributable to the petrol and glycol fumes seeping into my practically air-tight Boulton Paul 4-gun turret, rather than the violent manoeuvres. I opened the sliding doors of the turret to let in the cool slipstream, otherwise I *would* have 'honked'. Nearly all the gunners who flew in the Defiant felt sick or were sick.

At 2.30 pm on Friday, 13 June, I was detailed to fly in Hampden

No. P.1313. The two morning details in that aircraft had, for some reason (superstition?), been cancelled by the pilots concerned. The aircraft had just been repaired and inspected after a 'prang'. My pilot, P/O Boxall, either unaware of the date or aircraft number, or just not superstitious, signed the form 700, and up we went. I wasn't at all nervous although I didn't like the Hampden very much.

I did pretty well on the course with one exception. We had just been given a lecture on how to give a lecture. The lecturer had told us that 'Marks will be given for the way the subject is treated and delivered. They will, on the other hand, be deducted for any showing of distracting idiosyncrasies such as smoking, swinging keys round the finger, juggling with a piece of chalk etc.' When my turn came I was so nervous at giving my first ever lecture, that I wandered to the dais smoking like a chimney and, throughout my delivery, unconsciously juggled with a piece of chalk!

The majority of us were billeted in requisitioned houses some way from the airfield, which meant a bus ride to and from the 'field morning and evening. But we had the delightful Dorset hills on our doorstep. On one of our walks, thereover, we bagged a hare. Carrying the carcass by the ears we were suddenly confronted by a gamekeeper who said that it was agin the law to shoot game on a Sunday. 'Game?' we echoed, 'but this is a rabbit.' He gave us a quizzical look, grinned and went his way.

Having qualified as gunnery leader, on 22 June, I returned to West Raynham with another thirteen hours flying recorded. Meantime, the squadron had completely converted to Wimpys under the command of W/Cdr Briggs. I felt like a fish out of water. The 'A' Flight Commander, F/Lt Freddie Craig (a New Zealander) approached me and said, 'I know you've finished your tour but how would you like to join my crew as first wireless operator?'

'May I think it over?'

'Sure. Sleep on it. I shan't mind if you decide against it.'

I liked Freddie very much but couldn't see myself liking the job he had offered. The thoughts of sitting in front of the radio unable to see what was going on outside and below; to watch the blinking green of a magic eye on the Marconi receiver for hours on end; to wonder whether the gunner in the tail turret was alert, all contributed to my decision to reject Freddie's offer. I filed my application to join another Blenheim squadron rather than go on rest. I heard later that the first casualty of the newly converted squadron was F/Lt Craig. His aircraft was seen going down in flames into the Bay of Biscay. The squadron had attacked in daylight the S and G which had been moved south from Brest to La Palice. Only one person was seen to bale out. It was later established that it was F/Sgt Hesmondhalgh (the first wireless operator) who spent the rest of the war in a prison camp.

On 1 July I was posted to No. 18 Squadron, operating Blenheims from Oulton near Aylsham, Norfolk. Why I went there I'll never know for I wasn't given a crew nor did I see an aeroplane. I spent most of the few days on the squadron's strength on leave. The balance of my time was spent wandering about the beautiful, but then uncared for, grounds of Blickling Hall where we lived. This magnificent historic mansion (the birthplace of Anne Boleyn, the second wife of that Mk VIII forebear of mine) and grounds are now National Trust property.

On 10 July, I was moved again to another Blenheim squadron, No. 21 ('YH') at RAF Watton, south-east of Swaffham, Norfolk. I was temporarily crewed up with F/Lt Waples and completed only one sortie with him (and the squadron). It was a shipping sweep off Texel, Holland.

I remember one sergeant pilot who did nothing else but brag about his low-flying prowess. He would relate how, when at FTS, he would bank a Tiger Moth over the waving golden harvest so that his wing tips would cut through the wheat. I also remember remarking to a colleague: 'He won't last long.' He didn't, for he hit a crane on a low-level mass attack on shipping in Rotterdam harbour. A great pity about the two men he took with him. The crews had, of course, to fly low to carry out their mission but it was also their responsibility to observe 'maintenance of aim' (*to attack the target without unnecessarily jeopardising the aircraft and crew*). Returning from that same sortie, one Blenheim had a piece of crane cable in its balloon-cable cutters on the wing leading edge; another had brick-dust on its bomb doors, while a third had telephone wire wrapped round its tailwheel. But they returned to tell the tale and to fight again.

On 17 July, the squadron moved to Manston to do much the same work as 101 Squadron had done. In fact most, if not all, 2 Group Blenheim squadrons took their turn to operate from Manston. The fighter squadron in attendance during 21 Squadron's stay there was No. 222 equipped with Hurricanes. I did not fly from

Manston on that tour for the simple reason that Waples had his own crew again. As far as I can remember they lost their lives there, for the losses were very heavy. On 25 July, the Squadron Commander, W/Cdr Webster, flew me back to Watton.

My unsettled existence was becoming monotonous. On 2 August, I packed my gear for the umpteenth time and moved on to another Blenheim squadron, No. 107, stationed at West Raynham's satellite, Great Massingham. With a completed tour (27 sorties) to my credit, I was crewed up with a pilot who hadn't operated at all. As he was the only pilot with whom I disliked to fly and whose flying left a lot to be desired, I'll refer to him henceforth as 'Fox' (F/O 'X').

The Squadron Commander was W/Cdr 'Bunny' Harte whose gunner, P/O Wewage-Smith, was an amazing character. He had served in the French Foreign Legion, was a fighter pilot in the Bolivian war and then returned to Europe to fight in the Spanish Civil War as an air observer. When greeted by one of the squadron IOs with 'Well, mercenary, what can I do for you this morning?' his reply was 'Mercenary I may be but I'll have you know that I'm doing this at strictly cut prices for patriotic reasons.'

The squadron's motto, *Nous y serons* (We shall be there) was most appropriate for its record of achievements during World War II was one of outstanding success and versatility. Practically every form of bombing attack, including smoke-laying, had been carried out in Blenheims and Bostons from bases in East Anglia, Scotland, Kent, Malta and Hampshire and finally from liberated Europe and Germany with Mosquitoes. Later in the war, No. 107 Squadron was adopted by the East Anglia town of Lowestoft.

Before I arrived on the squadron, one of its pilots, P/O Bill Edrich, went out with his crew one morning, sank a 5,000-ton ship off the Norwegian coast (for which he was awarded the DFC) and rounded off his achievement by making sixty runs for the M.C.C. at Lord's the same afternoon.

One of the squadron personalities during my term was Sergeant Dickie Leven. He was a pilot of outstanding quality and possessed a keen wit. He looked no older than 16 yet he was a very mentally-alert 20. Before he flew on operations, he would drag up a stool to the battered upright piano in the mess and proceed to beat out a horrible dirge. It was the same piece on every occasion. The cries of derision from all present merely bounced off him. He was later awarded the DFM for his many cool-headed accomplishments.

My first flight with 'Fox' was a practice bombing exercise against the dummy ship target in the Wash. It shook me to the core. So shaken was I in fact, that I told him what I thought of his flying whereupon he threatened me with arrest on landing.

The plan was to split the fire power of an enemy ship or convoy by making a simultaneous attack from both beams. At first sight it seemed a good scheme. Two aircraft at a time would attack the target with 11 lb. practice smoke bombs. They would approach the dummy ship together, at nought feet, split up one wheeling to port over the water, the other to starboard inland. Both would then come round onto the target in the hoped-for simultaneous attack. It was very difficult to time accurately. Each pilot would point the nose of his aircraft at the right-hand side of the target (one aiming for the bow, the other the stern). As the wing span of the Blenheim was fifty-six feet and the dummy ship only about 150 to 200 feet long, there was no room for misjudgements

We were on the first run, approaching from the sea, and the haze over land completely swallowed the other aircraft. Flying low over the water Fox was, I noticed with alarm, aiming for the centre of the ship. Two aircraft had already collided head-on while practising that fraught procedure and with that in mind I watched with baited breath. As we neared the ship, its black and grey diagonal markings standing out clearly against its misty backcloth, the other aircraft appeared, pulling up from the other side of it. It was heading straight for us. Fox made a fast climbing turn to starboard, evading collision by a few feet. He radioed for another attempt. Much the same happened again. In spite of the warm, hazy summer weather, I felt cold shivers nipping up and down my spine; I just couldn't stop myself switching on the intercom after the second ill-timed attempt and saying: 'You were heading straight for the other aircraft again, you stupid clot.'

'Any more of that, Henry, and you'll find yourself under close arrest when we get back,' he replied heatedly. I didn't answer, just got off a quick prayer or three. 'I'll show them how to bomb a ship,' he continued, and then pulled the aircraft round in bloody near a stall turn. He aimed the Blenheim at the distant target and, like an angry thwarted schoolboy, he pressed home his lone run on the target ignoring the fact that the other Blenheim was in the vicinity. It was, to say the least, a frightening and juvenile exhibition by a pilot one which I'd never experienced before or since. As might be expected my thoughts were a mixed, apprehensive bag as we flew back to base. Nothing more was said about my outburst, perhaps his conscience had pricked him. My navigator, Sergeant 'Mac' Smith had said over a pint that evening: 'You took the words right out of my mouth. What a crazy thing to do.'

A couple of days later, Fox asked me whether I had a small haversack and a revolver.

'We aren't issued with revolvers,' I told him coldly, 'and what do you mean by a small haversack?'

'Well, something to carry your small kit, spare socks, underwear, shirt, shaving gear etc.,' he elaborated.

'Are we going somewhere, then?' I asked.

'No, but if we are shot down we'll need things like that to help us to escape. I have two revolvers, I'll lend you one of them.'

'Thanks. The revolver might come in handy,' (for Dickie Leven, I thought, when he next sits at that bloody piano), 'but with due respect, I've never taken small kit with me yet and I don't intend to start now. I always go with the intention of coming back.'

He didn't broach the subject again.

My first sortie with Fox was a 'circus'. That term applied to a high-level, daylight attack when the bomber formation was escorted by fighters. Because of the limited range of the Spitfire and Hurricane, the targets were usually confined to the North of France. So, on 14 August, we were briefed to ginger up the dock area of Boulogne. Our rendezvous with the fighters, three squadrons of Spits and three of Hurribuses (close and high cover), was over Beachy Head.

A newcomer to the squadron and operationally inexperienced, my pilot was to be almost last to take-off. This was fortuitous for he made a mess of it. We gathered speed as the aircraft bounced across the grass when, suddenly, the engines lost their power. It became ominously quiet. Engine cuts at take-off and their dire consequences quickly flashed across my mind. We stopped with a squeal of brakes in front of the far hedge. Turning the aircraft he started to taxi back to the take-off point.

'What went wrong? ' I asked.

'It's all right, I forgot to close the gills and put down flap,' he answered with a nervous laugh.

All right! Little did he know that his flying was becoming as good as any MO's laxative. From that day on I made sure that such an essential part of his cockpit drill had been carried out, since I could see and check both the engine gills and flaps from my turret. Getting off at the second attempt we caught up with and plugged the hole in the already-formed-up squadron. Climbing to our operational height of about 12,000 feet we ate up the miles to the south coast. Nearing Beachy Head I looked round for signs of our close escort. The sky was, with the exception of our twelve Blenheims, empty. A couple of minutes later the air was full of aircraft; Spitfires and Hurricanes were neatly arrayed on our flanks, a most comforting sight. Thus integrated, we crossed the Channel on a glorious August afternoon. The high cover could not be seen for, naturally, they had selected an altitude which did not produce condensation trails and so betray their position.

We dropped our load plumb on target and wheeled out of the flak bursts onto a course for home. This was my first experience of bombing at high level in daylight. It illustrated, too, that on night operations the darkness had kindly concealed from us the worst of the heavy flak for, over Boulogne that afternoon, the sky was one mass of ugly black smudges. As the saying went, 'none of our aircraft was missing' and we landed back at base after three hours flying.

Three days later we were subject to a snap briefing. Three crews (including ourselves) were to fly out in advance of the squadron to Malta. We were to fly alongside No. 105 Squadron ('GB', commanded by W/Cdr Hughie Edwards, VC) until Bunny Harte brought the rest of the squadron out. On 17 August, we flew down to Portreath, Cornwall. Our load did not include bombs, merely three crew, one ground crew chappie who sat next to the pilot, our personal gear (limited to 12lbs each), escape kit, spare wheel, boxes of engine and other spares, a water tank and auxiliary fuel tanks to enable us to cover the extra long journey for each leg of that trip was well over 1,100 miles.

At 7.40 pm we arrived at Portreath which was situated on the delightfully rugged Atlantic coast of Cornwall. We slept the night in a bell tent with earwigs as company. The insects weren't responsible for my restless sojourn that night, it was the noise of German bombers which pounded Falmouth (twelve miles away on the south side of the Cornish peninsula), coupled with the excitement at the thought of being in Gibraltar the following evening, if we got there. Both legs of the flight to Malta were to be counted as sorties.

At briefing early next morning, we were told to fly at nought feet from the Scilly Isles to a point off Cape Finisterre at the northwest tip of Spain. Then to climb to 10,000 feet and fly south (outside Spanish and Portuguese territorial waters); to nip round a left-hand bend at Cape St Vincent and begin to reduce height when off Cape Trafalgar as we approached the Straits of Gibraltar. '...this is to prevent your being mistaken for enemy aircraft approaching the rock, not to conceal your whereabouts from enemy agents in Spain because they will have already tabbed and recorded your presence to Berlin before your wheels touch the runway,' said the IO. To approach Europa Point with wheels lowered and to flash the letters of the period. 'When you get a green, go round to land. Do not hug the escarpment which is on the east side of the rock, because of the turbulent eddies which can be dangerous... Watch your landing as the runway is a short one...do not stray over the Spanish frontier which is only a matter of yards from the runway, otherwise you might get shot at...'

Those heartening words of advice were still ringing in my ears when we took off at 10 am. Clearing the jagged cliffs we got right down to skim the Atlantic swell and set course for the Scillies. This, our first turning point, was to be the last friendly territory (apart from Gib.) we would see for well over 2,300 miles. It wasn't long before we sped over that lonely clump of gnarled islands and, adjusting course a few degrees to port, we began the 450-mile crossing of the Bay of Biscay. We traversed this vast expanse of water at nought feet simply because the enemy had it under constant surveillance from the air and sea. A quick radio message from, say, a patrolling Fw. 200 Condor, a ship or submarine, would soon bring a pack of long-range fighters on the scene. The Germans were, at that stage of the war, very keen to prevent reinforcements of any kind from reaching the Mediterranean theatre. We saw nothing. It was a boring journey until the hilly coastline of Spain rose through the haze on the horizon.

Before climbing up into the clear blue sky, Mac checked the landfall and verified that we were off Finisterre, dead on track. Levelling out at 10,000 feet, a magnificent view of Spain and Portugal spread away beneath our port wing. It was a sun-drenched vista I didn't tire of looking at. Oporto, hugging the mouth of the Douro river, we had passed when the port engine began to splutter.

It picked up again but a few minutes later, coughing and banging, it sounded more like a veteran car on the Brighton road than a radial engine of nearly 900 horsepower. Fox asked our mechanic passenger whether he could effect repairs if we had to land. 'I expect we can find a suitable stretch of beach on which to land, if need be,' he added optimistically.

'That's just asking to be interned,' chipped in Mac.

'Henry, you'd better get ready to jettison as much of the gear as will go through the camera hatch but not until I give the order.'

He managed to keep the aircraft in the air for the rest of the trip but its recalcitrant engine gave us intermittent heartburn all the way. Power had to be reduced for minimum cruising speed and thus the journey took longer. Before we had rounded Cape St Vincent, I found myself in the uncomfortable position of bursting for a leak. The usual receptacle was missing from the aircraft but I had observed the omission before leaving England and had thoughtfully taken along an empty lemonade bottle. It was duly filled and corked before being dropped a couple of miles to join the indigenous sardines. I had long since learned my lesson – the hard way – of *not* 'aiming' through the camera hatch (a hole about one foot in diameter covered with a removable perspex plate) for on one occasion when I had been caught short, I got the lot back in my face!

We had reduced height when nearing the Straits and, as briefed, approached Europa Point with our 'legs' down. I flashed the letters on the Aldis lamp and we got a green in return. Peeling off to the right, we made our approach to the eastern end of the runway on the north side of the rock. Fox had obviously forgotten the warning of air currents up the escarpment, for we flew too close and bobbed about like a cork in a rough sea. However, for that mental aberration he must be forgiven for nursing those spluttering 'pots' for the last 500 miles or so of our journey must have been fatiguing. (We found out later that the rest of the squadron, when they eventually flew out, were told of an airfield in Portugal where they could land should they find themselves in trouble. Repairs would be made and the aircraft allowed to get off again.)

We made a low motored approach to the runway the threshold end of which was two or three feet above the sandy beach. Making doubly sure that he got his wheels down right away, he narrowly missed breaking the aircraft's stern frame since the tailwheel only just cleared the lip of the runway before it touched. We taxied to the control tower and switched off. Opening my hatch I climbed out into a blast of sultry late-afternoon air. Looking up at the towering rock I was amused to see its peak smoking like a chimney. The cool Atlantic air meeting the warmer Mediterranean air produced a continuous stream of small fluffy cumulus clouds.

The sun was low by that time for we had taken ten minutes under eight hours for the trip. Some of the resident ground crews were on the spot to put chocks against the wheels, fit the undercarriage links, replenish the tanks and to tell us to 'get our knees brown.' Fox reported to the control tower to inform the duty officer about our faulty engine and to find out where we were to mess and kip for the night. Mac and I were shown to our quarters, a bell tent near the runway, this time filled with flies, millions of them.

Next morning the fitters stripped down the faulty engine and found that there was a lot of work to be done. We wouldn't be getting off that day. The chief 'plumber' was incensed with the condition of the aircraft we had brought with us. 'The bloody thing should never have left England,' he had said. However, Mac our 'erk' passenger and I made the most of that break to get our knees and most other parts brown. We spent the bulk of our time sunbathing on and swimming from the small piece of beach at the Mediterranean end of the runway. I take to sunshine like a duck takes to water and during the three days we spent on the rock I had acquired a healthy tan. So much so that when I was invited to an Army sergeants' mess for a drink ('Pop in for a jar on your way back to the airfield. It's near the cemetery,' invited my Army drinking companion in town) I was greeted with 'Wogs aren't allowed in here, get out.' The white silk shirt and white shorts I had bought in town (to tide me over until I was issued with khaki) accentuated my tan and with nothing to indicate that I was 'Breeteesh', let alone a sergeant, the lack of hospitality was understandable. However, I was spotted by my newly-acquainted buddy and we concluded the evening with a riotous party. While there one of the RA chaps told me that, not long before we had arrived, a Wellington had strayed over the Spanish frontier and was fired upon. This had been too much for members of the Black Watch who, on their own initiative, had opened fire on the Spanish gunners. Only hurried diplomacy had saved the day.

Getting fed up with lounging about on the beach, the three of us decided to go for a ride in a large yellow rubber dinghy (salvaged from one of the many crashed aircraft at Gib.). As we paddled out into the Mediterranean, a current took hold of our frail craft and began to tow it towards the fence which marked the boundary of 'no man's land' across the narrow isthmus. We paddled furiously but made little or no headway against it. Mac dived overboard and swam for the beach. I thought he was going for help but not a bit of it. He lay down on his towel to resume sun-bathing where he had left off. When things looked really black, I yelled to him 'Hey, come on in and help me to swim the dinghy back. Charlie boy here cannot swim and they'll be seeing the whites of our eyes soon.' He saw our predicament and swam out. Leaping overboard I took hold of one of the dinghy ropes, Mac another and between us we got back to the beach, exhausted but safe. What had worried Mac and me most was being stung by Portuguese men-of-war, of which there were plenty that day. Even the tough Army lads who spent a lot of their time drilling inside the rock, wouldn't go in the water when those horrible hydrozoa monopolised it.

The town/port of Gibraltar sprawls at the western foot of the 400-foot-high rock. Its character is composed of many facets. Its residents range, in Darwinian fashion, from Barbary apes to Admirals of the Fleet. I didn't see the apes nor did I mix in exalted circles but my impressions were, nonetheless, as varied.

Walking down the main street one's nostrils were assailed by many smells from garlic to sickly, overpowering perfumes. Each doorway exuded its own aroma into the hot, dusty street. One's eardrums vibrated from the noise of car, bus and lorry doorpanels being beaten by impatient fists (horns and hooters were then banned). Sailors, soldiers and airmen weaved through crowds of gesticulating Spaniards the majority of whom came over the frontier each day to work. We were pestered by flies and street hawkers. 'You buy good silk scarf?' 'You like for lady good perfume?' and so it went on.

I was taking it all in for it was, apart from my visit to the Isle of Man, the first time I'd strayed from England's shores. I remember seeing *Rebecca* at the local 'flea-pit'. When the lights went up during the interval, slap in the middle of the film, there was a mad rush to buy soft drinks and fruit. I sat there on a hard wooden seat in a hot and rancid atmosphere sipping lukewarm lemonade (ugh!) and chewing almonds.

As the food in the mess was inadequate and poor, we topped

up with fresh fruit which was plentiful and cheap. I recall buying peaches at 6d. per pound while a weighty bunch of grapes cost but a few pence. The one thing that was expensive on the rock was beer. If I remember correctly, I paid 5s for a large bottle of beer in the Victoria Hotel. Fresh water was at a premium and we washed in sea water which, we found, was quite a performance using ordinary soap.

Anyway, it was an entertaining and educational break in our journey to Malta and who knew what we were to meet there?

On 20 August, at 9.45 am, we took off on the last leg of our journey. We hadn't been flying for more than forty minutes when the port engine started to play up again. We returned to Gib. Eventually we took off, at the same time, on the 22nd and that time we made it – just.

The first 750 miles went smoothly enough but as we neared the Tunisian coast we put the nose down to fly low over the flat-calm sea. In order to avoid detection by an enemy fighter screen which operated between Pantellaria and Cap Bon, we had been briefed to fly at nought feet over that section, turning starboard at Cap Bon. We turned all right, and to starboard, but at Cap Farina and so into the Gulf of Tunis, a navigational error we didn't spot until we noticed that the horizon ahead and to each side of us was no longer a straight line. Our limited fuel capacity demanded a smart reciprocal if we didn't want to swim the last fifty miles or so to Malta.

Later my radio packed up on me hence no morale-boosting bearings which were so necessary over wide-open, landmarkless sea. Malta is a comparatively small island, and a few degrees off course might have meant our overshooting it and winding up in the drink. Mac had, however, recovered from the stream of abuse that had been flung at him after his first navigational blunder; he found the right 'road', the pilot had 'blue on blue' on his compass and in the late afternoon we crossed the Maltese coast and landed at Luqa. The trip had lasted seven hours five minutes.

Hungry and tired we followed, for what seemed an eternity, a small bus to a very dispersed dispersal point. The airfield itself presented a most depressing picture: the twisted, charred geodetic remains of Wellingtons and other aircraft, littered the field. It was a sorry sight and not at all inducive to nonchalance.

The ops room at Luqa was underground and by the condition of the rest of the airfield it was undoubtedly the best place for it. At interrogation we were asked for our escape kits. The kit consisted of a flat tin (the size of a flat fifty cigarette tin) containing foreign currency, water-purifying tablets, matches, Horlicks tablets, compass, silk maps and other useful survival/escape items. I had left mine tucked behind the IFF set in the aircraft. 'You'd better go and get it before it's too late,' I was told. Wondering what he meant by 'too late' I surfaced and hailed the duty bus driver. He raced me out to the aircraft. Clambering through the hatch and down into the stuffy semi-darkness I felt behind the set – it had gone. It was too late. The driver told me on the way back that to leave anything loose in an unguarded aircraft was simply asking for it to be swiped, and pronto. How right he was for we hadn't left our machine more than fifteen minutes previously.

Mac and I were given temporary accommodation in a stone hut near the airfield. The sergeants' mess, served by Maltese stewards, consisted of a large marquee on the airfield. If an air-raid warning sounded during 'elevenses' or lunch, we just had to wait because the stewards went to earth faster than that. Even our assurances that it was only a high-flying Italian recce aircraft would not prevent them from dropping what they were doing and making a bee-line for the nearest shelter. Understandable I suppose for they had had a helluva pasting.

A couple of days later we were moved to more permanent accommodation in a fishing village called Marsaxlokk, four miles away to the south-east of Luqa. Not, however, before we suffered our first casualty. When the sirens blew their tops during our first night on the island, we made for the air-raid shelter (its exact location having been mentally and indelibly noted). We didn't quite know what to expect but with the blitzed state of the airfield we decided that discretion was the better part of valour. One of the lads in his eagerness to get as much rock as he could between his head and the island's surface, fell down the concrete steps and fractured his collar bone.

My first experience of a Maltese bus journey will remain in my memory until I die (and if this book is published, it will be recorded for all posterity). The driver, sitting well to the left of his steering wheel (a custom which didn't inspire much confidence) raced through the camp gates and in a swirl of dust hurtled down the hill towards Gudja. He negotiated bends at breakneck speed to the cacophonic accompaniment of about six different motor horns.

I

1 The Bristol gun turret (two .303 Browning machine guns) as fitted to the Blenheim Mark IV

2 The graceful lines of the 'short nose' Blenheim (Mark I)

3 The baby 'dustbin' and author

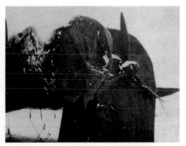

4 The nose and engines of 'R' Robert
   protected from winter weather

5 The Handley Page Hampden

6 Blenheim Mk IV of 107 Squadron

7 HMS Kenya

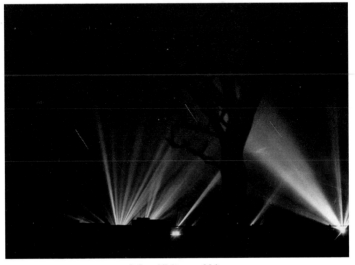

8 Searchlights over Malta

9 The Avro Tutor training biplane

10 Blenheim IV of 13 OTU Bicester

11 Junkers Ju 88

12 Air to air shot of Blenheim IV

13 The Blenheim Mk V, Bisley

14 Bombing up a Boston III

15 'Shiny D' at Hartford Bridge

16 Dr Garbett visits RAF Melsbroek. Author third from right.

17 Pep talk by Air Vice-Marshal Basil Embry,
Brussels

18 The crew of 'Shiny D',
G/C W.L. MacDonald, DFC, (centre),
F/Lt. S. Adams (left)
and the author (right).

19 Boston IIIAs taxying for take-off

20 The author receiving his DFC from
King George VI

21 Group Captain L. M. MacDonald
and W/Cdr Paddy Mahar

22 Air and ground crews of 'N' Nuts, 88 Squadron. Author (2nd from left),
F/O A.F.W. Valle-Jones, W/Cdr I.J. Spencer and F/O G.E. Ploughman, Butch in front.

23 The 'emblem' of 'N' Nuts

Even dear old Chesty couldn't better that display of driving. Rounding one corner we saw coming towards us a herd of goats; they covered the road from wall to wall. Our driver pressed on regardless and without slackening speed, all the while playing his horns fortissimo. Like the waters of a Biblical episode the goats parted; we were through, leaving behind us a fist-shaking goatherd and an unbroken mass of goats. The age of miracles, once again.

On through Ghaxaq (my pronunciation of that would make a Maltese Cross) and down into Marsaxlokk; the bus was thrown sharply to the right to race along the bay road (bordered on the seaward side with laundry-strewn barbed wire) scattering some pretty nude chickens in its wake. We pulled up in a cloud of dust outside the mess having completed the journey in a little under eight minutes. After that showing of recklessness, we actually looked forward to the comparative safety of the next shipping strike. We also felt that something very strong to consume in as many seconds as our journey had taken minutes, was the order of the day.

The RAF unit at Marsaxlokk comprised a dozen or so small stone buildings, a hangar and a slipway. In the hangar was kept a Heinkel 115 floatplane which we often saw being wheeled down the slipway and into the bay. When its engines were started, it taxied round to the adjacent St George's Bay from whence it began its long take-off run towards the open sea. It needed a long run, too, for when we watched it go off one evening, it made three attempts before it finally staggered aloft to pass the lighthouse at Delimara Point. We never found out what that German-built aircraft did although it was rumoured that a French pilot took it on secret missions to somewhere off the North African coast. One day it took off never to return, at least not to Marsaxlokk.

During our few leisure hours, mostly in the evening, we entertained ourselves with mah-jongg or ping-pong and sometimes cards. We also swam in the bay. At night our bodies would leave a phosphorescent wake as we revelled nakedly in the delightfully warm water which at that time of year averaged 78°F. On our rare stand-downs we took a rowing boat out into the bay. It wasn't the native dghajsa which had to be 'pushed' with oars but a plain, common-or-garden row-boat with a roundel on its prow instead of a staring eyeball. Tying the painter to one of the large Sunderland flying-boat buoys, we stripped starkers, cooled the hot metal by splashing sea water over it and lay there soaking up the ultra-violet.

There was a constant stream of luzzus (fishing boats) going by, usually with a husky female as part of its crew, but our nakedness did not inhibit us nor did it seem to worry them.

One afternoon two of us took the boat out to watch the antics of Maltese divers whose job it was to inspect the anchorage of each Sunderland buoy. In exchange for some cigarettes, we were offered the opportunity to go down into the clear water. The navigator I was with accepted with alacrity and, as there was only one spare suit, I sat there under the boat's awning watching the proceedings with interest. Robbie climbed into a frightening amount of gear. He was finally fitted with lead-weighted boots and, after having the valve system explained, a helmet cut him off from the outside world. Over the side he went falling off the ladder's slimy iron rungs to sink in a mass of bubbles – there, but for the grace of God... I watched his progress through the glass panel of a viewing box. He looked an ungainly monster and certainly out of his element. He stumbled over rocks, stirred up the sand and woke up the odd octopus a couple of fathoms down.

When he was fished up and decanted from his rubber suit, sweaters etc., I was offered the chance to go down. I declined for the simple reason that I couldn't face wearing all that gear in a shade temperature of about 92°F. I have regretted that decision to this day.

In the evening, if we felt peckish and/or thirsty, we walked along the bay to the village. The only reasonable place where one could eat was the Honeymoon Hotel the proprietor of which, Mr Smith, was an ex-Royal Navy man who had married a Maltese girl and settled on the island, long before the war. He was quite a character and we often exchanged stories over one of his recommended concoctions. My favourite dish at his establishment was a Spanish omelette which Mrs 'Smudger' cooked very well. I've tried many times since to match their quality without success. A little further along the bay was the village's largest bar – really only a small bistro. It was there that we tried the Arab drink *arrack* and discovered its potency. Sleeping off its effects was not easy, for the 'biddy' remained quiescent until a drink of water or tea the next morning stirred it into action once more.

A limited amount of entertainment was to be had in Valletta. Two places stand out in my memory, the 'Gut' and the Monaco. They were not cinemas or theatres but a rather dubious alley and a restaurant, respectively. The Gut ran parallel to the main street,

Kingsway, and it was made up of a string of bistro-type cafes and bars. They bore exotic names like 'The Egyptian Queen', 'The White Star' etc. In most of them a musical instrument or band could be heard grinding away in their efforts to attract more custom than the place next door. Touts, sitting on the steps outside such places, would yell as we walked by 'Come in Air Force, lovely girls, music, cheap drinks...'

At the Monaco (overshadowed by the Opera House) we were still able to buy the odd steak, although the island by that time was beginning to feel the pinch of blockade. While I liked the Monaco's generally clean atmosphere, I found it most disconcerting to have my legs whipped from under the table every ten minutes by enthusiastic bootblack boys. Nevertheless, when descending the stairs to the bar, we cooled off with a delicious John Collins flavoured with real lemon juice. We broke into a sweat again though when the most attractive, vivacious waitress came prancing in. Kissing the already lipstick-smeared poster of Winston Churchill, which was stuck to the door's blackout baffle, she gaily went about her work. She was a capable linguist, too, commanding four languages.

If we missed the last bus out of town, we'd hire a gharry or karrozzin, as the four-wheeled, one-horse carriage is called in Malta. One evening Chuck Whiddon (a Canadian W/Op. AG) and I were walking down to the bus terminus when there was a dull thud. Looking round, for my companion's conversation had stopped suddenly, I saw Chuck flat on his back on the pavement – out cold. He wasn't sloshed. either. We had both been so engrossed with the wonderful view of the Grand Harbour below us that Chuck had walked straight into a lamp-post.

The three squadrons at Luqa at that time were Nos. 38 (Wellingtons), 69 (Marylands) and 105 (Blenheims). No. 38 Squadron, whose members were mostly Australian, flew their Wimpys at night on what we termed the 'milk run' mostly to Benghazi and Tripoli. No. 69 Squadron, whose American-built Maryland B.1. aircraft had been stripped of armament, flew on high-level reconnaissance sorties. They could, we were told, show a clean pair of heels to contemporary Italian fighters. It was 69 Squadron's job to seek out enemy shipping for the Blenheims to attack.

When first arriving in Malta, we were told by some of the older hands what had been going on there. There was, for example, the attack by three Blenheims: before breakfast they located and sank three schooners anchored in the Gulf of Sirte. Those wooden-hulled ships carried supplies (mostly fuel and water) along the African coast to the advanced positions of the *Afrika Korps* and the Italian Army. The three schooners in question had dropped their 'hooks' in shallow water, and in a position which they had apparently thought safe, for their decks were deserted. When the Blenheims arrived on the scene they picked one ship apiece and sent each to the bottom before the crews could muster on deck. For the chaps (whose nerves were getting ragged round the edges) it proved a stimulating tonic.

Another story concerned an attempted attack by E-boats on Allied shipping in the Grand Harbour. That daring raid took place on 27 July 1941, but the Axis security must have faltered somewhere along the line for the whole scheme was in Allied hands twenty-four hours before the attack took place. Every possible gun was brought to bear on the harbour mouth, their crews having been briefed to shoot only when the E-boats had passed the mole at Ricasoli Point and had entered the harbour, proper. The resulting massacre can well be imagined.

Our first sortie from Luqa was on 25 August when we had a fruitless search for shipping off Lampedusa. This was followed on the 27th by a much longer flight (five hours) looking for shipping west of Crete. It was a boring flight; I just sat there looking at the vast expanse of flat-calm sea and cloudless sky.

There wasn't even a seagull to poop off at. I then made a vow that if ever I was wealthy enough to be able to afford a Mediterranean cruise, I'd go somewhere else.

The following day we went to the same area and that time we got ourselves a 'bite'. A row of merchant ships broke the horizon and into the fray we flew.

On 30 August I clambered into my turret for my thirty-fourth sortie. We were going out on a lone recce flight in place of a Maryland, since 69 Squadron had no spare serviceable aircraft other than those already on a mission elsewhere. I wore the usual clothing: open-necked shirt, shorts, Mae West, socks and shoes which had, up to then, been quite sufficient. Instead of the normal low-level flight we had been briefed to fly at 10,000 feet, which I thought would be just right, not too hot and not too cold.

'We have received a report that two large Italian troopships have left Taranto heading south-east to Benghazi,' the IO explained. 'If and when you see them, don't approach too close. Stand off, note their position, approximate speed and direction, also the number and type of any escort vessels and/or aircraft. You'll probably see a Cant seaplane in the vicinity but leave it alone; keep at a distance, get off your report and return to base. All we want is the "gen" radioed back to base so that we can get your squadron off to attack. Smith will pass the details to you, Henry, which you'll Syko, then transmit it as quickly as you can.'

Off we went into the blazing sun of early afternoon and set course to the north-east and the Ionian Sea. It seemed ages before we reached the search area but it wasn't long before an excited shout from Mac announced that the ships had been sighted.

'There they are, at eleven o'clock. They've no escort. What a plum target for the lads,' he added regretting that we had no bombs on board. The two large liners made excellent targets and presented, as far as we could see, little opposition.

'I'll work out the position and other details for you Frank, just hold your horses.'

We continued to circle at a distance, and I watched the enemy's progress with fascination. Fox piped up with 'I'm going closer to see whether we can get some more "griff".' We didn't argue; he was the captain, even if he was disobeying instructions. He most certainly wasn't improving the situation by making our presence too obvious. As we got closer I saw, patrolling at about 5,000 feet below us, a Cant 501 seaplane.

'Okay Frank, I've got the gen, pop up and get it,' said Mac.

'Yes, I will if somebody else watches that "eyetie" flying-boat down there. It may look harmless but it carries at least three gun positions,' I answered.

'All right, Henry, I'll steer clear while you're doing the coding. Let me know when you have finished sending the report and we'll turn for home,' said the skipper.

'I guess that we can do that right now,' I answered, thinking that we were pushing our luck a little too far since both ships and aircraft must have radioed for help.

'We'll hang about until you get the message off just in case they ask for other details,' countered Fox.

Lowering the turret seat, I crawled out and forward, stretching across the 'well' to take the piece of paper which Mac held towards me. Sitting on the IFF set I began the coding of the message. That done I clambered back into the turret and switched on the transmitter and called base. I got no reply. I called again, several times, but still received no reply although the transmitter seemed to be working all right. I decided to broadcast the message, and sent it about six times, but again received no acknowledgement from base.

We turned for home. Having circled the ships for some considerable time, Mac had a job to work out a course for home with any degree of accuracy. However, he was confident that we hadn't strayed too far from our original arrival point and gave Fox a course to steer. We knew that Malta was but a speck in a vast expanse of sea and that it was better to err to starboard of track than to port, since to miss the island to the south would mean ditching through lack of fuel and the possibility of inhabiting a dinghy for days under a fiery sun.

Fox was obviously jittery because about ten minutes or so before ETA he said, 'We should be in sight of the island by now, so we must be south of course. I'm turning due north.'

'I should wait another five minutes; it is hazy and I'm sure that my course was bang on,' argued Mac.

I tried the radio again to see whether we could get a bearing, but still no joy.

'I'm turning now,' said Fox, 'we can't risk It.' So much for his confidence in Mac. It really was uncalled for, as he hadn't even allowed for the normal extra five minutes or so beyond ETA. So, due north we flew on and on and on. Suddenly, in the haze dead ahead there appeared the grey outline of mountains and there ain't no mountains on Malta.

'Know where we are?'

'Allowing for the fact that my original course was all right,' said Mac, scathingly, 'they are the mountains of Calabria.'

'And where may that be?'

'The "toe" of Italy. We'll need to fly a reciprocal for Malta,' said Mac, urgently, for we were nearing the end of our fuel.

'I'm not going to lose sight of land now,' said Fox, obstinately. 'We'll follow the coastline to Sicily, then turn south. Meantime you'd better send an SOS and put the IFF to stud 3, Henry, the petrol gauges are hovering near the empty mark.'

When earlier we had left the ships behind us, Fox had reduced height to about 1,500 feet for it had been surprisingly cold at

10,000 feet. I had to pull my woollen socks over my knees for I was perished in that draughty turret.

Prudently, Fox put the nose down and turned to port. We flew low over the water following the Italian coastline which looked ominously close. When we saw land ahead, and the familiar mass of Etna, we again turned port and flew about four miles away from and parallel to the Sicilian coast. I kept my eyes glued to the sky, for Sicily was 'loaded' with fighters. As we sneaked between some enemy warships and Catania, with our propeller tips clearing the water by a matter of inches, one could sense the tension in the aircraft. We just prayed that our adversaries were myopic, for it was like trying to hide behind a shadow in the middle of a desert. The pains were brought on a bit more when we saw the balloon barrage ascending over Catania. They had seen us but miraculously no fighters appeared on the scene.

When we pulled level with Syracuse, the intercom came to life.

'How many miles to Malta, Mac?'

' 'bout eighty-five,' was Mac's pat reply.

'The tanks are nearly empty, I think it would be wiser if I dropped the wheels and landed in Sicily. Better to be a PoW than die of thirst in a dinghy...'

That statement brought forth an instant yell of disapproval from both Mac and me. While I agreed with the 'dying of thirst' bit, I certainly didn't wish to end up in a cage.

'For Christ's sake no,' yelled Mac, 'we haven't got far to go and we've only been airborne for just over six hours, the gauges are probably faulty and we should have enough juice to get us back. Even if we do come down in the sea a mile or two from Malta, the air sea rescue boys will be out looking for us...' 'If my SOS signals haven't been received, there is every chance that the IFF will have been picked up,' I butted in.

'Okay, but get that dinghy ready to launch and make sure that the rations are secured to it, Henry. Mac, fill your shirt with every Very cartridge you can lay your hands on and, at the first splutter of an engine, wrench the Very pistol from its mounting,' were Fox's rational instructions. I didn't tell him that I had already tied the dinghy release cord to the ladder and that all was ready for a hasty evacuation after ditching, if it came to it. Thank God his thought of capitulating hadn't been too strong, though our howls of anguish must have helped to sway the issue.

So prepared, we pressed on into the hazy twilight. We passed the lighthouse at Cape Passero and as land fell away behind us, Mac gave Fox his last course for home. Apart from looking at the sky for fighters, I kept a good lookout ahead, eagerly hoping to spot the friendly, rocky outline of Malta poke itself above the horizon. We had, by then, just under sixty miles to go and there wasn't as yet a faltering note from the engines. We hadn't by the way, flown at all in the Blenheim (N.6183) which had given us so much trouble on our journey from England.

During those next twenty minutes, the tenseness had intensified to a degree where it could be cut with a knife. At any minute we expected to hear the choking cough of engines as the last few pints of petrol were consumed by thirsty cylinders. The fuel gauges were registering 'empty', but they were obviously faulty. We knew that our maximum duration had a little while to run provided the pilot hadn't used too rich a mixture. The sun's disc had already dropped out of sight like a red-hot coin into a distant slot. There was a shout from Mac – 'Land ahead.'

'But,' argued Fox, 'there are several islands…it can't be Malta.'

'It can't be anywhere else,' answered Mac, annoyed but confident. 'What you can see are the islands of Gozo, Comino and the higher ground of the main island.'

'All right, I'll take your word for it; you'd better put a cartridge in the Very pistol for we'll be going in over Valletta.'

'But it's taboo to fly over Valletta,' said Mac.

'I know it is but we haven't got the reserve of petrol to make detours, that's if we ever reach land.'

We did make the coast and flew in over Valletta's neighbour, Sliema. Mac fired the colours of the period which happened to be red/red. We learned later that many of the inhabitants had mistaken our colours for incendiaries and had gone to earth. Fortunately for us no guns were fired. We could see the flarepath ahead but Fox didn't wait for a green nor did he bother about landing into wind or even on a runway, he just came over the nearest fence, across wind, ignoring the red being flashed frantically on an Aldis, and the red cartridges bursting in the air. The nav. lights of a fully-laden Wimpy were just lifting over the end of the runway which we were about to cross. No. 38 Squadron were going off on their milk run so no wonder we were being given reds. Traffic control knew that we were a couple of hours overdue but they were not aware of our dire predicament with regard to fuel and that we might drop out of the sky any second.

Fox bumped the Blenheim down on the rocky ground and we shot across the runway in use. Watching from my already opened hatch I saw that we were heading straight for a bombed up Wimpy standing on its dispersal. I shouted a warning to Fox as he appeared not to have noticed it; he immediately applied starboard brake and opened up the port engine. Our port wing sliced the air close to the Wellington and we slewed round to head for the open airfield again. As Fox throttled back the port motor a blast of flame belched from the exhausts (a common occurrence). Whether he mistook it for a fire I don't know, but his next action was to get out of the cockpit, slide down the port wing and fall off. Mac, too, came slithering down the starboard wing and dropped off its trailing edge. Henry was still standing there in the hatchway of a runaway machine doing about 25 mph but not for long. I pulled my helmet off, climbed the ladder, nipped smartly over the side onto the wing and leapt off. I saw the tailplane coming straight for me, I ducked and scrambled up to run clear after it had whistled over my head.

There followed the most amazing sight of a crew-less Blenheim spinning round on one wheel, going too fast for anybody to get near it let alone climb in to switch off the engines. A crowd gathered. A staff car appeared out of which leapt the AOC, Air Vice-Marshal Hugh Pugh Lloyd. A crowd of Maltese danced up and down with excitement. Meanwhile, the ground crew made several attempts to straighten the machine. They placed a coiled rope on the ground and their ingenuity was rewarded when the tailwheel was successfully lassoed. The Blenheim started to run forward but before it could do any damage, a fitter had climbed into the cockpit and switched off. I doubt whether anybody present had seen the like before or since.

Fox was placed under close arrest. Mac and I wandered back to the ops room for interrogation. I had my knees and hands dressed for they had been lacerated a bit on the hard rock.

My radioed report had not been received nor had my SOS (the only time I ever had cause to send one, too). They had, however, picked up the IFF emergency signal but assumed that we had 'gone in' when it faded out. This had happened when we came down to nought feet. Altogether, then, even though we hadn't been spared the drama, it had proved an abortive sortie. We had been aloft for six-and-a-half hours, had been two hours overdue and when the tanks were dipped, it was found that there was enough petrol left for only three or four minutes flying!

The signals officer took me out to the aircraft to find out what had gone wrong with the radio. I felt very small when he switched on and obtained perfect contact with base station for both transmitter and receiver worked without a hitch of any sort. I protested that it hadn't been like that in the air. He gave me an old-fashioned look as much as to say 'as a wireless operator you'd made a good cook and butcher'. However, I was vindicated, and apologised to, a day or so later when another crew had the same trouble with that aircraft. The radio could not be faulted on the ground but, when airborne, it mysteriously cut out.

At the end of that nerve-shattering flight I had flown just over forty-six hours with Fox during which time I had learned that, in order to maintain any measure of sanity and peace of mind, one needed complete confidence in one's driver. Enemy action could almost, in fact, be considered as a secondary cause of demoralisation. On so many occasions had that pilot put years on Mac and me. Apart from the cases I've mentioned, there was the time when we nearly decapitated the crew of a gun emplacement at one end of the main runway at Luqa. Taking off a fully-laden Blenheim in the thin air of a very hot day required every inch of the runway. We had got unstuck but Fox had pulled up the flaps prematurely; the aircraft sank alarmingly so that it almost scraped the ground, until it had gained sufficient airspeed to climb away.

I did the next two operations (after Fox's arrest) with another crew the pilot being F/Lt Alan Ballands. I was my old self again in the turret of his aeroplane. Both trips were of short duration and in each case took place off the Sicilian coast. On the second flight we ventured into the 'closing jaws' of enemy territory; our task was to locate and sink a couple of merchant vessels which had been reported heading for Messina. As our four aircraft headed north, the gap between Sicily and Italy narrowed until we could almost reach out and touch either side. We had no fighter escort and thus were extremely vulnerable although not one fighter came out to challenge our presence. Discovering that the ships had already reached the security of Messina harbour, we turned about and came home. Our orders had been specific: not to attack if the ships had reached port.

On the 12th, life again took on a sombre hue because Fox was brought back to fly. There was an acute shortage of crews at Malta hence that decision. My next trip with him (we didn't do any practice flying at Malta because of the drastic fuel shortage) was, for the want of a better word, a snorter. Eight aircraft, six of 105 Squadron and two of 107 Squadron, were on the battle order. The Maryland chaps had reported a large convoy heading for Tripoli which was escorted by eight destroyers and a squadron of Macchi 200 fighters. As the RAF fighters based on Malta were strictly defensive, we would have to attack that heavily defended convoy without protection. 'It's suicide,' said Alan Ballands. We all agreed. The squadron commander argued with the station commander that heavily escorted convoys should be attacked by the Wellingtons and Fleet Air Arm aircraft at night and that such attacks were a drain on his crews and aircraft. The Group Captain argued that 'there was a war on' – fair enough. The Wingco argued that the Blenheims wouldn't get anywhere near the ships for they would surely be shot down by the destroyers and fighters before they could bomb making it a wasted effort. The AOC was called for to act as arbitrator. We, meantime, sat there sweating on the top line while the verbal battle was going on.

The Group Captain won. We were to go. We went. Flying in echelon starboard, we began our square search. Several legs of the search had been completed without sighting a thing and we turned onto our last leg for home. Our fears were beginning to lessen with every mile flown, when over the R/T the leader reported 'Turning port, convoy sighted on horizon at nine o'clock.' My head whipped round to the right; yes, there they were, a long line of indistinct grey, mist-shrouded ships. The aircraft wheeled round in a shallow turn for we were very close to the water. Something had got hold of my insides and was twisting them into a knot; this was it. 'Say your prayers, Henry,' I murmured to myself.

The convoy was not in the position reported; it must have altered course after spotting the recce aircraft for they were steaming near the Kerkennah Isles, off Sfax in Tunisia. As we neared it the large troopships and merchantmen towered above the flanking pencil-thin destroyers. I didn't at first see any sign of fighters but as we drew closer I saw some of them skulking about above the convoy. The flak started to pour towards us, the larger calibre shells biting into the sea around us sending up columns of dirty-looking water. Then the light stuff began to fly in all directions, a dazzling criss-cross of fire guaranteed to scare the pants off the toughest soul. It seemed impossible to penetrate and live. As we passed one destroyer I raked its decks until my guns seized. I saw two Blenheims disintegrate in a ball of flame. We were through, by some miracle, and on our way back closely followed by a few last-minute shells. I can't quite remember whether it was three or four aircraft we lost on that 'do', but I do know that one of the crews was picked up by a British submarine because they were apprehended by service police in Valletta when they were on the way back to camp. Their crime? Being improperly dressed!

The following day, in the same aircraft that a couple of weeks earlier had pirouetted on the airfield, we went in search of a tanker off the Greek coast. That trip lasted fifteen minutes short of six hours. It was uneventful and the radio worked!

My last operation from Luqa took place on 19 September. It was my thirty-ninth. We attacked a schooner near Buerat el Hsun on the Tripolitanian coast. When we had finished with the ship we flew along the coast for a while, with, beneath us the clear, pale-green shallow water and to our right the desert and a few isolated barrack buildings which I had the pleasure of raking with my twin Brownings.

* * *

Between flights I had suffered from a dose of 'Malta Dog' (a form of dysentery) and a bout of sandfly fever. For the former complaint the doc. had given me a potion which he had termed 'liquid cement'. That jollop enabled me to fly without causing embarrassment to myself, my crew or the ground crew! The latter malady I would not wish to have repeated. I stayed in bed with my head wedged between stacked pillows, for the bite of that minute insect produced a headache the like of which I'd never known. Merely to bat an eyelid made my head split with sickening pain. I was dosed and slept it off.

One of our favourite pastimes at night was to sit on the steps of our small barrack blocks as soon as the air-raid sirens sounded. Draped in blankets, for the temperature dropped significantly at night, we sat there with the attentiveness of a first-night audience. We usually had a fifteen to twenty minute wait for our radar picked up the enemy bombers as soon as they took off from their Sicilian bases. We could hear our own fighters taking off from Ta' Qali, a few miles to the north-west, and climb to circle the island waiting to pounce. Only the bravest of Italian crews ventured over

Malta; the rest, we were told, dropped their bombs in the sea and took a devious route home to fill in time. The few that did cross the coast were not met by a hail of gun fire (unless it was too cloudy for fighter/searchlight affiliation) but by a mass of searchlights. We watched tensely as the beams groped for a victim. Once they had picked up a bomber, about three beams held the luckless aircraft while the others were doused. The fighter boys could be heard racing across the sky and then followed the exchange of fire: white tracer from the fighter versus the larger calibre pink tracer from the bomber's rear gunner. A strike on the bomber could clearly be seen for it was like a brilliant flash of sparks. While I was there I saw two Italian bombers plunge in flames to their doom. After the all-clear had sounded we returned to our beds, scrutinised the sheets for marauding lizards, adjusted the sandfly nets and fell off into a satisfied night's sleep.

W/Cdr Bunny Harte and the 107 Squadron crews had, by that time, arrived at Luqa. I was called into the CO's office one morning.

'How many sorties have you completed, Henry?'

'Thirty-nine, sir.'

'The MO has recommended that you go on rest. In fact,' he added as an afterthought, 'I'd forgotten that you had done a tour without rest when you joined the squadron.'

'That's all right, sir. In fact I wouldn't mind carrying on as long as it's with another pilot.'

'Yes, I understand,' was all he said.

On 26 September I and several others from Luqa (mostly from 105 Squadron) were told to pack our kit and report to the orderly room after lunch. We were going back to England. It was wonderful news since I had long ago given up hope of ever seeing home again.

In those days one had to take whatever was going in order to get back to the UK: a Sunderland flying-boat, a submarine or any one of a variety of surface vessels.

A large convoy had just arrived in Malta and part of its naval escort was in harbour preparing to return to Gibraltar. Arriving at one of the docks, we were ushered to a gangway up which we scrambled carrying our kit. Assembled on the aft deck, we watched the approach of the captain and a small knot of officers close on his heels. With his hands clasped behind his back, he bade us stand easy.

'You are aboard HMS. *Kenya*, a light cruiser. Accommodation will be found for you but it is of necessity limited, so do not expect too much. One of the hangars will be set aside for your messing as unfortunately, there isn't room for you in the petty officers' mess. The kit that you don't require will be stowed away but you will be able to get at it for your warmer clothing when we berth at Gibraltar.'

He then went on to say that while we lived on his ship, we must do what we were told for we were under naval jurisdiction and we had to play a part in defending it. Volunteers for various action stations were called for. At the request for two gunners I stepped forward together with another gunner. Seamen were detailed to show us to our respective quarters and to where we might have to 'fight'. I was shown to the torpedo workshop wherein were three or four low-slung camp-beds. Dumping my kit and other bits onto one of them, I was led away to be shown where my action station was. As my guide led me up a companionway, he told me that while we sailed through the Mediterranean, action stations would be piped at dawn and dusk irrespective of whether there were signs of the enemy and whenever else it was deemed necessary. To reach my post I climbed sundry ladders onto the searchlight and auxiliary compass platform at the base of the aft mast. Then up another ladder to a small roped-in platform on which was mounted a Lewis gun. Looking down and aft I could just see two armoured turrets, from each of which sprouted three 6-inch guns. Below me were four anti-aircraft turrets each equipped with, I believe, two 4.0 guns. There were also some multiple pom-poms (commonly referred to as 'Chicago pianos'). Amidships was the hooded aft funnel, the top of which seemed only a few feet above the level of my platform. Beyond that was the launching ramp (on which was one of the two Walrus amphibian aircraft carried on board), two recovery cranes and the two hangars the starboard of which was to be our mess. The closed doors of the other concealed the second Walrus. Forward of them was the taller of the two funnels, aft of the bridge; then the superstructure, draped with Carley floats and surmounted by the forward mast. Up front, but unseen from my gun position, were the two forward 6-inch gun turrets.

I returned to the workshop, circumnavigated the large 21-inch torpedo which was lashed to its fore-and-aft mounting in the centre of the 'shop, unpacked the few things I would need on the first part of the 'voyage' and took the rest on deck to be stowed away in one of the holds.

One of my RAF colleagues, John Turner (a sergeant pilot) had been delegated the magazine as his action station. Whenever the pipes called us to stations, we would all strike up with 'Remember the *Hood*, Johnny?' He would reply to our unkind taunt with a scowl and a vehemently tossed 'sailor's farewell'.

When *Kenya* had been victualled, the mooring hawsers were cast-off and we steamed slowly towards the open sea. We hadn't reached the harbour mouth before the air-raid sirens ashore began to wail. There was a scuffle on deck and what at first looked to be a disorganised rush hither and thither, turned out to be the usual pace at which the Navy operated every man knowing exactly what he had to do and doing it at the double. I was most impressed. All sorts of peculiar whistles were being sounded. A passing petty officer, with a friendly pat on the back which nearly sent me over the side, said 'Action stations matey, hop to it.' I doubled smartly to my bunk, grabbed my tin hat and ascended to my Lewis gun, clamped on the magazine and waited for action. None came. We sailed out of the harbour and headed round the north of the island. The all-clear we didn't hear but when night had fallen somebody bawled through a megaphone for me to come down. I joined the rest of the RAF contingent in the hangar, sat at a plain wooden trestle table and wrapped myself round a steaming mug of black tea.

As we mooched about deck, trying hard not to get under the feet of our hosts, we passed near a grating in the deck from which wafted the delicious smell of baking bread. We often stood near that spot, like Bisto kids, getting a foresmell of lunch. The food was very good but didn't vary much and was mostly out of a can. Who cared, for the sea air whetted our appetites; whatever was served went down a treat. In the evenings we entered the seamen's canteen where we could buy a few cheap cigarettes, chocolate and soft drinks. We also played tombola which helped break the monotony.

At dawn the following morning action stations was piped and up aloft I went. I was met by a sight I shall never forget. We led, in line astern, three other cruisers and four destroyers behind which the pending sunrise was turning the eastern horizon into a beautifully vivid multi-coloured backcloth. As those silhouetted ships proudly cut the water, signals lamps flickered their messages from bridge to bridge. I felt like singing 'Hearts of Oak' and breaking into the hornpipe. It was a very proud moment for me to be associated with the Royal Navy and some of its might.

When that Mediterranean dawn had fully blossomed, I tore myself away from a magnificent sight for I was hungry. Breakfast went down well even if naval tea was thick enough to support a spoon. Later that day the rest of the Mediterranean Fleet joined us. I counted 34 ships, all naval vessels, including *Ark Royal*, *Prince of Wales*, *Repulse*, *Ajax* and *Cossack*. There were carriers, battleships, cruisers and destroyers whichever way one looked, the major units being encompassed by the fast, manoeuvrable destroyer flotilla. *Kenya* was flag-ship for we had Admiral Burrough on board. In her pinkish Arctic camouflage, she looked out of place among the sombre grey and black livery of the other ships. When the sun got unbearably hot, I repaired to my bunk and lay there reading until the sound of distant explosions, mingling with the discordant sound of pipes to action stations, had me on my feet in a jiffy. Whether there were aircraft about or not, I had to obey the summons. The explosions had been distant depth charges; there were enemy submarines in the offing. No serious attack developed, however, for it was too powerful a force to reckon with, in daylight, anyway. That night, enemy bombers were picked up on the radar scopes but we were hugging the North African coast and they didn't fly far enough south to make contact. We were told the following morning that *Kenya* had narrowly missed colliding with the *Prince of Wales* during the night. We, in our ignorance, weren't surprised at that piece of news when, all day long, every ship in the convoy zigzagged all over the place.

At the close of the second day out from Malta, we broke off from the main Fleet and carried out a small exercise using the Walrus aircraft. It was catapulted from the ship and then stooged off on a recce flight. When eventually it returned, the curving wake left by its heeling parent served as its landing run. Taxiing up to our lee side, one of the aircraft's crew stood astride the top of the mainplane (this looked pretty hazardous to us), secured the crane cable to four hooks on the wing surface and the Walrus was hauled up and inboard. Later that evening we put in to Gibraltar. Our decks were lined by the ship's company while the screeching of pipes echoed across the harbour.

We were informed that liberty boats would pull away at about 6 pm and that we could have short shore leave. We were anxious to buy a few last-minute gifts and cheap cigarettes (they were limited on board) and some fruit. Fortunately, the shops kept open quite late and we managed to get all we wanted and could afford, plus a few drinks to compensate for our spell on a 'dry' ship.

Quite a few Army chaps came on board that night and the poor devils were accommodated down below the water line. During the night we were awakened by the Tannoy over which a broadcast told us that we were putting to sea forthwith (at 0445 hours). We hadn't been able to get at our kit, as promised, therefore still wearing tropical clothing we were carried out through the Straits into the chillier Atlantic. When the lights of Spain had sunk below the horizon, our mission, to find and subsequently sink an enemy supply ship somewhere off the Azores, was made known over the Tannoy. The following morning, side by side with another cruiser HMS. *Sheffield*, we ploughed through a heavy Atlantic swell. Both ships rolled a lot; from my bunk in the torpedo workshop, it was most uncomfortable to watch the heaving horizon appear over the coaming, move up and up until it disappeared above the top of the door then back again. The best thing to do, so we were told, was to ignore it. When we visited the heads we saw several airmen and many soldiers heaving their hearts up. I was grateful to be a good sailor.

The days that followed brought many false alarms from our advanced 'eye', the Walrus. That aircraft was too flimsy and vulnerable to venture very close to an armed merchantman but off it went every few hours to scout ahead. On one occasion we caught up with and challenged a lone vessel which turned out to be British registered and on its way to South America. We too were alone (*Sheffield* had left us the previous day to make its own search), but there was a vast difference between an armoured, powerfully-armed cruiser capable of 28 knots and a 12-knot tramp with only a couple of smallish guns mounted on her unarmoured decks. I raised my tin hat to those chaps, tanker crews in particular.

At each report of a ship ahead action stations was sounded. I climbed up into the rigging with my heart in my mouth perhaps because I dwelt on the days when one's adversary aimed for the masts first before getting down to the task of piercing the hull.

When 'Enemy depot ship with submarine alongside has been sighted, prepare for action,' came over the Tannoy, I felt the familiar flutter of fear. This was it. While my heart was doing a couple of Immelmanns, my imagination conjured up the scene which might ensue. Never having been in action with the Navy it was easy to get the wrong picture. However, when the pipes called I doubled to my station with an Irvin jacket over my thin shirt, nothing over my knobbly knees, a tin hat strapped securely under my chin and 1/2 lb. of cottonwool stuffed in each ear. Certainly I was nervous but I had lots of company around or rather below me, which is always a psychological comfort.

When I reached my little platform and had slapped a magazine on the Lewis, I quickly surveyed the horizon ahead. Yes, there it was, the tell-tale smudge of smoke marking the position of our still invisible target. With 'full-ahead-both' telegraphed to the engine room, *Kenya's* bow cut the water fiercely at about 27 knots, to close with our victim. Black smoke poured from the forward funnel and whipped over my head, swirled down to kiss our wake, then swept away to be dissipated behind us. The supply ship had also got up steam and bravely tried to get away.

With a deafening roar the first salvo of 6-inch shells from the forward turrets sped on their way. A cloud of acrid cordite-laden smoke came aft but the superstructure had shielded me from the guns' concussive blast. A few seconds later three spouts of water indicated that aim had to be adjusted although the first sighting shots had been close. 'Any moment now,' I thought, 'their shells will be slicing through the air...' but we must have been out of range. Meantime, the two front turrets continued to hurl their deadly salvoes across the rapidly diminishing stretch of sea between the target and ourselves. The shelling was effective; the target was ablaze on the poop. Two of their boats got away while the shelling continued with thunderous encores. As we drew closer to the stricken ship, I nearly had heart failure when the 6-inchers below me joined in. I got the full blast then and my tin hat went sailing down to the deck narrowly missing an officer. Looking up he shouted 'You may come down from there, your services won't be needed in this action.' Thankfully, I descended and made my way along the port deck as they were firing off the starboard side. I was met by the sight of another RAF gunner rooted to the deck, his face the colour of chalk and with a finger, buried to the first knuckle, in each of his ears. It was Gerry Quinn, DFM and bar! As the guns fired, a heavy metal hatchway that wasn't properly secured lifted from the deck to come crashing down again. The din was appalling. There was a sudden loud hiss, then another – they're firing back, I thought, but it was the sound of compressed air as two torpedoes were fired. 'Torpedoes away,' I heard faintly through my cottonwool We moved across to the starboard side to watch; one torpedo hit the already battered and blazing ship amidships just as another boat was pulling away. The depot ship (it was a tanker – the *Kota Pinang* – for refuelling U-boats) exploded into a boiling column of black smoke from which emerged an assortment of flying debris. Then there was nothing except for the couple of boats which had got away earlier.

'We shall not stop to pick up survivors,' came the mystery voice from the Tannoy, 'as there is reason to believe that the U-boat got clear and is still in the vicinity.' A very wise decision as it would have been madness to stop; the survivors would be picked up by their own submarine(s) later.

We turned in a wide arc onto a northerly course for home. It had certainly been a spectacular experience. I had by that time become hardened to the tragedies of war and therefore felt no compassion for those who might have died in that action. We had eliminated a source of danger to our own shipping which had suffered a terrible mauling at the hands of the U-boats. War was war; it was kill or be killed and it was no earthly use getting emotional about it.

We heard on the BBC news that evening '…an enemy supply ship was today sunk by the Royal Navy in the Atlantic…' We also heard, from one of the seamen in the torpedo workshop, 'That's how the Navy sinks a ship…' Whereupon, one of the mathematically-minded members of our contingent replied, good humouredly: 'Jolly good show, Jack. Most impressive. But just for the record, we have been sinking ships, too. In fact it hasn't been unknown for an aircraft to sink a ship with one 250 lb. bomb, which costs about £45. Your colleagues have just pooped off about 50 6-inch shells, about £25 each, I suppose, and two tinfish, one of which missed, each costing about £3,000. Sum total £7,225. Hmmmmm. Most impressive.'

An amusing tailpiece to that action: more than eighteen months later, when I was undergoing an aircrew medical, they fished from one of my ears a small piece of cottonwool. No wonder I never heard my friends when they asked for a loan!

The further north we steamed the colder it got for it was after all October and we were still in tropical gear. Our tan was wearing thin, too. I had hoped to preserve mine (when I left Malta I was almost black) in order to impress the opposite sex but it was not to be. All that I retained from that Mediterranean sojourn were, apart from a little piece of fluff in one ear, a store of vivid memories, some cheap cigarettes, a pair of white silk pyjamas, some green lemons, a tin hat with its Malta 'tortoiseshell' camouflage and a Maltese vocabulary consisting of three words: *Sahha* (goodbye) and *grazzi hafna* (ta).

Eight days after steaming out of sunny Grand Harbour, we steamed into dreary wet Gourock, west of Greenock on the Clyde. After our kit had, at long last, been extracted from the bowels of the ship, we hurriedly changed into warmer blue and disembarked. Hanging about in a fine drizzle on the quayside for what seemed ages, HM Customs finally caught up with us which was my first experience of their prying and chalky ways. That was followed by a nightmare, all-night journey by troop-train to an overseas reception depot in Lancashire. Arriving in the early hours, it took us all our time to convince those officious pen-pushers that we couldn't take our respirators with us for we had been allowed no more than 12 lb. of personal kit (other than what we stood up in). We were then given a long-awaited meal of lukewarm beans on 'paving-stone' toast and a mug of tea that would have tanned a hide *and* put the Navy's brew to shame.

The following day, after hours of time-consuming form-filling, we were issued with railway warrants to our units and, with abounding benevolence, sixpence subsistence allowance was given to each of us. With that princely sum in my pocket and a few 'pagoda' sandwiches, I had to travel right across the country to East Anglia.

When I got back to base I felt very lonely. It was strange and sad not to see familiar faces in the mess. I learned that dear Chuck Whiddon and Mac had 'bought it' with Fox on the very next sortie after I had left. It would have been my fortieth and very last, sortie had I stayed. Their aircraft had been hit when running-up on a ship and with full bomb load they had crashed in flames right into their target. There, but for the Grace of God…

I later ascertained that practically the whole of 107 Squadron had been wiped out in the months they were there. Bunny Harte was officially credited with sinking four ships before he was reported missing. The squadron adjutant, Tony Richardson, wrote (among other things) a couple of books of verse about the squadron's personalities: *Because of These* and *These – Our Children*. In the former there appeared the following tribute to the squadron commander:

IN MEMORIUM: WING COMMANDER
F.A. BUNNY HARTE, DFC

Now that your course is run, what sign or token
Shall such as I pass on to whom remain,
To those who've never heard your slow words spoken,
To us who'll never see that smile again?

That slow, sweet smile and brown, grave eyes in laughter
Your measured walk and trouser-pocket hand
Still will you weigh your words before and after,
Discussing flights across the Promised Land.

What message may I signal to those others
But that the tragic triumph of your end
Has set you evermore among your brothers,
Who loved you once on earth and called you friend?

The Squadron returned in January 1942. While operating from Malta it accounted for over 30,000 tons of shipping sunk and a further 16,000 tons damaged. But it had cost dearly for, apart from the one or two odd crew members (including myself) only three of the original crews returned. Other 2 Group Blenheim squadrons shared similar achievements and suffered similar fates while at Malta. Their work, nevertheless, contributed in no small degree to ultimate victory in North Africa and the war.

After a most welcome spell of leave I was posted to No. 13 OTU, Bicester for my first rest, on 29 October 1941. In the capacity of gunnery leader (with the rank of F/Sgt) I settled down to a dull routine as instructor on armament training. My log records the fact that I didn't fly for the five months October/ December 1941, January/February 1942; 150 days of boring anti-climax.

At the end of my third year with the RAF I had accumulated just over 420 flying hours, plus 190 hours with the Royal Navy. I had also survived some pretty close calls and to mourn the loss of many wonderful friends.

CHAPTER 4

March 1942/43:

First Rest – Search for dinghies – Second tour – New aircraft

How refreshing it was, after that long break, to get into the air again. On 19 March 1942, I had my first ride in the latest version of the Blenheim, the Mark V or Bisley, as it was called. It was different in that the nose had been rounded off and the characteristic 'greenhouse' front of the IV had largely disappeared. It was a heavier machine and the gunner's turret had been modernised. There was no longer a draughty aperture around the gun barrels and the turret structure and controls had been altered considerably. I must confess to a feeling of claustrophobia (even if it was a little warmer) within its structure and preferred the old, cold but nonetheless efficient turret of the IV.

From then on I enjoyed pretty continuous flying. One or two of the trips brought on pangs of nostalgia: a spot of low-level practice bombing on the dummy ship in the Wash; a formation flight to Yatesbury after which we landed at Boscombe Down and Thruxton. Two days later we landed at Yatesbury.

It was early in May when I scrounged my first-ever ride in a biplane, an Avro Tutor. I persuaded W/O Morrison, a gnarled, tough Scot, to get me away from the blackboard since the weather was too good to be entombed in a classroom. I asked him to demonstrate some real aerobatics. We took off into glorious sunshine; sitting there in an open cockpit I revelled in every second of the flight. There was no need for recourse to Mitty, for below me were green fields; the slipstream was whistling through the flying/landing wires; the engine was ticking over rhythmically and the air was like champagne.

We flew around for a while when, over the Gosport tubing (there was no radio), the scratchy indistinct voice of the pilot informed me that we were '…going down to land for a moment.' We touched down on a strange airfield and, with the engine ticking over, the pilot climbed out of his cockpit, saying 'Must have a leak.' It was, to say the least, an incongruous situation. I sat there while he made water over the port wheel of the undercarriage, on a strange airfield, in the middle of a flying programme by Wellington aircraft which took off either side of us. It would shake him, I thought, if I opened the throttle and made him run for it. Before he climbed back again, he leant over the side of the cockpit and checked my straps. He told me that he couldn't have done any aerobatics as he hadn't done his straps up but that we would get off and do some.

Off we went again, doubtless leaving behind us a traffic control officer just putting down his field glasses and scratching his head in puzzlement. Climbing up to about 7,000 feet, the Gosport crackled the information that we were about to loop. The nose went down and the Tutor gathered a respectable airspeed before the stick was pulled back. I felt 'g' pressing me down in my seat as the nose reared over the horizon and pointed to the sky above and then over. For a moment I hung on my straps, the throttle was closed and with an almost silent motor the nose dropped towards the ground below before the Tutor flattened out with the accompanying 'g' once more. Apart from the dust which came off the floor and the Gosport tubing hanging out of the cockpit when we were inverted, I found the experience electrifying. Every minute of that loop, and those that followed, was superb. I had no qualms, just the initial instinctive gripping of the underside of my seat when upside down, but I soon learnt to trust the straps.

After a few more loops and spins, I was offered the controls for a while. I found them to be almost as sensitive as those on the Link trainer but the fact that I was airborne made the comparison difficult. I'd say that it felt 1,000 per cent better than sitting in a wooden box full of instruments.

At the end of May I again scrounged a trip in Tutor K.4811 that time for an hour's aerobatics with P/O Vivian. I realised two things after that flight: first, how apt was the expression 'in a flat spin' for we went through those motions several times; secondly, how pilots differ in their choice of aerobatics.

The classroom work I had to cope with, meantime, was boring to the extreme but it had to be done. It wasn't made any easier with the pupils' restless anxiety to move to a squadron. I don't know whether it was to escape the tedium of ground instruction, or the urge to charge willy-nilly into action, but it had to be faced and all of us had to endure the more boring aspects of training. There were a lot of Commonwealth chaps coming through OTU at about that time and I found that the Aussies were the most impatient of them all almost to the point of blatant inattentiveness. They were keen enough and intelligent but out-and-out rebels in the classroom. All I could say to them was 'I know how you feel, but remember that it isn't just your life at stake but those of your crew and not to overlook a bloody expensive aeroplane. Everything you are being taught here is for your benefit.' They agreed all right but it was always an effort to hold their attention during the duller aspects of training.

In the practical field one got the occasional non-mechanical type (referred to earlier). A gunner came back from his aircraft one day bemoaning the fact that he couldn't cock one of his guns. I jumped on a bicycle and went out to the machine, climbed into the turret and took one look at the offending gun. Immediately the cause of his trouble stared me in the eye; the reflector sight cable was wedged in the cocking-stud slot and had nearly been severed by the frantic pulling of the cocking toggle. Had this occurred in action he might have been a dead duck.

We had a lot of fun in the sergeants' mess at Bicester. Two great friends, Reg Goode and 'Tupp' Tuppen and myself were on the entertainments committee. Two incidents arising from that work bear relating for we, at any rate, found them amusing. The first could, in fact, have had unpleasant repercussions but for a slice of luck.

We were putting the finishing touches to the stage arrangements in the upper dining hall of the airmen's mess where, that evening, there was to be a dance. Reg, Tupp and I had borrowed an amplifier and microphone and had wired the whole apparatus at the side of the stage. We noticed that there were two large horn-type loudspeakers mounted high on the wall. Ideal, we thought. Assuming them to be part of the stage equipment (ENSA shows were given in the hall below), I found a ladder and carried the amplifier leads up to one of them. I couldn't remove the existing leads for they were soldered, so just attached ours to them. Switching on to test whether the microphone was correctly positioned and so eliminate feed-back howl, Reg (who was to be MC) took over. He was about to recite a monologue from his not-so-clean repertoire when two WAAFs appeared with their tea. This was indeed fortuitous for us as you'll see. Dropping his original intention, Reg called us over and the three of us did our imitation of the then popular radio show 'ITMA'.

'Hey, Lefty, look at dem goils,' boomed from the 'speaker and reverberated round the empty hall. That noisy repartee went on for the best part of twenty minutes but it was all good clean stuff.

Switching off, we dusted our hands professionally and went back to the mess for tea. As soon as we entered we were greeted with 'Wonderful broadcast you made but you aren't going to be very popular with the Station Master.'

Naturally, we thought they were pulling our legs but similar remarks were made by every NCO who came in the mess. There was no mistake about it they were deadly serious. We had been broadcasting over the station Tannoy system! We decided that something had to be done and quickly. Reg went off to the signals section to scrounge a 'speaker, while I went to the hall to disconnect from the main circuit. It had been an understandable error since Tannoy 'speakers were usually of one pattern, a square box with TANNOY slapped over its front panel. I'd certainly never seen the horn type used before.

When we had put things right and tested for sound, we went back to the mess. Any minute now, we thought, the 'phone would ring followed by a summons from the adjutant to march down and see the 'old man'. Reg, Tupp and I kept bursting into laughter, for it really was funny to picture the afternoon peace of the Group Captain's office being shattered with 'Yea, he's a gwate guy, gwate guy...' in a raucous Bowery accent followed by a string of impersonations of other Tommy Handley characters to flex his eardrums. But while we acquired for ourselves the title 'Tannoy Kings', we didn't hear a squeak from SHQ. The Station Commander must have been away. We blessed those WAAFs who had so beautifully timed their entry to prevent us from going on the air with unexpurgated versions of *Eskimo Nell*, *Salome* or *The Good Ship Venus*.

Ironically, a few weeks later both Reg and I were interviewed by the Station Commander, Group Captain Kyle, on the occasion of the recommendations for our commissions. That tough Australian had betrayed no sign of having discovered our names in his black book before firing the routine questions at us.

The second incident involving the entertainments committee was, I thought, even more amusing. Knowing that there was going to be a WAAF social in the mess. I had returned from leave earlier than usual. As soon as I set foot inside the mess Reg and other committee members approached me with broad grins on their faces. I thought to myself 'ullo, 'ullo, what's all this, then?'

'Frankie boy,' Reg began, with his most disarming smile, 'You are performing at the social tonight.'

'Performing?' I asked, apprehensively, for one of the facets of my character was a built-in stage fright. 'And what, may I enquire – er, I'll have a large gin, please – am I threatened with?'

'We have rigged up the most wonderful surprise item which will slay 'em in the aisles and you are going to take the part of Ali Ben Henry.'

'I'm what! Ali Ben... Now just a minute, who said that I'd fall for that?'

'Just a moment, calm down, we're all taking part so let me explain...' and as Reg went on to outline the scheme, I ordered more Dutch courage to be poured. Actually, it was a stunning party piece which had been suggested by a New Zealander (he had seen it performed at home) and the plot was as follows: I would be draped, toga-fashion, in a sheet, while a one-piece earphone would be concealed by a puggaree. From the earphone two wires would be threaded under my clothing and divided so that one went down each of my trouser legs and attached to the back of specially-prepared boots the soles of which were covered with a piece of metal gauze. I was to be ushered in to the strains of special music (potentates for the use of) and to climb up onto a table to face my audience. I would then sit on a chair which had been placed in such a position that two metal studs protruding through the table top would fit nicely under each boot. From the studs, wires (concealed from the audience by drapes at the table front) ran round the edge of the large anteroom to the stage at the back of the audience. On the stage, concealed behind the glare from a battery of hand-held Aldis lamps, was the New Zealander with a microphone (connected to my earphone) and powerful binoculars. Reg was to collect from the audience and hold aloft, various personal items which I would then proceed to identify. I was, by the way, to be blindfolded. It sounded so simple that I couldn't very well refuse to participate, so I ordered another stiff gin.

When the appointed hour arrived, a roll of drums and an announcement from Reg got the assembly squatting on the floor facing my chair. Only half a dozen of us knew the secret of the trick we were about to perform. With the smell of grease paint up my nose I walked in and bowed to the mob. As I did so my turban nearly came adrift but Reg secured it with the blindfold (checked for efficacy by one of the audience). I was guided up some steps to the chair on the table top and sat down squarely hoping that my boots were making contact.

Another roll of drums preceded Reg's next announcement: 'Ladies and gentlemen, we have with us tonight Ali Ben Henry who will amaze you with his powers of extra sensory perception. In a few moments I'll come down among you and ask for something from your pockets or handbags. Ali Ben will then tell you what that object is. I might add that no code will be used. Thank you.'

I heard it all, in a muffled way, but could hear nothing over the earphone. I then heard a distant voice saying 'Ali Ben, can you tell me what I am holding in my hand?' I damned well couldn't as there wasn't a squeak from my informant. I had to say something so, while gently moving my feet about trying to gain contact, I said 'Ze object iss a leetle cloudy,' still playing for time as I didn't want a flop on my hands, I continued 'I weel haff to meditate for a jort while.' My boots touched something for there was a crackle in my ear. I groped a bit more until, at long last, the circuit was closed. 'Can you hear me? For God's sake, can you hear me? Lift your right hand a little if you can hear me,' a voice said with a tinge of panic in it. I lifted my right hand and said 'I am beginning to see more clearly, pleece giff me a few seconds.'

I heard Reg cut the band who had been helping me to concentrate with a loud rendering of 'The snake charmer from old Baghdad' – and he again held up the first object; the binocs were trained and the 'gen' was whizzed down the wires to my ear: 'It's a ticket of some sort,' I was informed.

'I zee a peeze of paper,' I began, 'Eet iss small and hass writing on eet...'

'I'll give you the number,' continued my 'spy'.

'Zair iss a number on zat peeze of paper...I sink eet iss 423147

'Ali Ben,' broke in Reg, 'can you tell us what the piece of paper represents?'

'Yez, I sink eet iss a ticket, maybe to zee zinema...yez, I can zee a prize on eet, two and seekspenze.'

'You are absolutely right, Ali Ben,' said Reg.

There was a soft murmur of wonderment, then applause followed by complete silence as Reg produced another item. The 'turn' went on for nearly an hour. I couldn't go wrong, although one or two small items like a well-worn foreign coin etc., called for some cautious 'near' answers which generally described them. But we succeeded, after the dodgy start, in bewildering them all.

When the show was over, Reg climbed up to remove my

blindfold. I climbed down as majestically as I knew how and thirstily made my way to change before getting at the bar. Over a pint of more-than-welcome beer I was besieged with questions. 'How the devil did you do it?' 'It's amazing!' 'Are you really psychic?' (the last from a wide-eyed WAAF), and so forth. I had never been so popular in my life. I didn't buy a drink for ages after that performance. I had to grin because the chaps who had done all the hard work getting the props ready, fixing the boots and other wiring, were ignored.

We didn't disclose the secret to anyone, more to preserve the fillip to our ego than fearing an unwanted anti-climax.

It wasn't long after that fabulous success, however, when our efforts were made to look puny by a couple on an ENSA show. A man not only got rapid identification of objects from his lady partner but she knew, and, what is more, could play on the piano every tune (except the Portuguese National Anthem which one wag asked for) that was whispered into the ear of her colleague by members of the audience. It was an outstanding performance. Ali Ben Henry fell from his pedestal that night.

Reg and I joined the station dramatic society. We started to learn and rehearse our parts in *I Killed the Count*. Unfortunately, so many of the cast were posted that it was decided to kill the production. It took too long to get new members and for them to start from scratch.

We also started to take German lessons which were given by one of the padres. We took to him from the outset, for he began the first lesson with '*Herr Ober, ein Glas bier, bitte.*'

Our interviews for commissions had gone off successfully as official recognition came through: F/Sgts Goode and Henry were to proceed on leave for the purpose of getting kitted-up as pilot officers. One is, of course, dismissed the service to rejoin as an officer. My number was whittled down from 637244 to 48844. Reg and I went up to London to spend the £45 allowance made by the Air Ministry. It was insufficient to buy everything listed (Dress kit was not included during war-time).

On our return to camp we found the experience of being saluted a strange one and rather shyly we entered the officers' mess. I was more than pleased to share a room with Bunny Rogers. He was, as I entered, grooming his large moustache with a couple of silver-backed hair brushes. He made me very welcome and showed me the ropes.

The first officers' mess party (a stag affair) I attended was astounding. Some of the quiet, efficient Dr Jekylls I worked alongside and under became veritable Mr Hydes. Although they didn't exactly resort to murder, they came close to it with some of the 'games' that were played. Broken bones weren't uncommon nor were broken windows, glasses and furniture. Footprints, in beer and soot, would weave a crazy pattern up the walls and across the ceiling. The evening was usually rounded off with a sing-song – a Bechstein grand surrounded by beer-mug-swinging officers, singing as lustily as they knew how. A Bavarian *bier keller* would have seemed like a deserted chapel by comparison.

In the years that were to follow I attended countless parties but the most outstanding of them all were in the RAF with operational stations proving the most hectic. I am reminded of the story concerning the young acting pilot officer at his first mess party. Being a gentleman, he approached a dowager Duchess-type of woman who had been surveying the throng through lorgnette with the utmost solemnity.

'Would you care to dance, madam?' he asked politely.

Looking him up and down as though he were a rotten piece of cheese, she coldly replied 'Thank you, but I am not in the habit of dancing with children.'

'I beg your pardon, madam, I wasn't aware of your condition.'

* * *

In June 1942, the pulverising 1,000-bomber raids took place. The first, Cologne being the target, was on the night of 1-2 June. At 7.30 am on the 2nd, I flew with P/O Vivian on a three-hour air-sea-rescue operation. We searched a section of the North Sea for dinghies. In order to muster that number of bombers, for there weren't enough front-line aircraft, OTUs supplied the balance. Many of the crews were only half-trained and some of the aircraft had seen better days. Before we took off that morning, we watched some of them stagger back to their bases nearby. I recall being told of the inexperienced crew from an OTU who, at dawn, had crash-landed their aircraft in a field. Scrambling from their machine they spotted a windmill nearby. They hadn't been at all sure of their position before letting down through cloud and so assumed that they were in Holland. It was decided that the aircraft must be burned, and then get clear quickly to start the long trek south into

Belgium where they'd contact the resistance movement. Firing a Very cartridge into the damaged wing fuel tank, the machine got blazing merrily and the crew crawled away along a hedge. They put in a few miles before the approach of two cyclists made them freeze into a ditch. As the 'enemy' passed, the escapees distinctly heard them talking fluent English. They had put down in the Fens!

We did three of those dinghy searches that month (and a fourth in January 1943), each counting as half an operation.

In July, memories were stirred again when P/O Alec Bristow flew me down to Weston Zoyland. On the way back, after putting in at Haddenham, I sat up front and had my first dual in a Blenheim Mk I.

Alec and his navigator were later to put up a good show after attacking, in their Mosquito, a target in Norway. On the way back they flew at nought feet over the North Sea and hadn't been at it for long when a large seagull crashed through the pilot's side of the windscreen and smashed into Alec's face, temporarily blinding him. His navigator had the presence of mind to grab the stick and pull the aircraft up a few hundred feet while Alec sorted his face out from all the bones, feathers and blood. His face was very badly cut and one of his eyes was puffed and closed, but it looked worse with the bird's remains spattered all over his front. The relative speed of the bird/aircraft had been reduced considerably at impact by the tough windscreen. This had saved Alec's life but for a few moments the situation had been fraught. At that height, and the initial shock it gave the pilot, the aircraft could easily have plunged straight into the sea. Nevertheless, they brought back the very draughty Mosquito to base and landed it without further mishap.

I saw Alec a week or so later and he still wore a 'shiner' to outshine all shiners.

Still eager to fly in new types, I got a ride in a Boston, a fifteen-minute air-test on 31 July. What a magnificent aeroplane it was. It was immediately apparent how much more powerful and manoeuvrable it was when compared with the Blenheim. A strange innovation was the duplicated flying controls in the gunner's cockpit, a stick and rudder bar, but no instruments nor could the gunner see where he was steering if he had to take control. Nevertheless, later in the war, there was the case of the French gunner who helped bring in a Boston when his pilot was badly injured and weak from loss of blood. The navigator called out the airspeed and altitude; the pilot was conscious and just able to move the throttles and select the undercarriage/flaps while the gunner helped with the controls. It was a highly commendable piece of crew co-operation.

In August I added to my growing list a Tiger Moth and an Airspeed Oxford. The former flight was a delightful hour of aerobatics and dual, and the latter a two-and-a-half hour trip: 'BAC checks at three different airfields.' There was a special BAC (Blind Approach Calibration) Flight attached to Bicester at that time. The pilot told me as we approached to land, 'These bloody aeroplanes are hell to three-point, they have to be wheeled in...'

There followed an interesting flight when we photographed (VLOs – Vertical Line Overlaps) six airfields. It was very draughty in the back with the camera hatch open. One of my jobs was to check that the camera turned over when the navigator operated it by remote control. Air-to-ground mosaic photography called for a steady course and, naturally, clear weather.

Eleven months after leaving Malta, I was posted to No. 114 Squadron ('RT') which was converting from Blenheim IVs to Bisleys. The squadron was stationed at West Raynham and I was delighted to be accommodated at Weasenham Hall once more, this time in the officers' mess. The squadron commander (who shall remain nameless) hadn't, as far as I can remember, operated much if at all. Nor had the majority of the crews. Many of the pilots were former Army officers, a grand bunch of chaps who, on qualifying as pilots, had transferred to the RAF. But the usual atmosphere and spirit of an operational squadron was lacking. A few of us 'old sweats' tried to infuse such a spirit among the newcomers. I was crewed up with the 'B' Flight commander, S/Ldr Tommy Thompson, and my navigator was F/O 'Twiggie' Branch. Between us we had more operational experience than the whole squadron put together. Twiggie, a tremendous personality, had to his credit seventy-seven ops. all of which were done in Blenheims in the Middle East, Greece and Crete (I believe with No. 30 Squadron?). He was a regular and had completed about 8 years abroad before joining 114 Squadron. Tommy Thompson had done between forty and fifty, and my score was forty-one.

Twiggie and I spent a lot of our off-duty time in the bar at Weasenham, the best place to infuse the spirit required. The young ex-Army chaps seemed, at first, a little shy of parties. We were at that time temporarily non-operational pending a move to North Africa together with No. 18 Squadron (whose CO, W/Cdr H. G. Malcolm, was later posthumously awarded the VC and whose name was given to the many RAF clubs throughout the Service). However, our efforts proved to be an uphill struggle, for the CO was not a party man, nor was his navigator, and he invariably went to bed at about 9 pm. It was almost unheard of, although it wouldn't have mattered a great deal had he not tried to dampen the spirit of the rest of us.

He certainly had it in for Twiggie and me since it was made quite clear that he was having his beauty sleep disturbed by our racket in the bar.

Apart from the bulk of the crews and our own pilot, the best supporter of our cause was Group Captain 'Paddy' Bandon. With some admin. friends, he would often come down to Weasenham and, with tunic comfortably unbuttoned, tankard in hand, he stood by the bar enjoying himself. He had a deep, resonant laugh which boomed and echoed round the panelled walls of the mess. In spite of his easy-going manner in the mess, he was deeply respected and was a magnificent CO. He ultimately reached the rank of Air Chief Marshal before his retirement from the Royal Air Force in 1963.

The day arrived when the squadron commander put his cards on the table. Twiggie and I were called, separately, into his office. I knocked and entered, stood by his desk and saluted, wondering what he was about to say.

'You wanted to see me, sir?'

'Yes, Henry. As you have only been back from abroad less than a year, I'm afraid that I cannot take you with the squadron to Africa. Branch, too, is not eligible, since he has been back in this country only a few months. You'll both be returning to Bicester. This I have arranged.'

I had expected something like that but I was nonetheless shattered, more so because he had made that little speech with his back turned towards me, looking out of the window as though ashamed to face me. Twiggie told me after his interview that he had received similar treatment. 'Apart from the stigma, I couldn't care less,' he said, 'there's no future with this squadron,' he added.

However, a day or so later when Twiggie and I were having a few farewell drinks in the main hall of the West Raynham mess, a steward came up to me and said 'Excuse me, sir. The Group Captain would like a word with you and F/O Branch. He is in the anteroom.'

'Thanks,' I said, putting down my beer.

When we entered the anteroom, Paddy was standing with his back to the fireplace. Taking a hearty swig from his silver tankard, he said to us 'I'm dreadfully sorry that you two are leaving us. I have a good idea why but I cannot very well oppose it. However, don't worry, I take a good view of you both and you'll be leaving here with a clean sheet. As soon as the two squadrons leave for Africa, I'll see what can be done to get you back here. Have a noggin...'

That was good enough for us; we were relieved that no black marks had been chalked in our dossiers. Apart from making some very good friends and having the pleasure of serving under Paddy Bandon, also seeing a lot of the 'Pheas' again, all we had to show for that month with 114 Squadron was a very thin bank balance.

After 18 and 114 squadrons had arrived in North Africa, we heard that they had received a mauling, one of the squadrons being practically wiped out when they were jumped by an overwhelming force of fighters.

When Twiggie and I got back to Bicester, we shared a room in Brashfield House. It was a small, expensively-built private-type residence standing in its own grounds at the back of the officers' mess. The downstairs floor was used as a club. There was a small bar, shin-dig space and a fruit machine. Fortunately for us it was used only on special occasions and at week-ends. We added to our list of friends a W/Op.AG, Colin Shevlin (Shev to us). He had just arrived in the UK from Kenya. The three of us had some wonderful times at Bicester.

My duties at OTU were many and varied, mostly gunnery instruction, aircraft recognition, clay-pigeon shooting etc. The aircraft 'recog' I coped with quite well, partly because I had a good eye for 'shapes' and also because my artistic talent enabled me to bespatter a large blackboard with a variety of significant aircraft 'bits' or, if you like, some of their salient recognition features. For example: the diamond-shaped tailplane of the Avro-Anson; the pronounced cutaway at the base of the rudder on both the Saro Lerwick flying-boat and the Heinkel 111; the bulbous nose of the Ju.88 and the similarity between the fin/rudder of that aeroplane and the Blenheim and so forth. There was also a special model room from the ceiling of which hung scale models of military aircraft of every description. I knew them by heart.

I came unstuck one day, however, when taking a visiting party of Air Training Corps cadets. I was soon to learn how careful one had to be when faced with those keen young men. Their knowledge of aircraft was astounding. They almost knew how many rivets there were in a Spitfire and what its designer had for breakfast on the day he conceived it.

Anyway, there I was...surrounded by a group of mustard-keen lads. 'What's that one?' I asked, pointing to a fighter which I thought to be an easy one for them to start with.

'A Dewoitine, sir,' was their quick-as-a-flash answer.

'Look again,' I said.

'A Dewoitine 550, sir,' they echoed. There was no doubt about their self-assurance.

'I think you'd better look once more because you're wrong,' I said, grinning at them.

'But it is a Dewoitine, sir. It says so on the bottom.'

My head whipped round and up. Yes, there it was, large as life 'DEWOITINE 550' marked on the underside of the model's fuselage. I didn't know where to put my face, for a moment.

'You're dead right. My mistake, I apologise. Should have looked more closely as somebody has changed that model for the Hurricane that usually hangs in that spot.'

D'you know, I'm sure that they didn't believe me.

There was a new Station Commander at Bicester by that time, Group Captain Arbuthnot. I was delegated to be his personal W/Op.AG. He was a very tall man with a soft, almost high-pitched voice. One of the ribbons on his uniform intrigued me. I hadn't seen the like before and found out that it was the Order of St John of Jerusalem. My first flight with him was in a Defiant. We went down to Boscombe Down for lunch. While there I remember being shown some tests which were being made with the mid-upper turret of a Lancaster. In it was mounted a 20 mm cannon its butt and muzzle protruding from the front and back of the cupola (the gun was about eight to ten feet long) while the gunner sat underneath it. The tail of the Lanc. had been jacked up and an armament boffin was firing the cannon into and through some railway sleepers which had been erected in the range's sandy butts. I believe that the tests were discontinued because of structural weakness.

I accumulated quite a bit of flying in October and on the 8th got me a ride in a B.25 or Mitchell as it was called in the RAF. It was the type of aircraft which flew off the decks of a US Navy carrier to bomb Tokyo later in the war. I didn't like the turret of that machine for, with ordinary flying clothing and parachute harness on, it was as much as I could do to squeeze through the very small space between top of fuselage and seat of turret, and I'm only a 5½-footer. How the bigger-built gunners got into the thing I cannot imagine. There was a very sad story of a Mitchell gunner who was trapped in his turret and died there. The aircraft had been badly hit by flak and, as it returned over the Channel, it was obvious that a ditching was necessary. Plenty of warning was given the air-sea-rescue organisation and they had a couple of launches on the spot when the machine hit the water. The pilot and navigator got out all right but the aircraft's back had broken and had trapped the gunner in his turret. He was sitting there watching the efforts of the rescue teams as they tried desperately to cut him free while the aircraft still floated. They couldn't cut through the aircraft's structure before it sank and down went the gunner in front of their eyes, by that time wet with tears.

I also flew a few times with the OC Operational Training Flight, S/Ldr Bob Iredale – a great personality who wore the dark blue uniform of the Royal Australian Air Force. Then there was an amusing ride with F/Lt Dickie Bird in a Miles Master II. We stooged up to Wittering, near Peterborough, – to do some BAC tests there. When we neared the area we saw below us, weaving in and out of cloud, a few Tiger Moths – doubtless pilots under training. 'This aircraft,' said Dickie, 'might easily be mistaken for a Fw.190, so let's come out of the sun and put the wind up 'em.' He pushed the nose down and made a mock attack on one of them. Its pilot soon spotted us and, using the manoeuvrability of his biplane to best advantage, quickly turned away below us and dived into cloud. It was an excellent piece of evasive action. Dickie said 'That's enough, I think. He should produce a jolly good "line shoot" in his mess when he gets back.'

The Group Captain's personal aircraft was a short-nose Blenheim and, naturally, it was kept in impeccable condition. My first flight in it was to RAF Hixon in Staffordshire. This was intended to be an away luncheon but when we landed there the port engine developed trouble and the G/Capt. spent a lot of time (until a tractor with tow-bar came out to assist) trying to taxi on one engine and opposite brake, an almost impossible task. It was pouring with rain, too, which didn't help matters. We stayed for lunch, tea, dinner and breakfast but managed to get off at 10 am the following morning.

The following day I had a very pleasant trip with the CFI, W/Cdr Mike Pollard, a young Canadian who, apart from being a very skilful pilot (and, I believe, a bit of a poet) had a grand sense of humour. I sat next to him, up front, in a Blenheim IV while my Flight Commander, Bob Iredale sat in the navigator's seat in the 'greenhouse'. First we landed at West Raynham for a few ales and lunch, then took off at 2.30 pm for RAF Feltwell, twenty minutes flying away. On leaving there, Mike took off straight from the control tower where he had parked. That last leg back to base was a riot. Mike, with his feet up on the instrument panel and stick between his legs, switched on his microphone and started to sing one of our favourite party songs: 'Oh the deacon went down, to the cellar to pray, and he got drunk, and he stayed all day...' Bob and I joined in. With Mike yawing the Blenheim all over the sky to the rhythm of the song we so lustily sang, it was one of those happy carefree occasions when one sensed the later brewing of a party.

At the end of the month I flew with the G/Capt. to Gransden Lodge, near Bedford. We left L.1285 to be flown back by another pilot while we brought back an Albemarle Mk I. That aeroplane was a peculiar contraption; whenever the undercarriage was selected 'up' or 'down' two small flaps opened up in the top of each wing, followed by two rods which bobbed up and down again before the flaps shut. That constructional oddity fascinated me. It was also the first British-built aircraft to be fitted with tricycle undercart. I wasn't terribly impressed with the machine except for the fact that the wireless operator's position was a pleasant one, right behind the pilot. I always liked to watch the 'driver' since I had a strong passion to drive and fly.

The Albemarle, having been found unsuitable for operational work, was to be tried out at Bicester as a possible training aircraft. As the Boston and Mitchell aircraft were coming into service with 2 Group squadrons, the Albemarle with its 'trike' undercarriage was possibly considered to be a suitable conversion trainer, and there were a lot of Albemarles hanging about doing nothing. Nevertheless, later in the war that aeroplane was used to good effect as a glider tug.

Before landing the Albemarle back at Bicester, the G/Capt. said to me, 'Henry, see if you can find the emergency hydraulic handle, the undercarriage warning lights aren't showing at all.' I hadn't a

clue where the emergency handle was as it was the first time I had
seen the aeroplane. Looking over his shoulder at the instrument
panel, I noticed that the undercarriage indicator was switched to the
'night' position which cut down the glare by means of a filter over
the lights. Leaning over his right shoulder, I moved it to 'day' and
the green lights shone brilliantly. 'The undercarriage is down and
locked, sir,' I said, little realising that I might be embarrassing him.
However, hunting for the emergency handle and then pumping it to
no avail would have been equally embarrassing.

One of the two Albemarles in use at Bicester was later involved
in an accident. It was standing on the grass, minding its own
business, when a Blenheim did a ground-loop on take-off and hit
the stationary Albemarle, practically severing the tail assembly
from the fuselage. Shev was in the Blenheim and while he got away
with a few bruises and abrasions, the pilot was badly hurt and, so
I'm told, died later. I also vaguely remember being told that the
wooden part of the tail was found to be badly affected by
woodworm, thus that accident might have prevented another.

On 6 November, I flew for the third time in the Tutor – 30
minutes of glorious aerobatics with F/Lt 'Tubby' Coombes (a staff
pilot at Bicester since I first knew the place who had moved up
from the rank of flight sergeant). The following day I did a Cooks
tour with the G/Capt. in an Albemarle; we got in forty-five minutes
local flying then flew down to Aldermaston before landing at the
U.S. Army Air Force base at Greenham Common, near Newbury.
The next day I had another forty-five minutes in the Tutor.

On 11 November, I went on attachment to the AFDU (Air
Fighting Development Unit) at RAF Duxford, near Cambridge.
There was no flying involved on the two-day course but it was of
great interest. We saw some excellent camera-gun film of bombers
being attacked by fighters (RAF versus RAF, of course) and the
evasive action that had been used during the attacks. How effective
that action had been was revealed by the ring and bead sight
superimposed on the film, since not many strikes were registered.
The four radial engines of the Stirling gave rise to much
apprehension among fighter pilots for, when that bomber began to
corkscrew, its slipstream produced a turbulent vortex, a deadly
weapon which fighter pilots came to respect. We had a wow of a
party in Cambridge before returning to Bicester.

Over the latter half of November, I flew with the G/Capt., Mike

Pollard and with Bob Iredale several times; only the best drivers for this chicken. I also had another session in the Tutor with Tubby Coombes. Landings were made and recorded at the following 'fields: Ford, Farnborough, Feltwell, Foulsham and Finmere. The last flight of the month was with the G/Capt. We went down to Stert Flats, off the north Devon coast, to drop four 250 lb. bombs, live. Later Mike Pollard took me on a proving flight in the Albemarle. His remarks about that aircraft weren't very complimentary, for it lost height with one engine throttled back and would just about maintain height with one prop feathered. This was my first experience of flying in an aircraft with a stationary 'fan'. It was odd to look out and see the blades swivelling at their roots and then to stop revolving – no windmilling, no drag.

Talking of feathering brings to mind the pilot I knew on 107 Squadron, later in the war. He, George Turner, was returning in his Boston from France when he spotted ahead and below a lone Mosquito cruising in the same direction. George put the nose down and wound up a decent speed. He then feathered one prop before sailing past the Mozzy. The pilot in the Mosquito nearly fell out of his seat when he looked to his right and saw George, two fingers raised, steam past in a 'slower' type of aircraft and with one of its props feathered.

I only got in five days' flying during December but in that time I chalked up flights in Blenheims Mk. I and IV, Tutor, Defiant, Beaufighter II and a Junkers 88. The latter entry was a prize one. That German-built, Jumo-powered bomber was one of a group of captured enemy aircraft which toured the country to give the ground defences at RAF airfields a bit of recognition practice. We circled Bicester and made various dummy attacks from many angles so that the gunners could familiarise themselves with the features of each aircraft; the 'circus' included an Me.110, He.111, Me.109 and the Junkers 88. They all bore, of course, military roundels but were escorted wherever they went by fighters. The Ju.88 (HM.509), flown at the time by F/O Llewendon, was far more manoeuvrable than the Blenheim and could turn within the airfield boundary. The whole crew sat up front as the fuselage of most German bombers was taken up by the vertically-stowed bomb load. I noticed a peculiar smell about the Ju.88 (and the other German aircraft I'd looked over), and I was told that it may have been the hydraulic fluid they used. Their hydraulic systems were reported to be far superior to those of British design, so it may have been due to that.

The Beaufighter was another addition to my list of types. This aircraft, the pilot told me, was apt to swing badly on takeoff and one must therefore have good brake pressure before attempting take-off.

On one of those five days' flying I had my first flight with S/Ldr Paddy Maher. He was a wonderful chap and a regular pilot of long standing. As far as I recall, he was the only pilot I'd flown with who wore the ribbon of the AFM. We flew to West Raynham in a Blenheim I. With the patience of an experienced and hardened instructor, Paddy bade me sit in the pilot's seat (the aircraft was, obviously, equipped with dual controls) and I taxied it awkwardly round the peri-track. He took it off the ground; I flew it all the way, getting in the odd turn; he landed it and I taxied round and in. How I enjoyed myself that day.

The little men who hammered on the inside of my skull during the throes of a post-Christmas hangover, were still hammering when I was posted to 107 Squadron (then commanded by W/Cdr Carver). The squadron had converted to Boston IIIs. Twiggie and Shev had crewed up with S/Ldr Ian Spencer and were also on 107 Squadron. Paddy Maher was my pilot and I had no qualms about the fact that he had never seen a shot fired in anger for his flying was beyond reproach. His excellent airmanship and placid temperament should make him a fine operational pilot and leader.

Our first trip from Massingham was almost a repeat, without the screaming abdabs, of my first trip with 'Fox', with the same squadron and from the same airfield. We did some low-level practice bombing on the ship target in the Wash.

While hanging about the airfield waiting to fly, operationally or practice, we held shooting competitions between pilots, navigators and gunners. Armed with 12-bores and plenty of cartridges, a clay pigeon trap was set up and we had six shots each. We all put sixpence in the kitty which, collectively, was a prize worth winning. I held high hopes of winning the 'pot' as I was a pretty good shot. As the competition drew to a close, I was level with another gunner. We both had five out of six. We shot again, I got five and he, six. I had a feeling in my water that he would collect because, before joining the RAF he had been a game-keeper!

We also used the 12-bores, and many other weapons, to keep down the stands of plover which threatened our aircraft every time we took off. We tried approaching them on foot but they got up long before we were in range. It was decided to try an approach using transport. The ambulance and fire tender were requisitioned, as were the flight vans. We drove slowly across the 'field with guns poking from every window, out of the backs and from the roofs of each vehicle. Strangely, the approach of our vehicles didn't scare the birds so much and we got right up to them before they took off followed by a hail of shot and shell. We bagged a lot that way, until they got wise to it.

Practical jokes were always part of a squadron's activities. Bobby Bance decided to have a bit of fun one day when we had finished shooting clay and real birds. He went to the roof of the office block near the control tower and dropped a Very cartridge down the chimney. It travelled down into the ops room stove where it exploded, filling the room with pungent smoke. The duty IO wasn't very appreciative of that joke, as Bobby found out.

All my flying for the month of January 1943, was with Paddy and on every occasion in Boston aircraft. We did one dinghy search in the North Sea on the 9th and two 'circuses' at 10,000 feet on the 21st and 22nd. The first was over Tricqueville in northern France, the second to Abbeville in the same area.

On the 25th we did some fighter affiliation with Typhoons from a nearby squadron. Some of the fighter pilots came over on the following Sunday to discuss the exercise. There followed a pretty hectic lunch-time session. After lunch, when they were about to return, they discovered that their CO's Hillman had been tampered with and was unserviceable. They borrowed W/Cdr Carver's car and we promised to get their's repaired and to return it that evening. It was as good an excuse as any to further the party and visit another airfield and, of course, to collect our CO's car.

The squadron gunnery leader, Ken (whose surname I forget), Bobby Bance and I pushed the car round to MT and got it mended. The three of us then set course for the Typhoon squadron's base at Matlaske, a remote war-time airfield tucked away in the north-east corner of Norfolk. I drove the car since the other two were a little 'high' and wanted to kip in the back. It proved to be one hell of a job to find the airfield but we got there in the end, pulling up outside the mess just before dinner. As we entered there was a howl from the bar, 'Come in you bomber types and have a noggin or six.'

After a pretty riotous session and dinner, it was decided to get going. I hadn't had too much to drink since it was obvious I'd have to drive – Ken and Bobby were in a fine old state. Ken had the ends of four severed black ties tied round his forehead, looking like a Greek beauty after being hit by a bus. Bobby, a 6-foot-4 burly rugger-playing type, was reeling all over the place. Agreed he was an excellent pilot but he was a menace at any party. When his ham-like fist smote one on the back, it was like getting a kick from a stallion rather than the friendly 'pat' it was meant to be. However, we said farewell about a dozen times after the usual dozen 'ones-for-the-road' and climbed into the Wingco's car. I hadn't moved into top gear before Ken and Bobby were snoring in the back. The fifteen miles or so I had to drive through dark un-charted, unlit, un-signposted lanes of Norfolk, proved a bit much for my somewhat beer-fogged sense of direction. I found myself approaching, on three different occasions Cromer, Sherringham and Wells. After about an hour's driving there appeared in the headlights a familiar cross-roads. It was about one mile from where we had started. Ultimately, I hit the Fakenham road and from there on it was plain sailing. At about 2 am I eased the Hillman through the large wrought-iron gates of the officers' mess at West Raynham.

It wasn't very many weeks beforehand that Bob Iredale had got himself spliced to the daughter of the owner of the Crown Hotel in Fakenham. The party that ensued was a wild one and was not, I should imagine, forgotten by the local inhabitants for many a year. In fact many wild parties were held at the Crown, some of them starting at breakfast time. Mike Pollard, I'm told, organised the squadron buses from West Raynham after the first 1,000-bomber raid and told the crews that a celebration would be held in Fakenham. A deafening shout of approval was followed by a hasty move to the transport. When they arrived in that peaceful, just stirring town, the crews battered on the back door of the Crown until the bossman opened up. He could do nothing else but let them in.

* * *

Group Captain the Earl of Bandon was replaced at West Raynham by Group Captain W. L. MacDonald. Paddy Bandon's pride and joy, the remnants of Snake-Hips Johnson's band (survivors of the Cafe de Paris bomb disaster) were replaced by a string quartet and the station's discipline was tightened up.

The squadron's crews, meanwhile, continued to travel to and from Massingham by bus. On the way back from the satellite one day, we decided to snowball the Land Army girls who were cutting down trees in a copse near the mess. The bus halted just before reaching the clearing from which we could hear the businesslike thwack of axe against timber. When several piles of snowballs had been made, an aircrew whistle sounded the advance; we attacked on a broad front but within five minutes it was like the retreat from Moscow, for we had been driven back, covered in snow, into the bus. Those girls were tough.

The squadron buses were sometimes taken further afield. A series of visits to power stations and factories were arranged. A lot of our targets before D-day were power stations in occupied territory and it was thought that the crews would find it useful to know the most vulnerable points. We were, for example, shown over St. Neots power station (we had already made several low-level dummy attacks there) and were told that it wouldn't make much difference to its operation if we knocked out the massive cooling towers. Those large concrete towers contained nothing but masses of spruce beams over which hot water poured and dripped to the base while a tremendous surge of cold air entered through the vents at the foot of the tower and rushed up through the spruce lattice-work. 'Aim for the power house,' we were told by our escort, 'the generators are the vulnerable pieces of equipment.'

Another trip we made was to the Air Sea Rescue base at Wells on the north Norfolk coast. It was a crisp, bright Sunday morning when we all boarded a high-speed launch bearing RAF roundels on its prow. As we sped out to sea, Bobby, Tommy Dunn, Twiggie and I searched the launch from stem to stern for the bar but discovered nothing that resembled it other than the possibilities of a first-aid box. The launch eventually arrived at one of the special rescue buoys anchored quite a way out to sea. Buoy is the wrong term, I suppose, since it was a floating one-room hotel equipped with a couple of bunks, a cooking stove, supplies, first-aid, wireless etc. If a crew had managed to paddle their dinghy to it, they could open the door of the buoy and enter, swig at the medicinal brandy, cook a meal and radio for help, in that order. However, we wondered whether that would be possible for an exhausted crew since it took two of us a lot of hard kicking to budge one of the two handles on the heavy water-tight door.

Apparently, the Germans had similar 'gadgets' off their coastline and both sides would sometimes make swift raids on each other's buoys and pinch the aircrew, if any.

When we got back to the peaceful, almost deserted Wells, we made for the nearest pub where some of our ASR hosts were entertained. Twiggie and I, having satisfied our thirst, felt a wee bit peckish, so asked the publican 'Where can we buy some seafood?' 'There aren't any shops open today,' he answered, 'but you might get something at Charlie's place down the street if you knock on his door.' This we did. We stood outside the quaint old cottage-cum-shop and waited for somebody to appear. The door was opened a few inches and Twiggie, his face always alight with a broad smile, asked whether there might be any cockles, shrimps, prawns, lobsters, mussels, crabs, whelks, winkles or oysters for sale. After scrutinising us for a few seconds he said, 'I may have a few mussels, wait a minute.' He came back with a small sack of mussels. Having paid for them and thanking him we repaired to the bus. In the bus on the way back, Twiggie and I were the only ones who ate some of them straight from the shell.

They were mad but delightful occasions.

I did no flying for the month of February as Paddy Maher had gone into Ely hospital with a duodenal ulcer. Paying him a visit one day, I found him chokka to the gills with gallons of milk and masses of boiled fish.

In March I flew once with Ian Spencer, Tiger Shaw and Jack Evans before being posted back to Bicester. I had come to the end of my fourth year with the RAF.

CHAPTER 5

March 1943/44:

With New Zealand squadron – Back to Bostons – Break with East Anglia

Back at No. 13 OTU, Bicester for my fourth spell, I was becoming not only identifiable with the district, station, and the more-or-less permanent staff but part of the furniture. Bicester had become the focal point around which my 'run-around' RAF career careened. All my promotions, and commissioning, had passed through its signals section; once more the Mess Secretary licked a newly sharpened pencil tip before boosting his bar stock. The Tannoy system was not, I believe, disconnected.

I was pleased to see many of my old friends there including Bunny Rogers and Mike Pollard. But I missed my bosom chums Twiggie and Shev. Mike Pollard and Bunny later crewed together when they joined a Mosquito squadron during which spell Bunny came to his untimely end.

My first departure into the air from that familiar piece of Oxfordshire was in a Boston with Mike Pollard. It put paid to my flying in March. April's flying programme comprised twelve 'up-and-downs', eight of which were uninteresting air tests of short duration. Paddy Maher returned to Bicester having left hospital with the warning not to start extinguishing the conflagration of his ulcer with buckets of beer and, on the 24th, he and I flew up to West Raynham. The following day, having spent the night in Norfolk, I was given a lift back to Bicester in a Lockheed Ventura. A souped-up version of the Hudson, the Ventura wasn't very popular with the operational squadrons who had recently inherited them. Whatever merits it had as a piece of airborne machinery, pilots weren't impressed. 'Fine aeroplane,' I heard one pilot comment, 'for carrying mail but as an operational aircraft I don't rate it.' The Douglas Boston was far superior.

In May I was slapped onto No. 72 Course going through Bicester. At the first intimation that this was about to happen, I felt my hackle rise. I did not crow, however, for I was told that it was to be for the last part of the course and that I'd be crewed up with an experienced pilot, F/Lt Court. We did some pretty long cross-countries together, in Blenheims, and by the 16th of May I had reached exactly 500 hours flying by day excluding exactly ninety-one hours night flying. The previous day I had enjoyed a pleasant thirty-minutes of dual with Paddy Maher in a Blenheim I.

On the 21st, I was attached to a heavy AA battery of the Royal Artillery on the Isle of Wight. Six of us went there and were made very welcome. We were shown the guns, predictor equipment and the Starboard Club at Seaview. Before leaving, on the 23rd, we were driven to the west side of the island to visit a light AA battery. They were in the middle of a shoot when we arrived, firing a Bofors and an Oerlikon at an aircraft-towed drogue. We were told that, once a week, the heavy and light AA crews swapped places for practice shoots with each other's weapons. Oddly enough, the heavy boys did better with the light guns than did the light boys and vice versa!

Two of us, the only gunners in our party, were invited to have a shot at the drogue with the Oerlikon; there was one magazine left. Having been so used to ·303 ammo, I noticed how large the shells looked. The method of traverse and gun elevation/ depression was demonstrated while I sat on the seat waiting to get cracking. Placing my shoulders firmly in the rests provided and squinting through an enormous cartwheel sight which, I remember distinctly, was broken at the bottom left and caused it to wobble almost uselessly at the slightest movement, I waited for the drogue to appear. When I fired the noise was deafening but how satisfying it was to bang away on a large-calibre gun. However, when one got beyond that size to the automatically-fused shells, slamming breech blocks, the rapping on tin hats or strings on one's legs being jerked, gunnery lost its attraction. It became too impersonal and scientific, almost like modern flying. Still, one didn't fire guns for personal enjoyment, or did one?

On 7 July, F/Lt Court and I were posted to No. 487 Squadron, RNZAF ('EG'), based at Methwold, Norfolk. One of its flight commanders, S/Ldr L. H. Trent, won the VC a couple of months previously when the aircraft he led were attacked by a superior force of FW.190s over, I believe, Ijmuiden. His aircraft was the only one to return. The squadron was equipped with Venturas in which, we were told, the squadron would not operate unless something 'big' was called for by Group. Large sighs of relief from Court and Henry and our navigator. It was also stated that the squadron, and its sister squadron No. 464 RAAF ('SB'), would shortly be converting to Mosquitoes. Grins from Court and navigator, scowl from Henry for the Mozzy carried a crew of two only; gunners were on the way out. Nevertheless, I did over forty hours flying in the Ventura, all peaceable flights covering every aspect of training. We survived the initial stages of circuits and bumps, by day and by night, local flying to graduate to a quick whip round Spalding/Goole/Leicester/Winchester/Reading/Cambridge in two hours forty minutes (British Railways please note).

The crews of both squadrons were a mixed bag. I remember getting involved in many poker games in the mess and my inexperienced 'poker ears' were assailed by a variety of accents yelling 'Ante-up, sport', 'You lousy bum', 'Get your thievin' hends orf, cobber – my kitty' and so on. I always lost.

On 20 July we moved to a new base at RAF Sculthorpe, an isolated site a few miles from Fakenham. Entering the Nissen-hut mess that evening, we made for the bar. Standing by it was our new Station Commander, Group Captain Pickard, and his grizzled Old-English sheepdog, Ming. Smoking his pipe, he nodded his acknowledgement to our 'Good evening, sir.' He watched us in silent amusement as we ordered 'Three large bitters, please.'

'Sorry, sir, bitter hasn't arrived yet.'

'Oh, well, what's it to be chaps? Scotch or gin?'

'Sorry, sir, no spirits in yet.'

'Christ, this bar matches the camp, empty and uninteresting.'

The G/Capt. butted in at that stage, 'I'm afraid that we have caught the staff unawares. The Free French left here a few days ago and left us nothing but a hogshead of red biddy. We'll have to make the best of it until supplies arrive.'

'Thank you, sir,' Court answered. The mess steward then added, 'I can get you a carafe of wine very cheap.'

'How much? ' we all said together.

'Two shillings…'

'Bring it on,' was the sharp cry.

With the Group Captain still watching us, we poured ourselves a glass of the 'stuff' and took a swig. The reaction from all of us was immediate and identical – 'Ugh…bloody hell.' It was so astringent that I spent the rest of the evening trying to untie my tongue.

'Perhaps a little sugar and warm water would help? ' suggested the steward, trying to be helpful.

'Perhaps some decent British hootch would help,' replied my

pilot, his face contorted like a ten-year-old prune. But there we were, landed with that ghastly potion which I was again to experience when catching up with the French squadron.

The G/Capt. had enjoyed that lively little scene for, he too, had obviously suffered. What a grand chap he was. He had fought his way through red-tape which had barred him from operating again in Bomber Command (he had completed ninety-nine operations on heavies). They had given him the newly-forming Mosquito Wing in order to keep him quiet. I had seen the film *Target for Tonight* in Malta and had enjoyed watching the locals bounce the energy out of their seat springs when the Wellington 'F for Freddie', flown by Pickard, unleashed its load on the target below.

It was Group Captain Pickard who later led the low-level Mosquito attack on a prison near Amiens. With great skill he and his crews knocked holes in the prison building and the walls surrounding it to allow the escape of many French prisoners held there by the Gestapo. After he had bombed, the G/Capt. flew around in the area to make sure that the job was successfully accomplished and quite possibly to cover the retreat of the escapers. He didn't return from that operation.

Meantime, the squadrons were taking delivery of Mosquito aircraft. It meant many trips down to the de Havilland factories at Hatfield where that excellent all-purpose machine was made. It also presented the opportunity for some of us to nip into London on short spells of leave. I had my first ride to Hatfield on 31 July 1943. On the second trip to de Havillands, I sat in the back with the Group Captain. He puffed away at his pipe while going through papers he had extracted from a bulging briefcase. The squadron CO, W/Cdr Wilson, was at the controls of the Ventura. After a while the G/Capt. got up and wandered forward. I saw him tap the Wingco on the shoulder for he wanted to take control. I also wandered forward to stand behind the pilot's seat and to watch the countryside pass by beneath us. Taking out 'George', the G/Capt. put the nose down and proceeded to do a wonderful piece of low flying. I saw one farm-hand leap from his tractor and fall flat on his face in the nearest and deepest furrow he could find at such short notice. I suppose that we flew like that for about twenty minutes before pulling up to circuit Hatfield. He made an excellent landing. When the engines had been 'killed' and we had climbed out, the G/Capt. turned to the Wingco and said, 'What a dull aircraft.'

On 3 August I had five trips in one day totalling five-and-a-half hours. At 9 am we took off for Tangmere. We left there at noon to land at base at 1.15 pm. At 3.45 we took off for Tangmere; at 5.10 we left Tangmere to land at RAF Tempsford, near Bedford, leaving there for base at 6.30 pm. I cannot to this day remember what we had been playing at.

On 7 August, I had my third trip to Hatfield and on arriving there the G/Capt. asked me whether I'd like a trip in a Mozzy. I leapt at the chance. We walked over to a shiny-new Mk VI; I scribbled its number, W.4052, on a cigarette packet to be logged later. I had a delightful forty minutes in that fast, manoeuvrable aeroplane. Its two Rolls-Royce Merlins hummed away as we plunged about the Hertfordshire sky. In a shallow dive I noticed that the ASI registered a bit over 360 mph. It was the fastest that I had ever travelled. He came in to make a long, low-motored approach and a perfect three-pointer. 'Now that is an aeroplane,' he said smilingly. I agreed with him and felt somewhat sad that I wouldn't be flying in them.

On my return from leave I went via Bicester. It was a better train journey and I knew that I could always get a lift back to Sculthorpe. There were plenty of training flights and I had many friends among the instructors. Paddy Maher, in fact, flew me back and I got in another forty-five minutes dual in a Blenheim I. I finished off the month of August with a flight down to Northolt.

On 21 August, I and others were in for a shock. With the Allied invasion of Europe getting closer, it was considered by the top brass somewhere along the line that aircrew, between and including the ranks of sergeant and flight lieutenant, should be taught a few of the rudimentary aspects of ground fighting and deployment of troops. Actually, the training we were about to receive came under the heading of 'Leadership Course'. It only lasted for a week but during that time we were put through the paces with so much vigour that at its termination we almost dropped with near exhaustion. Nevertheless, some of us enjoyed it all.

That concentrated 'semi-commando' course, as we labelled it, took place at RAF Swanton Morley, in Norfolk. We were issued with Denim overalls and a rifle but we took our own tin hats. Each day was a full one; up early, very early, for PT, then back to our quarters for a shower and change into battle dress before making the longish walk to the mess for breakfast. Back to change into Denims; on parade to be drilled and to take it in turn to drill our mixed (in rank, not sex) squad. Our instructors were mostly RAF Regiment NCOs. We had armament instruction on various light automatic weapons, including the Sten and Bren, and the already familiar (to me) Browning. As I was proficient with the latter, I assisted the instructor. It is no idle boast that, in those days, I could strip a Browning in about forty seconds, blindfolded, and reassemble it in a few seconds over that time. I did it so often when instructing at OTU and had handled the gun for over three years, that even now, twenty years later, I'm sure I could put up a reasonable time after a refresher dummy run.

We were lectured on how to deploy troops for, while we might be efficient where flying was concerned, we hadn't a clue on the soldiering side as up to then it hadn't been necessary to know. But after D-day it was on the cards that the RAF personnel on forward airfields would need to know something about the subject in case the enemy turned round and overran them.

Our instructors demonstrated how effective camouflage could be. They also showed us how to sneak up from behind on a sentry without him knowing it. In order to demonstrate that there was no catch to it, volunteers were called for to stand sentry. 'Only turn round and challenge if you really hear or sense anybody approaching,' they were told. Whoever stood there with his rifle, all ears and with twitching nose, heard nothing and was overpowered without making a sound; his rifle was grabbed at the same time as the throat was encircled by an arm. Some of the tricks of the trade seemed rather brutal but the sound advice that '...if *you* don't do it the enemy *will*. It's your life or his...there's no alternative...' made a lot of sense.

Half-way through the course we were further put to the test: a mock battle on nearby heathland made our rigorous PT and other physical activities pale into insignificance. Dressed only in our underwear and Denims, tin hat, boots and webbing, we proceeded to the battle arena, about two or three miles away. I had been lent a pair of Army boots by a colonel who wanted them broken in. Thus equipped, we marched 300 yards and doubled 100, all the way. The peak of physical fitness I had attained back at Cardington had long since been frittered away but I managed to cope all right, I had to.

When we reached the 'front lines' we charged about, leaping from bush to bush firing off blanks at the 'enemy' who sometimes didn't play fair and wouldn't fall down dead! When I say charged about, we *were* under control, making quick advances under covering fire. I had a go on the Bren and found it a beautiful weapon, much better than the crude but effective Sten which we had fired on the Swanton range.

When fighting had finished we advanced for about a quarter of a mile until halted, temporarily, by a river. 'In you go. Keep your rifles above your heads, they're useless when wet,' our NCO roared. In we leapt, up to our armpits in water, weeds and waterboatmen. Just as well it was August. Squelching up the opposite bank we made our way back to camp in much the same way we had come. It had been a pretty tough day for us softish mortals but worse was to come.

We were given a dummy run round the specially prepared assault course. Halting at each of the twenty or more obstacles, we were told and shown how they were to be tackled on *der tag*. The first of them blocked the narrow lane and approach to the course. It consisted of a pyramid of coiled barbed wire. 'I want two of you, the first two will do, to double forward, grab the bottom coil of wire and lift. Stand with your legs apart so that the others can crawl between them and under the wire. Don't worry about the barbs, just grab the wire quickly and you'll find it won't hurt. If you're squeamish and start picking a spot to lift, you will get cut to pieces. In any case there won't be time.' We stood there stunned; grab the wire it won't hurt was a masterly piece of understatement – or, as we preferred it, 'famous last words'. 'The last two under the wire,' he continued, 'will repeat the performance so that the first two can come through.'

I was lucky to be somewhere in the middle of the group on both occasions and wasn't called upon to do the wire-grabbing act. The next obstacle was a high brick wall over which we clambered like a bunch of ruptured ducks. That was followed by a long belly-crawl under about 100 square yards of corrugated iron sheeting which was supported, about eighteen inches from the ground, by a host of miniature pit-props. While we negotiated that hazard, making sure that our rifle muzzles weren't scooping up a ton of mud, our instructors amused themselves by throwing thunderflashes under the low 'roof'.

For our next trick we had to rush across a large expanse of open ground. Covering fire was given as we ran, in small groups, at the stoop until we reached the edge of a sand quarry over which we leapt come what may. There followed sundry other obstacles to be climbed, vaulted, jumped or crawled through. The grand finale was a river which we crossed, Tarzan fashion, by swinging on a rope. Crashing through some bushes as though we really meant it, we re-crossed the river by means of a slippery tree trunk off which three of the course fell, to the amusement of all.

At the end of the week we went over the assault course in deadly earnest. There were time records to be broken and I think we either got within seconds of the record or just pipped it.

Needless to add, there was a wow of a party at the end of the course. I had certainly learnt one thing: that even the most arduous tasks could be pleasant if one approached them in the right spirit. The warrant officers and flight sergeants who took umbrage at being drilled by mere sergeants were miserable throughout that concentrated week. The four of us who shared the same attitude, that of making the best of it, had a cracking time.

We returned to our respective units feeling fit and ready to organise the whole station at the first sign of trouble. When I got back to Sculthorpe, I was pleased to learn that, with effect from 2 September, I was posted to No. 107 Squadron (for the third time), stationed at RAF Hartford Bridge (better known today as Blackbushe), near Camberley and London. At long last I got away from East Anglia and its poor communications with the outside world. No. 107 was equipped with Boston IIIAs which had twice the power, carried twice the bomb load, but had only half the duration of the Blenheim. I crewed up with S/Ldr Jack Evans and on the 6th we took off on a new venture, that of smokescreen laying. The aircraft had been prettied up with black and white bands over and under each wing and encircling the rear part of the fuselage. From the bomb bay there protruded four nozzles each connected to a canister and from each of which 1,000 yards of smoke could be spread.

We were told at briefing that HM minesweepers were dodging about off the French coast near Boulogne. This was a ruse, it was said, to make the enemy think an invasion was due in or near that area. The Supreme Commander of the Allied Expeditionary Force, 'Ike', wanted Adolf to start gnawing at his rugs again and to throw in his rapidly diminishing air force so that Fighter Command could further its diminishment.

The smoke-laying, at nought feet, was a great success even if we gunners did get a fair amount of the chemical down into our lungs. We repeated the operation the following day, and on the 9th we continued to play on the enemy's nerves by carrying out a 'baiting' circus having with us an escort of nine squadrons of Spitfires. Our target was the airfield of Monchy Breton, in northern France. Actually, there was nothing on the airfield but it could be quickly stocked with fighters if the balloon went up and would be an additional thorn in the sides of an invasion force. But the primary aim was to tempt into the air the remnants of the *Luftwaffe*. Not a one came up to challenge us. I'll always remember that trip not because of the flak they lobbed at us but for what might have been waiting for us on arrival. On the approach to the French coast, some silly clot had his intercom on transmit and the following is roughly what went out over the air:

'Eh, Bill.'

'Yep?'

'What's our target?'

'Monchy Breton airfield.'

'Are we bombing from twelve thou.?'

'Yep.'

'Where do we cross the coast?'

'Just south of Gris Nez.'

'What's our ETA?'

'1440, roughly.'

'Thanks.'

The whole squadron heard it and quite possibly every German monitoring station within range. Nobody could get through to tell the offenders to 'belt up' for when on 'transmit' one was cut off from any incoming broadcast.

Another type of operation carried out by the squadrons was to fly at nought feet to a point on the French coast, then fly along the beach for three minutes (equivalent to about twelve to fifteen miles) looking for shipping. When the three minutes was up the aircraft turned out to sea and home. On one such trip a crew were stirring up the sand with their prop-wash along a strip of French beach when they spotted a German sentry.

'Give him a short burst,' said Jock to his gunner. The gunner obliged. Said sentry stood his ground in the best Teutonic manner, with spurts of sand dancing round his feet. This was too much for Jock, he wheeled the Boston round to make another run. 'Bomb doors open, prepare to bomb,' he shouted down the intercom, 'We'll move him.' And so that lone man, conscientiously watching for signs of invasion, became the target for 4 x ¼-ton high-explosive, delayed action bombs!

On the 11th I flew with Teddy Brice (with whom I shared many pleasant hours on the Isle of Wight, back in May). I also got airborne with the other flight commander, Ian Spencer, who was shortly afterwards promoted to W/Cdr. In fact I joined his crew when Shev was away ill. He took command of No. 88 Squadron, one of the three comprising No. 137 Wing, 2nd Tactical Air Force, at Hartford Bridge. The third Boston squadron was No. 342 'Lorraine' (Free French).

On 20 September we flew up to RAF. Turnberry, on the coast of Ayrshire. This beautiful part of west Scotland was to become, on the morrow, the scene of a Combined Operations exercise when a small invasion fleet, enveloped by RN and RAF laid smoke-screens, threaded its way up the Firth of Clyde, past the Isle of Arran and up into the Sound of Bute. We flew above it all taking official photographs. At 5 pm that afternoon we took off to return to warmer climes, back to the scenically uninteresting Hartford Bridge flats. We got back in ninety minutes.

On 1 October we led twelve Bostons on a low-level formation practice which lasted two hours. I hadn't tired of that type of flying; it was still as thrilling as my earlier experiences. In fact more so with a dozen aircraft threading their way between the trees.

On the 3rd I took part in the briefing which led to my first sortie with Ian Spencer, Tony Valle-Jones the navigator and Gerry Ploughman the under-gunner. Well, it wasn't quite the first for we had to turn back at the French coast because both our engines were cutting and that wasn't desirable when flying at nought feet. It was annoying but couldn't be helped. The rest of the squadron pressed on to the target, the power station at Saumur on the Loire west of Tours.

On the 8th we led three squadrons on a high-level (12,000 feet) attack on Poulmic airfield at Brest. There was plenty of excitement on that trip. Our escort consisted of eleven squadrons of Spits but they weren't keeping close formation with us. In fact I could only see a few of the squadrons and they were mere specks above and behind us. Near the target I spotted a Dornier 217 and a couple of Ju.88s, but they were a few thousand feet below us and presented no threat. The flak over the target was

pretty thick but we bombed and retired unhurt. Our bombs got
pretty close to the four main hangars (one hit the corner of the
NW hangar and an aircraft between them got a direct hit), but a
great number of the squadrons' 500-pounders overshot into the
fields. The French squadron managed to plant their bombs mostly
in the sea. I have since wondered whether it was due to their
natural dislike of bombing their own country, and people, or to
bad bomb-aiming.

To the east of the airfield was a seaplane base, and as we passed
over it a Dornier flying-boat was seen to alight on the water, its
position clearly marked by a white foaming wake. On the way back
we landed at Exeter.

In the evening papers there appeared a short reference to the
attack:

'Bostons escorted by Spitfires attacked the airfield at Brest in
the afternoon. Three Me.110s were destroyed, all by one
squadron, in this operation.'

On 22 October, I did my last sortie with Ian Spencer before Shev
came back. That trip was a snorter. The target was the aero-engine
works at Courcelles in Belgium. Thirty-eight Bostons, led by W/Cdr
R. G. England of 107 Squadron, followed by No. 342 Squadron
whose leader was W/Cdr de Rancourt, and then 88 Squadron led by
our aircraft (Ian Spencer). As a matter of interest, one of the French
navigators taking part in that operation was F/Lt P. Mendes-France
who was later to head one of France's post-war governments.

The briefing was the usual sort of thing and deserves no special
mention. The first aircraft was to take-off at 13.45 hours. The
flight plan was to fly north for a while, to avoid overflying
London, then due east over Suffolk to cross the coast at Orford
Ness. Crossing the North Sea we were to make a landfall on the
Dutch coast north of the Hook, then to turn south over the Scheldt,
on into Belgium and the target.

The plan of attack was for the leading six aircraft, each armed
with four 500 lb. instantaneous bombs, to climb to about 1,000
feet just before reaching the target area. After bombing they were
to get down on the 'deck' again, out of the lethal flak. The
remaining aircraft, each carrying four 500lb, 11-second-delay
bombs (a hazard for straggling aircraft) would thus have their
final run-in clearly pinpointed and, it was hoped, they would be
able to strike while the ground defences were still reeling or

possibly gauging at the retreating leaders. All aircraft would then head north-west to exit near Ostend.

It sounded a straightforward enough operation with the minimum of risk. The intelligence people had told us that the point of crossing the Dutch coast had been carefully selected because it was practically undefended. That sort of statement, as did some of the Met. forecasts, invariably invoked raised eyebrows, knowing smiles or whispered 'Famous last words.'

We were also informed that, at nought feet, enemy radar could not detect our approach until it was almost too late for them to slip one up the breech, or words to that effect. The fact that the North Sea supported shipping wasn't mentioned. But we knew by experience that thirty-eight aircraft, heading east and running over or near an enemy ship would automatically set the alarm bells a'ringing, radar or no.

The moment had arrived to start engines. Crews were in position; pilots checked their controls, instruments and intercom; navigators, in their confined nose compartments, made last-minute checks of flight plan while we gunners checked the radio, the electric traverse of our twin Brownings and saw that an ammunition belt was clipped firmly beneath each breech-cover.

As each of the seventy-six 1,600-horsepower Wright radials was started, the collective roar from scattered dispersals reverberated across the Hampshire countryside. With the intermittent hiss of brakes, the first Boston, gently rocking on its tricycle undercarriage, moved out on to the perimeter track. The CO of 107 taxied round to the threshold of the main east/west runway, closely followed nose-to-tail by the other thirty-seven aircraft. It was a magnificent sight.

On the dot of 1.45 pm the first machine began to roll, then the second and third at twenty-second intervals, until the whole thirty-eight aircraft were wheeling in the circuit like migrating geese. Drawing together in closer formation, we got down nice and low and set course on our first leg. Skimming over the rolling countryside of Berks, Bucks and Herts through to Suffolk, we roused all beneath us. People ran into the streets, lanes and back-yards. Having satisfied themselves that we were 'goodies' they waved their encouragement. Maybe the farms we thundered over were left with heaps of chicken feathers, addled eggs and curdled milk.

There is so much to see and hold one's attention when flying at nought feet that in no time at all the coastline flashed beneath and astern of us. With the obstructionless sea out front, each aircraft had its nose eased down that bit more. I depressed my guns and, making sure that no other aircraft was in the way, fired a short testing burst into the sea off the port quarter. In order to minimise the risk of hitting others' slipstream and then the sea, we were flying in echelon starboard.

The North Sea crossing was only about 100 miles, but even over that distance a couple of degrees off course could give a landfall error of several miles. Check! That's exactly what happened to us. We crossed the Dutch coast twelve miles from the so-called defenceless point which had been so carefully selected for us. We went slap bang over a heavily defended area.

Looking forward was not easy for the Boston gunner, but as we approached the coast I saw, on the port bow, the unmistakable funeral pyre of an aircraft, a pillar of black, oily smoke, then another. The leading squadron had caught it badly (four out of the leading six were shot down) and we had yet to cross. As we flashed over the coast a little to the south of the worst flak, I saw two aircraft burning on the ground (one on a sandy beach the other in a field). But at 230 mph one is over and pressing onwards with no time to stare and brood over such tragedies, only to scan the sky for fighters while the emotions of fear and excitement vied for first place.

We had turned south and were soon crossing the Dutch islands of Walcheren and Noord Beveland. Nearing the Belgian frontier, the leading aircraft put up hundreds of birds. When startled, a flock of birds will often rise quickly to 100 feet or more and then dive to the ground again. We had been briefed on this ornithological trait with the advice that it was safer to overfly rather than underfly them. However, this was not always possible, least of all with an unwieldy formation such as ours and we went straight through them. A little later Tony excitedly burst through on the intercom with 'We've been hit.' Immediately I conjured up visions of a flaming engine supported by a perforated wing. However, all that happened was the penetration by a medium sized bird through the perspex of Tony's greenhouse, and its remains had finished up behind one of the two sheets of armour plating. The hole it left admitted a fair-size gale which, apart from giving Tony an eyeful of dust, blew his charts into scattered confusion. Otherwise, the aeroplane continued to function to specification and we pressed on. We none of us knew that a bird had caused the damage until we landed. As for the draught, Tony had nothing to worry about since I had a built-in draught in my open cockpit which remained my companion from 'chocks to chocks'.

Approaching the target area we found ourselves weaving an erratic course through a forest of slag heaps while a worsening industrial haze didn't help matters. This was unexpected as we had not been briefed as to the type of terrain in that area. The two remaining lead aircraft climbed to bomb. We looked ahead for the tell-tale signs of their bombing and saw none. Meanwhile, navigators hurriedly consulted maps to see whether they could locate the target but the slag-heap maze and the haze had thrown us off track. When ETA had arrived and gone, the leading aircraft wheeled to starboard and set course for home. The Boston's duration was a short one, and thirty-odd aircraft milling about at nought feet looking for a target while dodging mountains of slag would be courting trouble.

On the way out we ran slap over Eecloo airfield. Its residents, not taking kindly to our intrusion, put on a brief pyrotechnic display for us. Hose-piped tracer streamed from all directions. An aircraft hugging our port wing tip was hit in the starboard engine the propeller of which was smartly feathered. Ian throttled back to keep the maimed aircraft company and to add our firepower to his should fighters appear on the scene. This was an imminent possibility for we had heard the French crews nattering to each other about 'chasseurs' in the offing.

The Boston had a pretty good single-engine performance and we soon ate up the kilometres that separated us from the coast. As soon as the coastline came into view, the pilots raked the buildings along the dunes with their four fixed front guns. Those harmless looking buildings were used as gun emplacements, all Belgians having been evacuated from the coastal belt. With little more fuss we were over the Channel, but well behind the main formation. We still had escort duty to perform as far as the Kent coast where we broke away to land at West Malling with our fuel gauges flickering around the zero mark. Our 'winged' colleague made for base as he hadn't used so much fuel on his one engine.

As soon as we had landed and the engines had been stopped, we climbed out, passed the cigarettes and took stock of the damage to

'N for nuts'. Coming through that flak blizzard had surely left its mark. No, there wasn't a scratch to be seen. The birds had, however, been more accurate. The remains of Tony's feathered friend we saw through the shattered perspex. One medium sized bird had got itself nicely condensed up one of the front-gun fairings, while two more had spread themselves round the 'pots' of the port engine but how they had slipped through the airscrew is and remains their secret.

The whole operation had proved abortive. In a little under three hours, six aircraft and their crews (19 men) failed to return and many others were damaged by flak and birds. Some bomb loads had been jettisoned into the sea but 107 x 500 lb. bombs were brought back. Not one was deliberately dropped on occupied territory.

*   *   *

All losses are tragic but the one felt most deeply by everyone was that of the leader of the operation – W/Cdr R G England, 107 Squadron. As Dickie taxied round on that fateful day, he was told that he had been awarded the DSO for previous achievements.

It had only been a week or so before the Courcelles fiasco that a few of us had been given a lift into Camberley in his Bentley, a vintage drop-head that gave off from a straight-through exhaust more than the accepted number of decibels. Because of the racket, we had been stopped by a member of the local constabulary who proceeded in the customary way.

'May I see your licence, sir.' Having scrutinised it he added, 'What is your name please, sir?'

'Wing Commander Richard Grenville England, officer,' our driver replied with a grin, 'but you may call me Dickie if you like.'

Such was the charm of that popular officer.

On 1 November I crossed the street, as it were, to join 107 Squadron for the fourth time. I retained my berth in a Nissen hut not far from the mess. Inside that corrugated shell my nerves were twice shattered. On the first occasion all but one of us were in bed. The last member came in around midnight; he'd obviously been tied up with some sidetracker in the bar. Eventually he got into bed but had omitted to switch off the lights. We bawled at him so to do but he ignored us. After more abuse and a few well-aimed shoes, he decided to do his duty but not the orthodox way. Leaning out of bed he fumbled for his Smith and Wesson ·38 and

let rip at the three or four lamps. The din was awful; his shootin'
was good; the lights went out; the whole camp sat up in bed. The
sharp-shooter, F/O Jack M—, was a young, fair-haired 'butter-
wouldn't-melt-in-his-mouth' type and was the last person I'd
imagine to take such drastic action. Surprisingly, nobody rushed
in to find out who had been assassinated.

The second incident also happened rather late at night. I was
reading in bed at the time, engrossed in an exciting short story about
destroyers and depth charges and submarines. I leapt a foot off my
mattress when I got the full sound effects in my ear; a clattering
crashing noise which began by my head and rumbled right along the
side of the hut. I thought that an aircraft had crashed right outside.
The racket defies adequate description. Some crazy loon had picked
up a stick and had run it along the hut's corrugations.

No. 107 Squadron was then under the command of W/Cdr Mike
Pollard. As I had virtually finished my two tours I wasn't given a
crew. My duties were varied and mostly to do with gunnery. I did no
flying for the months of November and December and, while this
was galling, it was I suppose better than being posted back to OTU.

On the first day of 1944 I had a ride with S/Ldr Reeve in an
Auster I a small, high-wing aircraft that was beginning to get
pushed when flying at 100 mph. Four days later I flew with my
eighteenth operational pilot, P/O Lawrence. It was a one-off
replacement-crew sortie. We took part in a medium-level attack
(9,500 feet) on a flying-bomb site in a wood near Marquenville. As
we crossed the French coast near Fecamp, I was asked how the
aircraft behind were positioned (they were stepped down in vics of
three). Lifting my head a bit too high and into the slipstream, my
tin hat was whipped off to sail down past, and narrowly missing, a
Boston beneath us. I was annoyed because it had been my line-
shoot souvenir battle-bowler from Malta, the tortoise camouflage
job. I often wonder who picked it up and planted geraniums in it.

On 1 February, Tony Valle-Jones and I made our way to
Harwich for a week with the Royal Navy. Volunteers from among
RAF aircrew officers had been invited (as part of one's official
leave) to join a ship. It had appealed to us both and it was agreed
that we would feel less out of place if we went together. On our
arrival at Parkeston Quay, however, we were separated for Tony
was despatched aboard a corvette and I marched up the gangway of
the destroyer HMS. *Montrose*. I was ushered aft to the wardroom

(what a contrast to that draughty hangar on *Kenya*). There were only a couple of officers present but they made me welcome and pushed the buzzer for the steward. I was asked what I would like to drink. Noticing that each of my hosts was clutching a glass of what appeared to be gin, it was an easy choice. Discovering that gin was 2d. a tot, I was ready to treat the ship's company. When the captain (I believe it was Commander Rolfe) and the remainder of the officers came below for their pre-dinner snifter, I was introduced and promptly put up a black by asking the gathered company to have a drink with the RAF. How was I to know?

I was, however, tactfully put in my place with 'We don't stand rounds of drinks in the Navy, old boy. Each drink that you or I or anybody has goes down on our respective mess bills,' whispered kindly in my ear.

The food on board was exceptionally good and it was a very pleasant atmosphere although at first, not being the Hornblower type, I felt a little like a goalkeeper behind a test wicket. It was, nonetheless, an agreeable change from the seething crowd of chaps in an RAF mess.

After dinner I was told that we would be putting to sea shortly and that when doing so I could use the navigation officer's bunk, as he would stay near his work and had a spare bunk in or near the chartroom. When *Montrose* was berthed I was given comfortable bunk in the sick bay and a cup of tea in bed the next morning.

That night we escorted a convoy as far as the Humber where, at 9 am, we anchored near a lightship. At 4.15 pm we set course once more to escort a south-bound convoy, returning to Harwich at 9 am on the 3rd. I spent most of my time on the bridge watching everything with great interest and, as once before, trying hard not to get under the Navy's feet. That night we moored to a buoy midstream in the River Stour, off Parkeston. There was an air-raid in the early hours and the ship's guns joined with the shore defences. The noise was deafening.

On the 5th, at 3.30 pm, we slipped our moorings and proceeded to sea via the zigzagging fairway passing Shotley Gate to port and Harwich to starboard, then the Felixstowe seaplane and air-sea-rescue base to port. We were about to begin an anti-E-boat patrol for a northbound convoy. That evening, after dinner, I had been left to my own devices in the wardroom. The Navy had work to do and they wouldn't hear of my suggestion that I might help out. Perhaps they thought I might pull out the wrong plug and sink their bloody ship. So I became a lounge lizard, propping myself up on one of the button-studded leather couches with the remains of a gin and The Illustrated London News. There was a sudden clatter of feet and a crowd of seamen began to advance on me.

'Excuse me sir, we'll be battening down shortly, so if you want to go on deck, better do it before you get locked down here maybe for several hours.'

'Thank you,' I said. 'What exactly do you get up to down here?' I asked, for I was beginning to doubt their motives as two or three of the lads were already rolling back the carpets!

'The magazine is under the wardroom deck, sir.'

As he said that I noticed one of the ABs had lifted what looked like a manhole cover and had descended down through the hole with an inspection-type lamp. I left them to get on with their work and to get as far away as I could from all that explosive. It was also getting a bit rough outside; every now and again the stern lifted partly out of the water and the screws thrashed and vibrated as they cut the surface. I didn't wish to be cooped up below in heavy seas; fresh air was the medicine for me.

Making my way forward I had to grab hold of a line, specially rigged during rough weather, and haul myself along to the companionway to the bridge. When I had reached its wet confines (it was protected only by tarpaulins round the front and sides), I stood by the Asdic in what looked like a telephone kiosk sunk into the deck on the port side of the bridge (I believe there was another on t'other side). From the 'kiosk' came a constant pinngggggg, pinggggg, pinggggg. The cold, fresh salty air and spray whipped into my face every time the bows buried themselves into a high sea. I was glad to have the warmth of my Crombie greatcoat. This was the life and I revelled in every minute of it. A large white mug of steaming beverage was handed to me and I confess that it was the only time in my adult life that I enjoyed cocoa; it was certainly more palatable than Navy tea.

The weather was too rough for E-boats, so our journey north was uneventful. The following morning, 6 February (having left the convoy), we steamed south for a small exercise off the Norfolk coast. 'At 10.30 am,' I was told, 'four of your aircraft are making an attack with dummy torpedoes. We are also having a short practice shoot, not at the aircraft but a parachute target which we fire ourselves.'

At the appointed time there was no sign of the aircraft. The Commander kept looking at his watch while impatiently pacing the few square yards on the bridge. In the Asdic 'box' the operator watched the instrument's pen-trace as it moved back and forth between pinggggggggs – it had nothing to do with the exercise, merely a routine chore, but it fascinated me.

'Not very punctual, your colleagues, what!' the Commander shot at me, not unpleasantly.

'We usually operate to within thirty seconds, sir,' I countered, defensively, 'perhaps they have been delayed by bad weather.' This was confirmed a few minutes later by signal; the aircraft had been delayed by fog but would appear on the scene very soon.

Meanwhile, the ship's company prepared for their practice shoot. There was one helluva big bang and all eyes turned to the sky. In a few seconds a parachute drifted down and 'guns' (the gunnery officer) on the deck below yelled out 'Fire, fire, fire.'

More noise followed by 'Check, check, check.' I was rather amused at those triplicated orders and thought to myself how silly they would sound over the intercom of an aircraft and how expensive they would be in a bar.

The aircraft arrived, made their attack (it wasn't a very accurate one) and buzzed off, leaving the Navy to retrieve the expensive dummy tinfish. Three were recovered but the fourth had been badly dropped and had gone down nose first.

As we moved off, half a dozen LCTs were about to cross our bows. The Commander was hopping mad and told a petty officer to sound off a warning. I was delighted to hear the shrill whoooooooop, whooop, whooop echoing across the water. The warning was repeated several times without effect and I itched to get my hands on that siren. It made no apparent difference to the course of the LCTs so the Commander called for the loudhailer and then proceeded to bellow a few scathing remarks at them. They heard his bark and heeded it.

We tied up at Parkeston; I settled my mess bill, conveyed my thanks to my hosts for a very pleasant week and rolled professionally down the gangway to catch a train for London.

When I returned to Hartford Bridge I found myself on the strength of Headquarters No. 137 Wing, having finished my two tours. I did no flying for the months of February or March, only the three flights in January since October. Some of that time had been usefully employed and some of it swallowed by leave.

One job I took particular interest in was helping to build and paint a new bar in the main mess. The mess consisted of a collection of interconnected king-size Nissen huts. The 'Boston Bar' took the form of a castle, two crenellated towers at either end of a twenty-foot bar counter over which was a portcullis. Above the portcullis was a panel upon which the crests of the squadrons based at HB had been painted, by my own fair hand. A navigator who was a dab-hand with a spray-gun, made an excellent job of sky and clouds over the curved ceiling, while others had a stab at the rural murals. Some tasteful light fittings in each corner and some comfortable furniture set the whole room off nicely. Once inside one would never associate the cosy interior with a Nissen hut. Visitors' comments were always favourable when they arrived, and when they left most of them were beyond comment; we were a hospitable bunch.

Another job we tackled ourselves in the mess was to build a fireplace in the main anteroom. This we soon accomplished but as soon as a fire was lighted, the smoke from it billowed back into the room. Obviously it needed an expert to work out the correct shape of the flue so that the smoke was carried up and out, not down and in.

On one of my leaves I joined Shev for a journey to Scotland. We had applied for a week's leave at Alastrean House in Aberdeenshire for Lady MacRobert had so very kindly placed that wonderful house at the disposal of RAF aircrews. Her three sons were killed in the air, two of them with the RAF during the war. In 1941 she donated £25,000 for a Stirling bomber, named 'MacRobert's Reply' which operated with No. 15 Squadron. In 1942, she made a further donation of £20,000 for four Hurricanes which were named: 'Sir Alasdair', 'Sir Roderic', 'Sir Ian' and 'MacRobert's Salute to Russia'.

We met Lady MacRobert on two occasions, the first was when we had a knockout competition on the putting green. I happened to play against her and, never having handled a golf club in my life, I lost hands down. On the second occasion we were all invited to her home at Douneside. Having been shown the prize Angus cattle, we entered the house where a large visitors' book was produced. The book was, however, different for she had had it marked, in numerical sequence, with every squadron serving the Allied cause. Every visitor signed his name against the squadron he represented and others he might have served on. After I filled in half a dozen blank spaces it became apparent that her ambition was to have a name against every squadron, for she was so excited and pleased.

It was altogether a wonderful week and we returned to Aberdeen most refreshed, that is before catching the London train. The twenty-odd hour journey south soon had us back to normal for we had to stand much of the time in a cold draughty corridor. Life became a little more pleasant when a female VIP, who had a whole first-class compartment to herself, invited us, through a ticket collector, to share it with her.

Between 20 and 22 February I received, c/o 107 Squadron, three teleprint messages from: Air Marshal Leigh-Mallory, AEAF, from the Air Officer Commanding Rear HQ, 2nd TAF, and from HQ No. 2 Group. There was also a GPO telegram from S/Ldr Jack Evans which read: 'Congratulations on your award well deserved and long overdue.' The others said much the same thing, without the overdue bit, but they were pumped over the wires automatically. I was, therefore, most touched to get those few personal words from Jack. Being awarded the DFC was indeed a thrill although I had some pretty strong feelings about its distribution. Awarded 'For Valour'; I felt that I had done nothing more than my job and, in any case, I'd been dead scared most of the time. Had they struck a medal for being messed about I *would* have been eligible for it, encrusted with bars and oak leaves. But there it was; it stirred up a jolly good party and it was a wonderful end to my fifth year with the Royal Air Force.

CHAPTER 6

March 1944/45:

Under canvas – D-day – To France To Belgium

My sixth year opened quietly for it wasn't until April 28th that I flew again, with Ian Spencer, getting in four trips with him during the day. It was about that time when I became a member of the Station Commander's (G/Capt. MacDonald) crew. Stan Adams, the navigator was an awfully nice chap but apt to be a little pompous at times. When I wanted a time check, for example, it was Stan's astro-nav chronometer, Air Ministry issue, upon which I relied, 'What's the right time, please Stan?' I'd ask.

'No such thing,' he would answer, '*the* time is 1433 and 35 seconds.'

'Whatteryermean, no such thing?'

'Time is always right, only the means of registering it are right or wrong.'

'Really!' I answered. He was right, of course, but he made such a meal of it. It was no gentle leg-pull, either, for he was deadly serious, in a pedantic sort of way. It happened every time I deliberately asked for the 'right' time. I bet that he used such accepted phrases as 'The kettle's boiling', 'My bath is running', 'He's got a temperature' and so forth. However, we got on well together and I found his transport useful for he had been issued with a 500 cc Ariel Service motorcycle.

When we lived under canvas at Hartford Bridge (a pre-D-day familiarisation exercise) Stan and I shared a tent. The tent site, which included a large marquee for our messing, was a long walk across many muddy fields from the main camp. It was good fun in a novel sort of way but it had its drawbacks. For one thing I ruined one of my best suitcases which had soaked up the moisture through the coconut matting on the grass floor of our tent. However, it wasn't for long and there was a good reason for preparing us in the event of a dire lack of accommodation when we moved across the Channel. As it happened we never saw a tent when moving to France.

I borrowed Stan's bike one evening on return from leave; I hadn't fancied lugging a suitcase across the fields. On the way back I took a slight bend too close to the grass verge and the bike slid from under me on loose gravel. The machine wasn't damaged very much but I was. I skidded along the road, face down, and picked up cuts across the bridge of my nose, my upper lip and my chin. The palms of my hands and both my knees were also badly grazed, and all the buttons of my best uniform tunic were ripped off – in fact the uniform was a write-off.

Some airmen, who happened to be walking down the lane, pushed the bike back for me while I called into sick quarters. An MO came along and stitched my chin by candlelight. He then proceeded to slap strips of plaster across my face making me look as though I'd been hit by a pantechnicon. The MT officer was next on the scene. He brought along a form which he filled in for me as I answered his questions. When completed and signed it was tantamount to a confession that I had no authority to ride the bike and had therefore damaged Government property without permission (with authority it was apparently okay!).

Three or four days later I got back into circulation, still feeling rather self-conscious with two strips of plaster across my face round the edges of which poked the whiskers my razor had been unable to mow. Creeping into the mess and the bar, I walked slap into the G/Capt. Sheepishly, I apologised for my misdemeanour, whereupon he said, 'That'll teach you to drive Service transport without proper authority, Frankie. Have a drink.'

Apart from the three Boston squadrons at Hartford Bridge, we had two Dutch squadrons using the airfield for a short time – No. 322 with Spitfires and No. 320 with Mitchells. Their crews were dressed in the uniform of the Royal Netherlands Navy. When we found out how much they were paid, we gasped; apart from their set pay scale, which was higher than ours, they received extra money for every flying hour. Operational flying was rewarded with about an extra 9s. 6d. per hour. We didn't see a lot of the Dutch chaps for they messed elsewhere, but we often saw in our mess Queen Wilhelmina and Prince Bernhard.

I flew with the G/Capt. for the first time on 30 April. Our Boston IIIA (BZ.331) bore a painting of Diana the Huntress (the name of Mac's charming wife) and, appropriately, the aircraft's letter was 'D', 'Shiny D' we called it.

Between 11 and 14 May, the Wing moved on detachment to RAF Swanton Morley. The crews lived in tents round the airfield perimeter. Living out of a suitcase under canvas was becoming a habit, but at least I didn't have to negotiate that assault course again.

One of our aircrew blokes, Stanley Devon, was a keen photographer (he gained many commendations and prizes as a photographer after the war, mainly when he served Kemsley Newspapers). He crept up on me one morning when I was attempting to shave, my mirror swinging round the tent pole in the fresh breeze while I chased round after it, the lather on my face beginning to flake off. He wanted to get a 'shot' of my ugly reflection and the real thing at the same time, trick stuff which meant nothing to me, so I told him to get on with it. The result was amusing.

Paddy Maher was with the Wing at that time and I was pleased to see that he had been promoted to Wing Commander. I never flew with him again, for later he took over a Mosquito squadron (107) and was killed in a flying accident in Germany about a year after that. Recently, I read in *A History of 107 Squadron* that Paddy (and his navigator, Ted Bowen) was taking off from Sylt when an engine cut. Nursing the Mosquito round the circuit, the other one failed. He tried to put it down between some houses but struck a flag-pole (erected to the glory of the German Reich), lost control and blew up on impact. Apparently had Paddy cleared his 'in' tray that morning he would have seen a signal grounding all Mosquitoes because of a series of engine failures on take-off.

I was getting more flying with Mac; when we were at Swanton, I flew three times on the 11 May, again on the 12th, 13th, 14th and 19th. Back at base again, we took a trip up to Little Warden, a USAAF base. Mac wanted to get all the 'gen' on the American flak suits which had recently been issued to our squadrons. Parking 'Shiny D', we were shown to the stores and made welcome by a technical sergeant.

'Come in fellahs,' he said. Stan looked at me, I looked at Stan, we both looked at Mac to see what his reaction had been. Mac's rank, equivalent to full colonel, demanded a little more than 'fellah' we thought, but he said nowt. Turning to Mac, whose four blue rings were clearly showing on his battle-dress epaulettes, the sergeant continued, 'Well buddy, how can I be of help?' We saw Mac's eyes do a couple of swift orbits but he didn't make a meal of the American. His reply 'We've come for a demonstration of your flak suits, *Sergeant*,' was, however, a bit frigid. Stan and I recognised the tone straight away and prayed that the sergeant would apply his brakes before going too far, however unintentional. I'm sure that Mac realised that there had been no intentional disrespect, just typical American goodwill, *absit invidia*. It was just as well he didn't use the favourite American expression 'OK Mac' for this would have severed the last straw. Instead he said 'Sure thing, I'll go get 'em.'

There were two types of flak suit; the pilot and navigator wore much the same, a front piece and a battle-bowler, for they were already protected at their rear by armour plating. The gunner wore a three-piece suit plus 'bowler'. I was shown how my bits went together. The fabric-covered steel strips (giving excellent flexibility) of both back and front portions buttoned at the shoulders, and could be released by ripping a quick-release tape. A sporran-type piece clipped on to the bottom of the frontpiece. The whole outfit weighed about 30 or 40 lb. The gunner of a Boston, if he was doing his job properly, had to stand most of the time while flying and the weight of the flak suit was just a bit too much for him after a couple of hours. It was, of course, a toss up between fatigue and the risk of puncture by steel or lead.

As it was compulsory to wear the stuff, I donned my suit of armour after climbing through the lower hatch so that Mac could see how obedient I was when he climbed onto the wing and passed my cockpit. But as soon as we were airborne I pulled the rips and let the whole pile of ironmongery fall to the floor. The relief I felt was, I imagine, akin to that felt by a corpulent woman having divested herself of a strangling corset.

After D-day, the radio in the mess did a roaring trade, especially with the French crews. We were all eager to know how the Allied front was moving although a few of us semi-privileged people could walk into the ops room and see the current situation chalked up in chinagraph on the talc-covered large-scale map. I shall, however, never forget the day when the liberation of Paris was so dramatically announced. I was standing by the radio looking out into the anteroom. There was a large circle of attentive faces; French, British, Canadian, Australian and New Zealand all agog for the latest news. After the pips the announcer, in calm measured tones, said 'It has just been announced that Paris was entered this morning by American troops; Paris is liberated...' There was a momentary pause, during which a pin would have been heard if dropped, broken by the first strident but stirring notes of the Marseillaise. Looking round the sea of faces I saw many an unashamed tear. I, too, felt a lump welling in my throat. It was truly a wonderful moment.

   While there were several differences of opinion between us
and the French, we liked the majority of them. Stan and I were on
great terms with the French ALO (Army Liaison Officer), Captain
Pierre L. Drefus. Pierre had been in Paris when the Germans had
marched in. He told us how mad he was when his property,
including a couple of prized motorcars, had been requisitioned by
the invaders. Before he left his beloved Paris to join the Free
French forces in North Africa, Pierre (himself an accomplished
racing driver) saw one of his best cars wrapped round a lamp-post
by a drunken German officer.

   Pierre's efforts to teach Stan and me some French were quite
amusing. I had had five years of French at school (as no doubt had
Stan) but what I had learned was rusty, in fact deeply corroded.
Nonetheless, having a musical ear I was always able to imitate
accents and made a better job of bonjour than Stan who made that
salutation sound like 'bonnjewer'. Pierre would tear at his thinning
hair and make Stan try it again and again. It was all good fun.

   Pierre was a magnificent bridge player and I often stood behind
him (he didn't object) to watch his masterly play. I also played a lot
of bridge and often paired with one of our two British ALOs, a
lieutenant-colonel (whose name I forget). One of his favourite
remarks when I ruffed our opponents' trick was 'Oh, *bien cracher*,
partner.' I got so used to that expression that I stored it away to use
when I wanted to express my pleasure in something 'well done'. I
should have known better, for the warning *Defense de cracher*
appeared in most forms of French public transport. However,
Henry put his dirty great foot in it a few months later when in
Brussels. On being introduced to a Belgian society lovely in the
RAF Officers' Club, I somehow brought *bien cracher* into the
conversation, purely meant to convey 'splendid' or 'jolly good' or
'wacco' or something, certainly not its real meaning 'well spat'.
She was, understandably, shocked at the expression used by that
vulgar little RAF man, anyhow that's how I read it in her face and
eyes. Her good breeding and my sincere apology prevented further
recrimination. I stuck to English after that, it was safer.

   Our other ALO was a Captain Cassidy whom we called
'Hopalong' or 'Hoppy'; he wore an enormous black moustache and
an air gunner's brevet, for (like Pierre) he took part, as under
gunner, in many sorties with the squadrons.

   When we flew (the G/Capt., Stan and myself, were officially on the HQ staff of 137 Wing) it was in an aircraft belonging to 88 Squadron and thus bore the letters 'RH'. Those letters, by the way, gave Shev the opportunity to make one of the most amusing 'cracks' of his career. We happened to be sharing leave together in London and one evening in a pub near Victoria station, we watched with interest the entry of two Chelsea Pensioners. With their scarlet tunics a'clank with medals of battles long past, they made their way to the bar. We stood them a pint apiece and, after the usual 'cheers', Shev said 'Why, what a coincidence. Didn't know you two were on 88 Squadron; haven't seen you about at briefing.'

The dear old chaps were, understandably, baffled for when they last saw action it was before Wilbur Wright got airborne at Kittyhawk back in 1903. Their raised eyebrows invited elucidation.

'Those letters,' said Shev, pointing to the metal letters 'RH' on the front of their black hats, 'denote 88 Squadron.' He went on to explain the squadron coding system. They were amused and delighted. No doubt they passed the information to their colleagues when they returned that night to the Royal Hospital.

There was rather a startling accident at Hartford Bridge one day. A Free French Air Force P.51 Mustang flew low over the airfield its pilot obviously showing off his skill (?), in the form of an unauthorised beat-up, to one of his mates on the French Squadron. As he scraped the 'field, his machine hit one of the French ground crews who was cycling across the centre of the runway. He was cut down and killed. The Mustang hit the ground wing-tip first, turned over to rip off the other wing while the fuselage hurtled along the ground like a zany-controlled rocket to finish up on the far side of the aerodrome. The pilot walked away from the wreckage with a few scratches.

Another incident involved two Bostons. One was approaching the main runway from the right direction, the other approached the same runway from the wrong direction. We stood there waiting for a glorious pile-up when the inevitable red Very cartridge was fired from control. The two aircraft then proceeded to change places and to repeat the performance. Each must have received a radioed instruction (meant for the one offending aircraft only) to go round again and make the correct approach, since it seemed impossible to make such a mistake in broad daylight and in reasonably good visibility. Eventually they sorted themselves out and landed into wind, one at a time.

On 12 June, D-day plus six, I did my first operation with the G/Capt. From the gaping bomb doors of 'Shiny D', four 500 lb. bombs fell 10,000 feet onto enemy transport concealed in a wood south of Caen. On the way to the target we flew over the Normandy beachhead. I'd never before seen such a concentration of shipping; vessels of every description were 'parked' haphazardly off-shore. It was, on the whole, a very quiet trip with only moderate heavy flak over the target. What a pleasant change it was to cross the French coast knowing that our own troops were down there, although we were still wary of the Royal Navy.

My last operation of the war (my fifty-fourth sortie with my twentieth operational pilot) was with F/Lt Pete Vickers, a Canadian. His navigator was F/Lt Turner, and gunner F/O Keith Kimber. I went as under-gunner just for the ride. It was a night 'do' with take-off at 1.30 am on 28 July and the target was a concentration of troops in a wood near Bretteville (between Caen and Falaise); the bomb load included 48 x 20lb anti-personnel bombs. I recorded the fact that it was a quiet trip.

I wasn't very happy about the under-gunner's position and it wasn't really necessary to carry one at night. I had to lie on my belly facing a gaping hole left by the open lower-hatch across which was clipped a single machine-gun. (As I only did the one flight in that position I am hazy as to the details of the armament and how it was fixed.) Anyway, it was bloody draughty and the dust from the fuselage floor eddied with every gust blowing into one's eyes; how I hated to wear goggles. Consequently, when Pete asked me whether I'd like to go again a few nights later, I declined. 'Sorry, Pete. I'd love to as an upper gunner but lying on the floor is a bit grim and a bit below my dignity,' I added, laughingly. They didn't return from that trip. My God, I thought, the number of times I have dodged the 'chop' because of a flimsy impulsive decision, and luck. They were a really fine crew and had got so close to the end of the war as, of course, did so many others.

My third and last flight for the month of July was with the Group Captain, a low-level to Stowmarket and back.

It was during the summer of 1944 that King George VI and Queen Elizabeth paid Hartford Bridge a visit. They came for an investiture because the flying-bomb menace made London a hazardous venue for such functions. The station was on parade, in working dress, and I stood in a long line of recipients. It was nice

to have my mother and sister there to watch the proceedings. I
expect that it was more exciting for them than myself. The Royal
party was late arriving, by which time 'erks' and WAAFs, who had
been on parade a long while, were falling like nine-pins.

When my turn came to step forward, salute and have my
'gong' hung, I was terribly nervous. But the King was very
friendly and put me at my ease when he asked, with a grin, 'How
long have you been air gunning?' I told him and he added the
customary congrats and handshake after hanging the gong. I
received something else that day which those attending an
investiture at Buckingham Palace never got, a photograph of the
actual ceremony. Each recipient was given a couple of prints (and
the negative) of the occasion – an excellent souvenir.

My first four flights in August were with the Wingco Flying,
Ian Spencer; the last four with the G/Capt. Between them they took
me to places like Castle Donnington, Greenham Common
(USAAF), Colerne, Benson and Finmere.

Ian Spencer had a pet on the station, a bulldog he called Butch;
a more languid dog I'd never seen. I had always imagined bulldogs
to roar about the place with large, blood-stained pieces of trouser-
seat between their fangs. Not a bit of it. Butch waddled
lackadaisically into the mess, made a bee-line for the rug in front
of the fire and pulled up his undercarriage. There he would stay,
occasionally lifting a bloodshot eye and dribbling jowl if anyone
came close enough to disturb his 'ugly-sleep'.

Butch featured on Ian's aeroplane; somebody had painted his
likeness with tin hat strapped on and holding a bomb. Underneath
the fierce portrait was a scroll upon which was nicely painted AVT
RVMPERE AVT STERCVS FACERE (the nearest that one of the
squadron's Latin scholars could get to a well-known service
expression). Below all that, were two rows of foaming beer mugs
instead of the usual little yellow bombs denoting the number of
sorties completed by that aircraft.

In September, I got off the deck only six times, all but two with
Mac. The exceptions were with W/Cdr Dickie North when he flew
me to Swanton Morley and back in a Boston Mk.IV (equipped with
two ·300 calibre guns). On the 27th, the G/Capt. flew Stan and me
to our base-to-be in northern France, Vitry-en-Artois. It was my
first time on French soil and it brought many new impressions. We
took off at 8.30 am and landed in that flat, uninteresting part of

France an hour later. Corporal Wally Palmer was there to greet us, for he had taken the Group Captain's Buick over in advance of the Wing. The S/Ldr Admin. was also there, fixing up accommodation and other details. Stan and I had many rides in Mac's luxurious limousine often with his pennant a'flying up front. I wondered how the 'old man' would react if I repeated the Bedford bus/Manston treatment on his paintwork? With a shiver, I hastily swept such a notion under a mental carpet.

As Stan and I entered the village we were stopped by a wee boy. With appealing eyes, just like Butch's, he held out his grubby paw saying *'Cigaret pour papa, m'sieur.'* Stan got his 'twenty' out and gave him one. He oughtn't to have done it for, from nowhere, hundreds of kids came at us, all screaming *'cigaret pour papa...'* We had learnt lesson number one. But it was a pleasure to do something for the people who for so long, had been subjugated. We did, however, wonder whether papa really got his fag.

Between 30 September and 28 October, Stan and I flew to Vitry and back four times with Mac. The Wing, comprising two Boston Squadrons, 88 and 342, and one Mitchell squadron, 226, moved over at the end of October. No. 107 Squadron had converted to Mosquitoes and had moved elsewhere.

Stan and I had the great advantage over the others in being able to bag the best accommodation in the village. The S/Ldr A. had been making an inventory of available billets and had told us that we could have a couple of rooms at Le Moulin, in the south-east corner of the village. It was the only place which had hot and cold running water as well as a pleasant view over the canal. We went down there with him. The owners, Monsieur and Madame Duflos (and their two middle-aged bachelor sons) were, at first, unhappy at the thought of their home being taken over again. They said, with a lot of gesticulation, that the Boche had kept them out of their chateau all the war and now the RAF wanted to do the same. They calmed down a little when S/Ldr A. told them that (*a*) he had official sanction to requisition any accommodation which the Germans had used, but no other, and (*b*) that they would only have two officers (Stan and myself) thrust on them.

We could understand their point of view but they had ample room: a lodge, where the family had lived during the occupation, and a small chateau where, latterly, the World War II *Luftwaffe* fighter ace, General Adolf Galland and his officers had lived.

(Incidentally, Goring flew from Vitry during the First World War.)
Stan and I were made welcome and were given a small room
apiece, each equipped with a wash-basin, and later some furniture
which we selected from a large warehouse near the village. We
entered and left the chateau by the back staircase and the kitchen.
In the latter we loitered to sniff at the stockpot, always on the
simmer and issuing mouth-watering aromas.

Stan still had his motorcycle so it was no hardship getting from
the mill to the airfield. As we flew back to the UK quite frequently
with the G/Capt., we asked the Duflos family what they would like
us to bring back from London (apart from coffee). A battery for
their electric clock; Savora *moutard Francaise* and some
'wooosoosoostersheer souse'. They were most grateful for our
gifts especially for the 5 lb. bags of coffee beans we got for them.
We were invited down for breakfast every morning. A large
steaming cup of good coffee, home-made bread and butter and
confiture and sometimes a new-laid egg, for they had their own
chickens. During the very cold winter, the hot coffee went down a
treat. It was good to see (and hear) dear old M. Duflos drink his
coffee with such gusto – from a desert spoon.

After we had been there some time, Stan and I were invited to
lunch. That day I'll never forget. Stan was a big man with a healthy
appetite but the Duflos spread soon had him (and me) tipping our
heads back for fear of overflow! Before lunch we had an aperitif
and a cigarette in the study. The six of us then sat down at the large,
heavy oak table upon which was placed the first course, a
magnificent omelette made with real eggs and ham. Stan and I were
about to say Grace and leave the table when the main course was
wheeled in: a large platter of roast chicken, French fried spuds and
a dustbin-sized container of fresh green salad suitably garnished
with garlic. We had a couple of helpings, not because we wanted it,
but because it was hospitably forced upon us. By that time both
Stan and I were wilting. Delicious white wine and champagne
helped a bit, but then came the large fruit pies liked so much by the
French. Not having a sweet tooth I tried to wriggle out of that
course but they insisted. Not to hurt their feelings I tackled a
massive piece which they put on my plate. It was delicious, as was
the second piece, but my eyes were beginning to stick out like
doorknobs. We rounded off the meal with fresh fruit, coffee and
cognac. We'd have been there until tea-time had we not excused

ourselves with *'Merci mille fois, Madame, mais nous sommes tres tard pour travail…au revoir, a bientot comme d'habitude.'*

Stan and I mounted the Ariel, its tyres almost flattened with our additional weight, and repaired to the mess at about 4 pm. There was a delicious steak on the menu that evening but we just couldn't look it in the face.

On one of our earlier visits to Vitry we took Pierre with us to act as interpreter. We met the local mayor and had a wonderful meal in one of the few cafes in the village. I wonder whether its proprietor is still there and whether he has the photograph I gave him and which he proudly placed on his sideboard as though I were his only son? Pierre told Stan and me that he was going to organise for himself a car. He asked the mayor if there was a collaborator in the district who owned a car. There was and Pierre went to see him. He told us that he had laid on the requisitioning of the man's Citroen. ''e was too frightened to refuse my demand,' said Pierre, with a smile.

The French were ruthless with those of their kinsmen who had bowed and scraped to the Germans. There was, for example, the case of the wine merchant in Douai who was approached by members of the French squadron. They wanted some supplies for their mess. There was a long queue outside the liquor-wallah's store when they moved in on him (after finding out that he had been a collaborator).

'We want a stock of wines for our mess,' they said, brusquely.

'But I haven't got very much and these people should be served first,' he answered nervously.

'These people buy only your cheaper wines. We want the better variety which we know you have hidden away.' The queue murmured its approval and encouraged their Air Force heroes to give him hell.

The merchant had no defence and led the 342 Squadron chaps to his vast cellar. They got all they wanted.

The airfield at Vitry was in a parlous state when the Germans had left, in a hurry. They had found time to damage the buildings and rip up some of the surface of the runway and hardstandings. We also suspected that the local people had been through the buildings, taking furniture and other fittings which they considered as rightly theirs. Anyway, an airfield construction company moved in and restored the station and got it into operational condition.

One member of that unit was a most amusing pilot officer.

Wearing World War I medal ribbons he was a born scrounger. He knew where to lay his hands on anything and everything, from supplies of timber, metal and furniture to Luger pistols, coal-scuttle helmets, ersatz soap and brand-new German refrigerators. One of the pilots took one of the latter home in the bomb bay of a Mitchell (it wouldn't fit in the Boston's bomb bay). The pilot officer would say 'Want some souvenirs? Sell you a refrigerator for 1s. 6d. There's an old Flying Fortress on the airfield, you can have that for 1s. 6d.' Everything was 1s. 6d.

We found some souvenirs when visiting the empty chateau where 88 Squadron crews were to stay. The place was in a shocking state; ripped mattresses all over the floor, masses of paper and rubbish of every description including pamphlets signed by his 'nibs' in Berlin. We found some candles with *Luftwaffe* embossed on them and some medals inscribed with '*Für kriegsverdienst 1939*', but we didn't find any gongs awarded to women for having mother hubbard families.

There were two rather amusing incidents at Vitry during our earlier visits the first of which involved a Dakota of RAF Transport Command. It landed late one afternoon and taxied to the apron. Having seen the aircraft circling and then making an approach to land (there were no traffic control facilities then), Mac decided to drive to the airfield to see what the score was. When the engines had stopped the door opened and the short ladder was clipped into position. There emerged from the aircraft a string of high-ranking officers of all three services. There was 'scrambled egg', 'fruit salad', red tabs, gold uniforms with navy-blue stripes – the lot. The only things missing were swords, spurs and a brass band. When that array of 'power' had gathered round the aircraft, the crew came out – the pilot was, I believe, a mere flying officer. He told the G/Capt. that he couldn't get through to his destination (Brussels) because of bad weather for even the birds were walking. If his passengers had had their way they would have pressed on but their rank was useless against the decision of the aircraft's captain. Mac agreed with the pilot.

'All I can do, gentlemen,' said Mac, 'with severely limited facilities at my disposal, is to organise transport for you.'

There was a general murmur of approval from the passengers and a sigh of relief from the Dak's crew (who would stay with us). Mac told Wally Palmer to lay on transport (I'm sure that he winked

at Wally). Twenty minutes later a three-ton Thornycroft trundled to
a halt before the august assembly.

'Gentlemen, I'm afraid that this is the best I can offer you under
the circumstances,' said Mac. Stan and I didn't know where to put
our faces for we could just imagine the reactions of that 'high-
powered' group during and after a seventy-five-mile ride over
cobbled roads, seated on hard wooden forms in the back of a
draughty exhaust-filled three-tonner.

As it left the 'field and turned onto the main road in the
direction of Douai, we all burst out laughing. Even if we had been
able to lay on accommodation, they wouldn't have accepted. For
them it was Brussels or bust and they got there – the hard way.

The other incident concerned an American pilot. He landed his
P.47 Thunderbolt one evening and asked for a bed. He had come
from Paris but couldn't make his base in the UK because of bad
weather. The following morning we went down to see him off the
premises. Before doing so, however, his aircraft needed topping up
with fuel. It was a messy and lengthy procedure without the proper
equipment. We had to decant 40-gallon drums into 4½-gallon
jerrycans, then lift them on to the wing. The fuel was passed
through a shammy-leather and took ages to deliver.

Standing with the American while the fuelling was in
progress, I noticed that the Thunderbolt carried a large auxiliary
fuel tank under its belly. 'Surely you have enough fuel to get you
back?' I asked him.

'That tank doesn't hold gas,' he answered with a sly grin, 'it
contains the payroll of a whole squadron, in perfume and
champagne,' he added with a low, almost villainous laugh.

'Fine,' I said, 'but what'll you do if the landing gear fails to
come down?'

'Only one thing I could do, with that valuable load, bud. I'd
come in upside down and pray mighty hard.'

We soon settled down on our new airfield and among the local
French people. Stan and I got about a bit and one day paid a visit
to Douai. We wanted to see some of the results of the bombing.
Wandering down to the main station and its adjoining marshalling
yards, we stepped down on to the track and walked along to the
goods sidings where twisted, entwined rails, deep craters and
rolling stock smashed to matchwood, was the staggering sight that
met us. Two through-lines had been repaired but the rest was left in

jumbled chaos. We then noticed some sour looks from two railway gangers, one of them weighing a heavy spanner menacingly in his hands. Stan and I made a wise retreat. We later found out that the people in that town were very anti-RAF because of the damage inflicted upon it. They cooled off when it was explained that most of the damage had been done by high-flying American Fortresses and Liberators. We pointed out the accurate bombing carried out by and TAF Bostons and Mitchells on the railway yards at Arras and targets elsewhere. The Arras yards had been well and truly pranged but the shops and houses alongside the railway were untouched other than a few broken windows. How were they to know that our 'GH'equipped Mitchells were the only aircraft allowed to bomb 1,000 yards ahead of our own troops from above cloud.

Some of the damage in the vicinity was appalling. When we later drove down to Amiens, we passed through the site of a small town which no longer existed. It was Doullens, and the area had been flattened by bombing and rocket fire. Craters overlapped each other and left a scene of desolation difficult to match anywhere, except perhaps on the moon. We were told that a German column, retreating through that town, had been bottled in by rocket-firing aircraft, then the heavies moved in and wiped them and the town out. It must have been terrifying. All along the road we saw signs of past battles; burnt-out tanks, guns, lorries and cars.

The only flying I got in was the occasional trip to the UK with Mac. In November, I flew back to Hartford Bridge in a Mitchell and four days later returned to Vitry in 'Shiny D'. In the back with me were our two ground crew who had gone over to the UK for the ride. It was on that return journey that 'Shiny D' became 'dirty bent D'. Arriving over the airfield, Mac prepared to land only to find that his undercarriage warning lights indicated that the nosewheel wasn't locked down. We plunged about the sky trying to get the leg locked home; sometimes the effect of 'g' helped to move the wheels just that bit extra. It could, of course, have been an electrical failure but it wasn't safe to take the chance with a 'trike'. Landing on main wheels only, the aircraft might somersault and receive more damage than a straightforward belly-landing.

After a fruitless attempt to get the wheel locked, Mac called up control and said 'I'm coming in, wheels up, on the grass to the left of the runway.' I, meantime, told one of the ground crew to sit on the floor between my legs and brace his head on the cushion of my stool. I would brace my head against the radio shelf, my Mae West collar protecting my neck. The other chap I told to lie flat on his back, head facing aft and with his hands clasped behind his neck. Thus prepared, Mac made his approach.

There appeared to be the whole population of northern France on the airfield to watch the Station Commander make a crash-landing. Actually, there was very little danger involved if done properly and the Boston's underslung engines protected most of the belly of the fuselage.

When the machine finally sank onto the grass there was a horrible 'groinching' noise from underneath as we slid along the ground – lumps of turf flying into the air behind us. The aircraft stopped in about 100 yards, which was some deceleration from about 100 mph touch-down speed. Quickly we scrambled out, just in case of fire, and stood there surveying dear old 'Shiny D'. The blades of both propellers were bent right back; the centre of the fuselage and the lower panels of each engine nacelle were torn and covered in mud. But the aeroplane still looked solid enough and repairable. Mac had really made a first-class job of that crash-landing.

Looking round I suddenly became aware of the masses of people; ambulances, fire tenders, flight vans – the lot. It was real VIP treatment, and yes, there was Wally waiting with the Buick.

It was in November that I had my first visit to Belgium. Three of us took a fifteen-hundredweight to Brussels to get some beer for the mess. Les Brotton, Stan Orski (whom Les and I called 'Baron') and myself were to stay in the big city for a couple of days (one night). Les was top gunner and Baron under gunner with Jock Niven's crew on 88 Squadron. Baron knew most of the people worth knowing in Belgium, for he was domiciled there before the war. Polish by birth, he spoke French like a native and was most useful on our shopping expeditions. He also was fluent in German, Italian and, of course, Polish. The visit to Brussels had been Orski's idea because among his many friends were the owners of a brewery there. They were both rich men and would, he felt sure, put us up for the night – if not there were always the transit hotels.

When we arrived in the city there was a tram strike in progress which made it easier for us to find our way about. In any case there were very few private cars on the road, mostly military stuff. Arriving at Vandenheuvel's brewery we were introduced to M. Descamps and Baron de Beco with whom we placed our order for a few barrels of wallop. Orski then took us back into town and left us in a large, almost empty restaurant while he buzzed off to make arrangements for the night. Les and I called the waiter and ordered coffee. *'Café ordinaire ou café speciale?'* he asked. *'Speciale, s'il vous plait'* I answered, for we didn't want any of that ersatz muck made from acorns or something. When the two filters came along he presented the bill. We nearly fell off our chairs, for each cup of coffee cost us about 19s. 6d. It was the most expensive cuppa I've had in my life.

Les stayed at the home of Baron de Beco while I went to M. Descamps' house on the Avenue Hamoir. It was a beautiful house. As I entered the front door I skirted a massive polar-bear rug for it looked too good to be walked on. At dinner that evening I had the company of another RAF officer, W/Cdr Denis Mitchell (who, in 1963, was promoted to Captain of the Queen's Flight). The Descamps' grown-up son and daughter, Paul and Monique, had between them taken some excellent film of the German exodus from Brussels. Their revealing efforts were shown to us in their home cinema, a magnificent affair complete with projection room, permanent screen and remotely-controlled curtains. There were shots of the fire in the dome of the Palais de Justice; of German troops scurrying away in every form of transport they could find while being jeered at by the population. Those scenes were followed by the first Allied tanks and military transport entering the city on that joyful early September day.

They received better than a royal welcome. Tanks, scout cars and Jeeps were one mass of people singing and waving, some crying with joy. Bottles of wine were passed from mouth to mouth and garlands of flowers transformed the battle-stained clothes of the tired troops. It was an experience they were never to forget.

*   *   *

My third and last flight in November was in an Anson when proceeding on leave via Swanton Morley. Mac had already departed for the UK prior to his posting. He was promoted to Air Commodore and was shortly to return to the Continent as Air Officer Administration, No. 84 Group HQ. In fact, on my return from leave he flew me back to France, on 5 December, in an Anson Mk X. It is the one and only entry in my log of a pilot above the rank of Group Captain. As we taxied round Lasham's peri-track, he told me that he'd never flown an Anson before. It didn't worry me though because he was a good pilot; the 'Annie' was a pretty docile beast and almost flew itself.

My only other flight during December, on the 23rd, was with F/O Andy Cole of 88 Squadron who flew me to Fersfield near Diss in Norfolk. I had been given Christmas leave and when I climbed out of the Boston great care was bestowed upon my two pieces of baggage, one piece being particularly heavy. Luckily there was no Customs check at Fersfield for my heavy case contained many bottles of 'Christmas spirit'.

I got a lift back to Vitry on 4 January with W/Cdr Dickie North, in a Boston. We took off from Hartford Bridge at 3 pm and I was back in the mess with the midday editions of the London evening newspapers at four o'clock.

Mac's place was taken by Group Captain Kippenberger, a jolly good CO although I once nearly came unstuck with him. Entering the bar one evening and feeling in good form, I saw somebody bending over a table looking at a magazine (rank on sleeves concealed). Thinking it was somebody else, I slapped the back heartily saying 'What about a drink you bald-headed old crow?' The G/Capt. looked up at me, stared rather hard for a moment and said, 'It appears that the drink is on you, Henry.' I couldn't buy it quick enough!

December and January 1944-45, at Vitry were two very cold months. Freezing fog in January was to give the Wing many grounded days and the Germans the opportunity to break through in the Ardennes. The news travelled fast for the Duflos family besieged Stan and me with anxious questions. Was the Boche returning? Would they be murdered in their beds? etc. We reassured them as best we could with smiles, limited French and plenty of gesticulation. The fact that we both wore revolvers (a standing order during the flap) didn't help to console them.

Just after the foggy period, the Met. boys dropped a clanger. A Mitchell was due for air-testing and its crew reported to the control tower for clearance. It was to be the usual fifteen-minute trip after a major inspection. The duty officer, who didn't like the look of the coppery, snow-laden front which was moving up from the south-west, rang the Met. Office. They said that it would be all right for a short flight. The crew, and the ground crew who went for the ride, clambered into their aircraft and took off. No sooner had their wheels been retracted than a blizzard swept across the field and swallowed them. The front, an extensive one, would take some time to move through so they had to fly across the Channel and land in England. They were there for a couple of days.

In the middle of January, a B-17 Flying Fortress Mk VII landed. Its American crew had just returned from a sortie over Germany and their aircraft had been shot up a bit. While it was being repaired, the crew stayed with us for nearly a week. They were given a small room in the mess (there were seven of them, two officers and the rest NCOs). I soon became friendly with the first pilot, First Lieutenant McCarty. He was an unassuming character and we had a lot of laughs together. When they were ready to leave Mac said to me 'Why don't you come back to England with us. We aren't allowed to carry passengers but we can slip you out through the hedge at our dispersal.' Thinking of another type in my log, and a spot of leave, I told him that I'd ask permission to go. Approaching Wingco Adams (W/Cdr Flying, 137 Wing) I asked him whether I could have a spot of leave and go back with the Fortress. 'Certainly, Henry,' he answered, 'but you'll have to find your own way back *and* get here on time.' I thanked him, and went away to brood over the chances of getting a lift back. I decided to have a shot at it and said to Mac 'Okay kiddo, you've got yourself a passenger.'

Just after lunch on 26 January, I made my way to the Fortress, threw my toothbrush in the rear door and climbed in after it. The crew were at their stations as I walked up the fuselage towards the cockpit. First and second pilots were seated and already running through their check-list for cockpit drill. Just behind the second pilot's seat was the base of the front-upper gun turret in which the sergeant gunner was sitting. I stood behind Mac watching everything with great interest. Looking out of the window I could see the RAF ground crew sweeping snow off the wing surfaces. The runways had been cleared of deep loose snow but there was a layer of hard-packed frozen snow on it. The sky was a filthy yellow, visibility about a mile and it looked as though it would clamp down at any minute. The four motors were started and Mac shouted to me 'Gee, you must have brought us luck to get us such a clean trouble-free start. This goddamned crew is the unluckiest bunch you ever did see.'

We taxied out on to the runway, turned into wind and after the final checks, the second pilot grabbed the four throttles in his big fist and eased them forward. We started to roll and gathered speed (without skidding off the runway, thank goodness) and parted cleanly from the ground. Climbing up through the murk we burst into bright sunshine and levelled off at about 7,000 feet. Having reached that height, Mac slipped in the auto-pilot, put his feet up and handed round the 'candy' and Camels. We stooged along munching and smoking and enjoying the view. When over the Channel, the weather cleared beneath us and we were able to map-read all the way to their base, at Lavenham in Suffolk.

Arriving over Lavenham, we lost height and made a run along the runway in use; the compass was set before we commenced a wide turn to make our final approach. While the vertical visibility had been good, the horizontal visibility was poor, but Mac approached on the pre-set compass heading hoping that the aircraft would be in line with the runway. On the final run Mac opened a side window and concentrated on the view ahead, while the second pilot called out the indicated airspeed in his loud Texas drawl. I thought, at first, that he was indulging in a bit of back-seat driving, but it was the American procedure (as it was in the larger aircraft of the RAF, I believe). Mac called for gear and flaps down, and out of the haze ahead appeared the sodium lights of the runway. Scraping the trees at the threshold, Mac put the Fort down gently on the runway.

We taxied across to dispersal and switched off, ninety minutes after leaving Vitry. No.4298014 stood there silently, the hot engine cowlings creaking as they quickly contracted in the cold air. Mac pointed to the hole in the hedge and said 'Get through there and you'll find yourself on the Bury St Edmunds' road. You should get a lift easily enough and then a train to London.' Thanking him, I said cheerio to the crew and nipped through the hedge.

I wrote to Mac later but never received a reply. I often wonder what happened to that great guy. Maybe the bad luck he said his crew were blessed with had got worse and they had been shot down. I still hope that he was just a bad correspondent.

I managed to get a lift back all right from the usual port of departure, Hartford Bridge. W/Cdr Sykes flew me back in a Boston IV, on 1 February. On the 9th, I got my posting through to SHAEF Air Information, attached to Headquarters No. 2 Group, Brussels. I was to become a penguin for a while.

My grand total of flying, from the day I took the plunge in the signals section at Little Rissington, was 723 hours 50 minutes. I had reached the rank of flight lieutenant and had reaped a large harvest of friends and experiences.

CHAPTER 7

March 1945/46:

With SHAEF Air Inf., Brussels – VE-day –
Press courier to Copenhagen – Into Germany –
Transport Command – Resign – Rejoin – On Lancasters

It wasn't long before I settled down among the chairborne although, strictly speaking, I didn't belong in their ranks for I got out and about quite a lot. My immediate superior, S/Ldr Bob Urquhart, was an experienced journalist. During the war he was a pilot on Halifax bombers yet he couldn't drive a car. He was, however, adept at the game from the back seat until the car was stopped and he was offered the wheel. F/O Tommy Thomas was the third member of our set-up and we had a floating section of RAF photographers including Frank Sharman from the *Sunday Pictorial*.

Bob was far from being a dour Scot, since he possessed an inimitable sense of humour, and his fund of anecdotes never failed to raise a good belly-laugh. He only told one story concerning his flying career and it bears relating. Apparently a Halifax he was driving swung off the runway at take-off and began a cross-country trip.

'...suddenly we swung off the runway and started across the grass like the clappers. While we were pulling back the throttles, pushing tits and stamping on the brakes, a bloke on a tractor hove into view, right in the line of 'fire'. He turned, saw us coming at him at a rate of knots, leapt off his machine and ran so bloody fast that he left his tractor way behind. We landed up in a ditch, shaken but unhurt, and the tractor driver – he's still running...'

It may not sound so funny on paper but when Bob told the story, in his broad accent, you could almost see that poor man scorching across the airfield and sense the atmosphere in the Halifax's cockpit.

Many years after the war, I had a letter from Bob which included an amusing corollary to that incident, and I quote it verbatim:

In your book you mention the story of how I pranged that Halifax at Topcliffe. Well about ten or twelve years *after* the war, during my 28 years as agricultural editor of *The Scotsman*, it had the most amazing coincidence. I had a company car but it was being serviced so I had to take the train to a sale of Highland cattle, the ones with the shaggy coats and long horns. After I had changed at Stirling I found myself sitting by a stocky, talkative, Yorkshireman.

I asked him where his farm was and he said, 'Oh, a little place you have never heard of called Topcliffe.' I told him that I knew it as I was stationed there during the war and asked where, exactly, his farm was. He replied, 'When you came out at the main gate and turned left at the village, where you chaps patronised our pubs, my farm was alongside the airfield.' I asked him if he remembered a Halifax landing on it in October 1942. He remembered, 'Too bloody well! It took them weeks to take it apart in sections with the four Rolls-Royce Merlins.' So I told him *I* was flying it or, rather, piloting it as I never got off the deck!

Now on the night before these sales the breed society always held a cocktail party in the Great Western Hotel, where I was staying. So, after taking my room, I went down to it. I had hardly got through the door when this Yorkshireman dashed up, grabbed me by the arm, and took me around the room telling people, 'This booger landed a bloody great bomber on my farm!' At each stop there was a drink but it was becoming like a 'dummy run' for Hogmanay and so, in self defence as I had a lot of work to do, I retreated to my room.

*   *   *

SHAEF Air Inf. was attached to HQ 2nd TAF but it answered to the Directorate of Public Relations, Air Ministry, headed then by Air Commodore Lord Willoughby de Broke. The unit, under W/Cdr Tom Guthrie, was situated in an office block near the Rond Point end of the Rue de la Loi, close to the delightful gardens of the Parc du Cinquintenaire. A little further down the road was the Residence Palace which housed Headquarters and TAF (Main and Rear).

It was in the Rue de la Loi office of Air Inf. that we, war correspondents (resident and transient) and visiting officers, irrespective of rank, were initiated as members of the bar. The member, napkin round neck, stood before a two-foot model of the *Manneken Pis* placed on the bar counter. The famous little boy's 'short-arm' was linked by tube to a rubber bulb at his rear. The bulb, filled with cognac, was squeezed with varying pressures so to fox the recipient. The object was, of course, to catch the precious liquid in the mouth, to waste as little of it as possible and to prevent it getting in one's eye and hair.

Our small off-shoot unit, under Bob, was attached to No. 2 Group HQ, situated in the Caserne de Cavalerie, on the Boulevard

General Jacques in the south-east suburbs of Brussels. It was about a mile away from the main office referred to above. SHAEF Air Inf. had its own car-pool and drivers and some of our motor-cars must have turned many an air commodore green with envy. It wasn't an uncommon sight, for instance, to see a group captain cycling about the caserne's network of roads, while Bob, Tommy or myself drove off in a 25-foot-long Cadillac.

Part of my job was to conduct war correspondents to RAF units in Europe, hence the luxurious transport. On other occasions I drove a Jeep to an RAF base in Belgium or France where I'd obtain stories about airmen and their work. Those stories were filed to Air Ministry who, in turn, passed them out to the local newspaper(s) concerned. It was, at the time, a morale-booster for the troops whose duties were arduous and so often unsung. Bombing up or re-arming an aircraft in freezing weather conditions on a partly destroyed foreign airfield was the lot of many armourers. Engine and airframe fitters and other ground crews had to work with limited facilities and spares, often to meet a ridiculous dead-line. All the ground crews, in fact, did a marvellous job of work under the rigorous conditions that obtained in those post D-day months. This fact I soon found out during my travels. When interviewing them, they sometimes were shy and nearly always modest when talking about their work. In fact it was a job to dig out the details. I was, nonetheless, very pleased to help publicise their efforts for they rightly deserved recognition.

Not being a journalist (as will have become apparent to the reader by this time), I found my job a little trying at first. Bob gave me a tremendous amount of help and advice. His objective criticism of my first attempts I found most helpful.

'They're too flowery, Franco,' he would say, 'you must remember that good writing is composed of simple English and the shorter the sentence the better. Don't hunt for the longest words in the dictionary. Be straightforward; tell your story sincerely and naturally.' All the while his blue pencil was hacking away at what I'd thought to be a literary masterpiece. I've always appreciated Bob's patience; though, during my six months with him he didn't turn me into a Fleet Street wonderman, he taught me a lot and made the job I was doing less exacting and more satisfying. However, I preferred the conducting-officer side of the job. It entailed more travelling, going to new places, meeting more people. It appealed to me then as it does today.

Our mess in the caserne was small but friendly, notwithstanding the barred windows which looked out on to the Champs des Manoeuvres. That stretch of open ground was used by HQ as a landing strip for small aircraft and we often watched our SASO do a couple of circuits in a Fieseler Storch which was parked there. My living quarters, upstairs, consisted of a large, bare barrack room which I shared with half a dozen other officers. We slept on camp beds and each 'inmate' was issued with a combined locker/wardrobe. The bar, on the ground floor, was small but cosy. A grand piano stood in the corner and some excellent caricatures, in colour, of 2 Group officers (done by a W/Cdr Bill Lord) decorated the walls.

The Air Officer Commanding 2 Group was Air Vice-Marshal Basil Embry and his two senior staff officers were Air Commodore David Atcherley (SASO) and Air Commodore 'Bull' Cannon (AOA). The SASO was known, like his twin brother Richard, as 'Batchy'. The Atcherley twins and Paddy Bandon formed a trio of legendary figures in the Royal Air Force, and it is the Service's great loss that David Atcherley lost his life in a Gloster Meteor over the Mediterranean after the war, while Richard Atcherley and Paddy Bandon have both retired. The illustrious RAF careers of the 'Batchy' Atcherley twins, have been revealed by John Pudney in his book *A Pride of Unicorns*. The mess contained many interesting types; there were the two Met. officers, W/Cdr J. Cumming (who was affectionately known as 'Charlie Cheese the Corned Beef Inspector') and F/Lt Jock Evans. I spent many hours listening to Jock playing Chopin on the mess grand. With the typical tenacity of a Scot he would practice for hours trying to perfect his rendering of the Polonaise in A. There were W/Cdr Digger Magill, S/Ldr Rufus Risley, Major John Pullan (our flak officer) and many other 'absorbent' gentlemen, as Bob would say.

Our catering officer, S/Ldr Cope, was most popular, too, for he spared no effort to provide us with the best fare. He did his job so well that he was later awarded the OBE. The excellence of No. 2 Group's messing became so well-known, in fact, that RAF officers from far and wide would pop in for lunch without invitation. I was in the cloakroom washing my hands one lunchtime when three strange young flying officers walked in. Batchy, who was also present, asked them who they were; were they on duty at 2 Group? 'No, sir. We heard that the food in your mess was so good that we thought we'd try it.'

'Then you can just try walking out again. This is not a public restaurant and we pay pretty high mess bills here but not to subsidise casual visitors, unless specifically invited with my permission.' The three of them left very sheepishly.

One of my favourite haunts in town was the RAF Officers' Club on the Avenue des Arts. It was the matter of a moment to walk down to the corner of the barracks, leap on a 24, 25 or 26 tram, and leap off again at the foot of the Rue de la Loi. Cars could be parked under the trees outside the club, at owners' risk. It was a risk, too, for in 1945 there was a fantastic black market value on a Jeep. Even the expedient of removing the steering wheel and hanging it in the club cloakroom (then a common enough sight) was known to fail for the thieves simply lifted the vehicle at the front end and towed it away.

I often visited the 2nd TAF Communications Squadron at Evere. Ian Spencer was its CO and Twiggie, Shev and many of my old squadron friends were there. They threw some pretty wild parties, too.

My old buddy, Reg Goode, I met on several occasions since he was a member of the crew which flew the C.-in-C. and TAF Air Marshal Cunningham, about the place, their aircraft being a plushly-furnished Dakota.

At the Comm. Squadron parties a very potent brew was concocted. It was called 'boonch'. To this day I've no idea what went into it but whatever it was it made Vodka seem like a kindergarten night-cap. It was at one of those orgies that I met a couple of charming English girls. They wore khaki and sported one 'pip' but were not in the Army. They worked with the Foreign-Office-sponsored Anglo-Belgian Liaison Unit. Jean and Eileen shared a flat on the Avenue de Broqueville (about a twenty-minute walk from the caserne along the boulevards General Jacques and St. Michel) where Bob and I enjoyed many parties.

The flat was about nine storeys up and, on a warm spring evening we'd sit on the window sill hugging a drink while watching Brussels light up. When the first Belgian prisoners of war and political prisoners returned, a fresh outbreak of hatred against known collaborators flared up. Fire engines raced all over the place, their sirens braying like demented asses and putting to shade the monotonous clanging of tram bells. Fires sprang up everywhere. There was no messing about; angry groups burst into the homes and shops belonging to collabs. and dumped everything movable in the street and set light to it.

Evere airfield, the home of 139 Wing as well as the Comm. Squadron, also housed a closely guarded squadron equipped with the Gloster Meteor jet. Nobody could get near the aircraft except the crews and VIPs. but I was lucky to get a close-up look-see and to watch a Belgian F/Lt put one through its paces. This was made possible when I was conducting officer to His Grace the Lord Archbishop of York, the late Dr Garbett. and a host of senior officers and padres. It was then a thrilling sight to watch the all-white Meteor flying towards us a few feet off the ground; all heads went back to gaze in amazement as it pulled up into a vertical rocketing climb to disappear, a mere speck, into cloud high above.

Taffy Langdon, one of our drivers, drove me up to Breendonck prison one day. Half-way along the road to Antwerp, it was, during the war a place of horror for the Belgian prisoners incarcerated there under the iron heel of the Gestapo. We were shown round by a Flemish guide and, even though he had no English or French, we sure got the gist of what he was saying – mostly demonstrating. For example, in the main building at an intersection of corridors, the four corners of the walls had been roughly chipped away leaving a face of jagged concrete. Apparently, if a prisoner or prisoners were near the spot when one of the prison guards or officers walked by, they had to turn and face the wall. If the Gestapo type had got out of bed the wrong side (which, it seemed, they invariably did) the prisoner's face was bashed against the sharp, knobbly concrete.

We saw some of the cells and the inscriptions written and carved on the walls; we gazed reflectively at the gallows in the yard outside, the wall against which many were shot, and the lime pits. That visit upset me and I wanted to get back to town and take the foul taste out of my mouth. It had all been horrible but not as bad as my later visit to Belsen and, to a lesser extent, Neuengamme (Hamburg).

The anti-collaborators weren't the only ones to create disturbances. I was putting some empty bottles out on the small balcony of Jean's flat one evening and found that there was little room left for them – the floor was one mass of empties (in fairness to Jean and Eileen, it was a long-term accumulation). Close by was the rubbish chute. 'Just the job,' I thought. 'No money on the empties, so let the *poussiere-homme* have 'em.' Opening the chute I let the first 'dead man', a Bollinger, go. I listened to its progress until the distant whisper of disintegrating glass told me that it had reached the bowels of the building. It was fun. There followed a couple of Gordons, a Bisquit Dubouche, a Nuits St. George, a brace of Liebfraumilch and sundry others until Jean came rushing out. 'Foot foot, what on earth are you doing? The concierge has been on the phone and is positively hysterical.'

'I'm only getting rid of a few empties, Jeannie my gal,' I answered, with a Veuve Cliquot poised at the mouth of the chute.

'Oh, please don't,' she appealed. I kept the peace.

'Tell the "hommess" that we're having a twenty-first birthday party and that it is an old British custom to dispose of bottles down rubbish chutes,' I suggested. Jean smiled and did that thing, but neither of us knew whether the concierge believed it.

The label 'foot-foot' which Jean stuck on me originated from one of my shaggy-dog stories. It was about the three rabbits, Foot, Foot-foot and Foot-foot-foot. As may be imagined, the continuous repetition of those names was tricky, but I managed to rip 'em off without ruining the story or tripping over my tongue. It was, to say the least, embarrassing to be called foot-foot. After I had been introduced by that name to Jean's family (who accepted it with only the barest flicker of an eyebrow) they passed it down the line of guests who visited them while I was there. On one such occasion the intro. was made thus: 'Oh, Brig. Pat, this is foot-foot, a friend of Jean's...' The Brigadier shook me by the hand and, quite seriously, said 'Howd'y'do, foot-foot.' I felt so small that I would cheerfully have climbed down into my shoes to regard him through the lace-holes.

While on the subject of names, I should briefly explain the use of 'Frank' in my story and 'Mike' on the cover. Simple. Until 1946, I had always been called Frank, Frankie, Franco (by Bob Urquhart). In that year I was posted to Nuremberg where I worked with the Press during the International Military Tribunal goings-on. Among the twenty-two nationalities I mixed with, there were at least five Franks (including Frank Faigl, a Czech captain from Prague Radio). I decided that it would obviate further aural chaos if I moved up one to my second Christian name, QED.

Between madhouse moments in Brussels, there was plenty of work to be done. I drove down to several airfields to get stories. I also re-visited Vitry on two occasions. While there I was fortunate enough to see the dress rehearsal and the actual ceremony to commemorate the First World War battle of Vimy Ridge. It was the first gathering there since before the war. The monument was not far away, between Arras and Lens.

Standing at the base of the towering white monument, we watched two columns of pipers march four-abreast from each side of the large stretch of well-kept grass below. Wheeling together, they advanced eight abreast towards the monument, to the thrilling sound of pipes and drums. The participants were mostly from Canadian-Scottish regiments and the bulk of them drawn from the front line in Germany. Practically every tartan was represented and bearded drum majors formed the front ranks. It was a splendid sight, even for a Sassenach.

One day, escorting a female war correspondent from a London evening paper and a male correspondent from South Africa, we left Brussels in one of our luxurious American cars. I was taking them to visit an RAF Wing at Cambrai in France. We didn't make it for, on the other side of Halle on the N7 to Mons, the driver stopped the car as the radiator was showing signs of boiling over. He lifted the bonnet and unscrewed the rad. cap nearly getting himself badly scalded as the boiling liquid gushed into the air. There was oil in the cooling water, too! Stopping every few miles to top-up, we managed to stagger back to the Air Inf. garage in Brussels. The driver told the mechanics what had happened and they got their heads together over the hot engine. A sudden stream of vile invective bounced round the walls of that cavernous underground garage when they discovered a cracked cylinder block or something. I went up to the lads and said, 'Please mind your language, there's a lady present.' 'Sorry, sir. Didn't realise he was a she.' The offenders were forgiven as Evelyn was wearing slacks and her close-cropped hair was covered with a beret.

One Sunday I was detailed to go to Liege to check on the preparations for an exhibition of RAF aircraft in the main square. I was told that the RAF officer dealing with all the local arrangements could be found at the Bon Marche. When I arrived I couldn't locate him, so l stood in the square, looking at a Spitfire, hoping that he would put in an appearance to see whether his exhibits hadn't been stripped or pinched. There was a tap on my shoulder. Looking round I saw a dear old lady giving me the kindly once-over. In stammering

English she said, 'Excuse please. We give help to a RAF man during ze war. He come down in parachute and we give him to ze resistance, *n'est-ce pas*. We like to know is he all right. His name was Smeeth and was in I think you call Bomber Command.' It was difficult to explain that Bomber Command was a large organisation and that there were as many Smiths as there were aeroplanes in it. However, I took her name and address and passed it through the usual channels. She was sweet.

About a month before hostilities were called off, I went into hospital for a week. I had fallen down a slit trench in the blackout (I was sober, too) and received a contusion of my port kidney. This I was unaware of until the following morning, although later that night I got the wind up when I passed blood in the 'Loo'.

At the RAF 8th General Hospital next morning, I handed a chit from the 2 Group MO to the duty MO. All it said was 'Ruptured kidney?' The MO told me that I should be on my back and not walking about like an idiot. How was I to know? I was placed on a trolley and wheeled round for X-ray. It was discovered that I had a badly bruised kidney and that I'd live. For seven to ten days I would be confined to bed and was told to drink about two gallons of water a day. 'Make it Guinness and I'll drink four,' I said, but it didn't wash.

Quite a few of the RAF officers would slip out at night. I always remember seeing a wing commander, with a couple of his friends, creep out of the back door, put a ladder against the rear wall, place some sacking over the jagged glass atop of it, over and away into town. You can't keep good men down.

The night before my discharge, I was told that I could have a pass-out until 8 pm. I telephoned Bob. He came down in a Jeep and we returned to the mess to get embroiled in a champagne-cocktail session. But as I hadn't consumed anything stronger than blackcurrant juice for over a week, I was the worse for wear when Bob and Tommy drove me back to the hospital at about midnight. They supported my unwilling frame and told me to bob down below the level of the window in the Service Police office at the main gate. We got by unseen and staggered down the antiseptic-smelling corridors. Apparently Bob had to tell me to stop singing. As we were passing the night sister's door (ajar) I chose to sink to the floor, two bottles I'd brought back for the boys rolling noisily over the polished lino. Sister Blake (a honey) was on duty that night and she would have merely wagged her finger reprovingly. Unfortunately, she had a visitor, a W/Cdr padre, who saw all. Luckily, my discharge papers had already got submerged in the welter of bumph passing through the hospital system and nothing drastic happened.

I left the following morning with a shocking hangover, leaving behind me two merrier-than-usual nurses and a not-so-bored Lancaster navigator who nursed a shrapnel wound in his thigh. Between us we had sorted out the bottles.

I was detailed off to drive to Paris in one of our Ford utilities. A New Zealand correspondent, staying at the Press Camp (Hotel Scribe), was waiting to be picked up and taken to the RAF station at Rosieres, a little to the south of Albert. On the way down I had engine trouble and it was some time before I got it fixed at an American unit. In consequence of that delay I pulled in to Paris too late to find my contact, W/Cdr Ian Ogilvie, at his office in the American Express building. I was told where he lived. Parking the car outside the hotel, I went in to find him and to ascertain where I was to stay for the night. The car doors were unlockable and, when I came out ten or fifteen minutes later, I noticed that a large parcel had disappeared from the back seat. I checked the rest of my kit and found that nothing else was missing. I drove to the transit hotel (the Bedford, near Madeleine), dumped my kit and parked the wagon somewhere safe. I then rang Bob.

'Wotcher! Had trouble on the way down. Arrived late, saw Ian Ogilvie at his hotel, when I came out I found that some miserable swine had swiped that large parcel you gave me to deliver,' I informed him, not wishing to beat about the bush.

'Do you know what was in that parcel?' he yelled.

'No,' I said. 'All I know is that I was looking forward to meeting the beautiful French actress you said it was addressed to.'

'It contained about £500 worth of gowns and things. I know it isn't your fault but there'll be hell to pay when the Air Ministry bod who sent it finds out. Okay, Franco, leave it to me.'

The parcel had come over on a Comm. Squadron aircraft (on the old-boy network) and had been stuck on top of a cupboard in the office for weeks, waiting for somebody to go down to Paris. I'd been that somebody and as Bob had said, I couldn't very well be blamed.

In April I flew to Croydon in a Dakota, landing at Coxyde in Belgium on the way. As we queued at Croydon's Customs bench, an officer in front of me said to the chap in front of him (whose baggage was already on the 'slab') 'Don't forget to declare all that brandy, old boy.' It was obviously meant as a facetious remark but it hit a vital spot, for the chap reddened, turned round and knocked the other's hat off. It fell to the floor and from it spilled half a dozen pairs of nylons!

I flew back on the 28th, my last flight during the war. It gave me a grand total of 727 hours and five minutes. It doesn't sound a lot but in medium-to-small aircraft it represented about 1,000 flights. Flying hours, like length of service, were often used as yardsticks of status. As for the former, one has only to compare the disparity of hours between, say, a fighter pilot and a long-range flying-boat pilot. The former's fewer hours were reaped in a cramped cockpit, mostly in the front line, with flights of short duration necessitating more take-offs and landings. The latter type would amass thousands of hours on long trips of anything up to, and maybe exceeding, eighteen hours. Moreover, he usually had a co-pilot as well as an automatic pilot, a galley and bunk on board, and plenty of room to stretch his legs. Many other comparisons could be made without necessarily disparaging the crews concerned who had their jobs to do. It was, however, galling for those who had seen shot and shell to be told to 'Get some hours in...' by a type with a bulging log book and little or nothing to show in the way of action.

Came the end of the war. VE-day in Brussels was something to remember. Celebrations came thick and fast and furious. In fact, a week before the big day we jumped the gun and stepped up our normal quota of parties. Bob, Tommy, Jean, Eileen and myself did a quick tour of some of the local bistros. As we entered each one Bob, in his broad Scottish accent, said *'Vive la Belgique, boissons sur la maison, s'il vous plaît.'* In most cases, when it was understood, we got our drinks on the house and the hospitality was reciprocated. We moved on to the next. Later, Bob and I were invited (not without misgivings on Jean's part) to the Anglo-Belgian Liaison Unit's celebration dinner. Jean was right – Bob and I got pretty septic.

Flags of all the Allied nations fluttered brightly from every building. It was a most colourful and joyful occasion. I remember driving through Breda and Tilburg a month or so earlier on my way to Gilze Rijen, when the Dutch were celebrating the liberation of their country. There were flags everywhere, too, but in every case they were Dutch. Not one Union Flag or Old Glory

did I see. Brussels' tram bells clanged more furiously than before
– if that were possible. The overflow of passengers hung
precariously by their fingertips. I was on the back of one (couldn't
get inside) when I grabbed at a rope to prevent myself from falling
into the road. I pulled the 'stick' off the overhead wire and the tram
stopped dead in its tracks!

Talking of trams, Batchy Atcherley led us all down to the Bois
de la Cambre tram depot at about midnight during one of the many
celebrations. He asked for a tram and driver for his officers. They
obliged. We hadn't got more than a couple of hundred yards down
the street when Batchy tapped the driver on the shoulder, told him
to stop, gave him a packet of cigarettes, led him to a seat and took
control himself. I wonder whether the people of Brussels
remember the occasion when a lone tram, full of RAF officers
singing bawdy songs to the accompaniment of a constantly
clanging bell, was driven by a tall, distinguished looking Air
Commodore all over their fair city?

In June I got in a bit more flying. On the 2nd, I flew over to
Croydon in an Anson and returned from there in a Dakota on the
6th. On the 20th, I flew over a thousand miles through four
countries. A Mitchell had been laid on for No. 5 PRS (an Army
public relations set-up) who wanted it for Press courier duties.
Twice a week that aircraft took off from Melsbroek, made four
landings elsewhere before returning to Melsbroek the same
evening. I managed to scrounge a ride on it. With F/Lt Walker at the
controls we took off at 8.15 am and landed at RAF Wunstorf, near
Hanover, seventy minutes later. We taxied round to control to see
whether there was any Press material and left again at 10.15. On
that first leg of the trip I was amazed to see the obliteration of
Wesel on the Rhine, and other bomb damage on the way, for this
was my first real daylight look-see at Germany.

Our next leg, to Luneburg, took only twenty-five minutes. As
we made our approach to land I noticed crowds of refugees or DPs,
a sea of white faces turned up towards us in a nearby barracks. We
took off again five minutes later for an hour's flight to Kastrup,
Copenhagen, where we stopped for lunch. I immediately fell in
love with Denmark. The people were so very friendly, so much so
that it was embarrassing to have autograph books thrust under
one's nose at every step.

After a plate of delicious roast pork at the airport restaurant, I managed to get a lift into Copenhagen, three miles away. On the way in I asked the Army driver where I could dispose of a few cigarettes, to get a few kroner to buy the odd gift. He said 'I'll buy all you can sell, sir. We are desperately low in cigarettes, everybody from the town major downwards is strictly rationed.' I sold him a dozen packets and he insisted on paying me what I considered a fantastic price. I wondered whether I had been unfair to accept his freely offered money but, when I later sold some packets to Danes, I knew that he could have recouped his money – plus – had he resold just a few of those packets.

That transaction had been carried out when we stopped the open Jeep in the Townhall square. A silly thing to do really, for crowds of people hanging about had seen it all. They also saw that the green signals satchel which contained the cigarettes was still bulky and they followed me down the road. I felt like the Pied Piper. Not a word changed place; I slipped a packet of ten into a hand, a note was slipped into mine. Nobody haggled and I didn't want to drive a hard bargain with friends. In any case, it was strictly against the law to do it, but they had been cigarettes issued on my own ration and which I had saved. When the last packet had gone, I made my apologies to the rest of the queue, then wandered round the shops to spend the loot. I managed to get rid of the money before we took off at 2.45 pm. It had been a wonderful experience to visit Copenhagen and to meet the people who were so genuinely pro-British. I didn't have time to visit the many places of interest in the 'Paris of the North', but I made up my mind there and then that I would return another day. I did, too.

Our next port of call was at Deventer in Holland. We landed there in ten minutes under two hours from Kastrup. At 5.50 pm we landed back at Melsbroek.

In July, Bob came to me and said that the Air Information Unit was being wound up, leaving only one or two senior PROs in Europe. 'You'd better apply for a posting now before you land a job in the stores, dishing out bloomers to WAAFs,' he said. I agreed. The thought of becoming a stores officer made me shudder a little. So I suggested that I'd like to get back to flying maybe with Transport Command. 'I'll see what I can do for you, Franco,' he said, and sat down at his desk to compose a letter to Air Ministry.

Meantime, I flew back to the UK on leave on 24 July. I got a ride from Evere in an Anson XII to Hartford Bridge (then renamed

Blackbushe). On the 31st, I got a lift back in a Dakota to RAF
Buckeburg, Germany. The Unit had moved up from Brussels to
Minden, in which town they resided at the Victoria Hotel, Tom
Guthrie having been succeeded by W/Cdr Tommy Wisdom. I was
intrigued with my new surroundings but disliked the unfriendly
atmosphere. We'd sit in the hotel lounge, drink insipid beer and
watch lorry loads of German PoWs returning home. The local
inhabitants cheered them lustily and threw scowls at us. I found out
later that Westphalia had been and still was a hot-bed of Nazi-ism,
the youth of that district, in particular. But we gave them no quarter.
I was, nevertheless, sorry to have to leave because I'd barely had
time to settle in before my posting came through. In early August I
got all my kit on board a Mitchell and returned to Blackbushe.
Before I had left, Bob had said to me 'Sorry to see you go, Franco,
but I've managed to get you into Transport Command. I haven't
written to tell them you're coming, I'll just let it happen.'

* * *

In the middle of August I reported to my new station, No.
1382 TCU (Transport Conversion Unit) at RAF Wymeswold, near
Loughborough, Leicestershire. The course started on 22 August,
but I didn't start flying from the satellite, Castle Donnington,
until 19 September.

I was crewed up with F/Lt Nigel Geere. A nice lad who hailed
from St Albans. He got me worried on one occasion, though, for he
told me that he had been grounded once because of double-vision.
Apparently, when he flew at night and made his approach to land
he saw two flarepaths and, what was more discouraging, he tried to
land on the false one, holding off at about fifty feet. Nevertheless,
he said that he had been cured. Thank the Lord, I thought.

My first three flights with Nigel were by day. The usual circuits
and bumps, overshoots, featherings, landing on one engine, etc.
Then we bashed away at the night flying. I must say that it was
pleasing to see the peace-time glow of light from towns and cities
all over the country as it was easier on the navigation. The Dakota
I liked very much. My previous flying in them was as a passenger,
and now I sat up forward in the wireless operator's 'office', just
behind the second pilot's seat on the starboard side.

I got in just over ten hours flying on those first two nights.

In October we stepped up our flying (from Wymeswold). On

the 3rd we went to Filton, Bristol (the home of the Blenheim), and then on to St Mawgan in Cornwall where we picked up seven passengers for Wymeswold.

On the 8th we did a seven-hour flight out into the Atlantic. During a break between my wireless broadcasts, I wandered back to the passenger compartment, sat myself down on one of the bucket seats and got out the sandwiches and coffee flask. Looking through the square windows I watched the silvery stippled sea a few thousand feet below. I hadn't been there five minutes before Nigel and the navigator came aft.

'Who the hell is driving? ' I exclaimed.

'George,' answered Nigel, with a smile.

'I only hope that George can spot other aircraft,' I replied.

The three of us sat there having our lunch while the Dak flew on by itself.

On the 11th we did another seven-hour-plus trip, from base to Sheringham to Landsend to base. We had to land by QGH as the weather had turned foul. A couple of trips later, after we had been out to Longships and Ballyquinton Point, we had to return because every time I switched on the transmitter, clouds of pungent smoke poured from the dynamotor beneath my desk.

On the 19th we took some ground staff on a Continental sightseeing trip. It was practice for us and there were seats begging, so why not. We went from base to the Naze/Haarlem/Rotterdam/Krefeld/Cologne/Essen/Amsterdam/Base, all in five hours fifty minutes. Our next four flights were at night, and I added another twenty hours to my night-flying total. In fact, when I had finished the course on 14 November (almost six years from the day I qualified as a wireless operator at Yatesbury), I had put in another seventy-three hours 'flying and my assessment read as follows: Average mark 'ground' 73.2 per cent; 'air' 72.5 per cent; equipment: SCR 287; Morse speed: 25 wpm – 61 per cent. Remarks: keen, alert and reliable. Has reached a high standard.

I proceeded on leave to await a posting to a Transport Command squadron. While at home, I received a signal saying 'Return to Wymeswold end of leave as wireless instructor.' I hit the ceiling. I didn't want to go back to Wymeswold nor did I wish to start instructing again. I rang the signals 'king' at Group.

'Why do I have to go back to Wymeswold?' I asked, testily, 'I was under the impression that I had qualified for posting to a TC squadron.'

'You would have been had your release group been higher than 27,' he answered.

'My release group?' I queried, 'What release group? I'm a regular and haven't got a release group.'

'Oh, I see. Tell you what, Henry. We're forming a new squadron at Full Sutton. It will be a VIP round-the-world squadron flying Lancastrians, operating on a slip-crew basis, with a nice slice of leave at the end of each trip...'

'Wizzo, that's the life for me, put my name down pleeeeeeease.'

'Okay, will do.'

Life was taking on a rosier outlook. At the end of December, I caught a train to York. It was a pleasant four-hour journey for I met an old friend in the buffet bar, where we stayed the whole time, swapping stories and drinks. In York I called into the George Hotel to find out where I could get a bus to Full Sutton! Needless to add, I stayed for dinner and a few more snifters, for it was cold outside. Twelve miles away, on a draughty slice of Yorkshire moorland, was Full Sutton. I wasn't impressed. The Nissen-hutted officers' quarters were about a mile walk from the mess (the airfield was a mile in the other direction). I found me a spare bed and slipped under the one and only top blanket (no sheets) on a night when the outside temperature was about minus ten degrees. I couldn't get warm however much I tried to withdraw my undercarriage into my stomach. Everybody else was asleep, possibly dead-beat from walking?

They were a grand crowd of chaps at Full Sutton which largely compensated for the bleakness of the camp. They included my pilot, F/Lt Denis Briggs (a double DFC) from Beckenham; Taffys Bruton and Lloyd (from Abergavenny and Swansea, respectively); Jimmy Doolin from Dublin; Jimmy Catlin from Bristol; Watkins, De B. Platts, Wolf, Roy Turner, Frank Hervery, Thomas and Jones, and Jimmy Mitchell from Glasgow. Mitch had done a lot of flying in the Far East and was a cracking chap, they all were. The majority of the crews had been hand-picked because of the work they would soon be doing, or hoped to be doing. In short, a splendid potential for a 'crack' VIP squadron.

The mess was comfortable, the food good until they made curry with ginger and put a bowl of mayonnaise on the wrong table and we ladled the stuff on our stewed fruit.

We flew in Lancaster aircraft which I liked very much. Unfortunately, I only flew in that type three times. Most of the work was done in the classroom. Having just qualified on American equipment in the Dakota, I had to start afresh on Marconi radio and its layout in the Lanc. It had been four years since my short course at Cranwell, and I had not used the equipment very much. The Boston was equipped with the American Bendix radio. I went through all the procedure once more, which did no harm. Then the rumours started. We weren't going to do that work after all and nobody really knew what was to happen. The weather was grim, the future unresolved. I felt so fed up with the indecision of it all that I applied for my release. 'Better to take the GPO certificate and become a telegraphist at sea, or something, than hang about in this God-forsaken corner of Yorkshire,' I thought.

I went on leave pending demob. While in London I began to put out feelers for work. Having liked the little I had sampled of Press work, and the people mixed up in it, I pursued those avenues. I might as well have tried the GPO for, to get something to fit my limited commercial qualifications, was damn near impossible. I rang the Air Ministry and spoke to Lord Willoughby de Broke.

'Any jobs going on the Public Relations side, sir?' I asked, hopefully.

'Well there may be, provided you don't mind going abroad possibly Japan?' he said, 'but I'm afraid that I cannot help you now as I am being bowler-hatted on Thursday. Get in touch with W/Cdr Caverhill at PR. He may be able to help.'

I thanked him and immediately contacted the Wingco for an appointment.

'Ah, Henry. Sit down. You want to get back into PR I hear. You're in luck as I've got a PRO going back to Australia on compassionate posting. How would you like to take his job at RAF Gatow, Berlin?'

'I'd love to sir. When do I start?'

'Better leave your home address with me and I'll let you know.'

'Can you fix it so that my application for release is cancelled, sir?'

'Certainly, I'll see to it.'

I was elated at the news and five days into my eighth year in the Royal Air Force, I leapt into a Dakota at Croydon and flew out to Buckeburg. I wasn't going to Berlin after all, but to the Air Inf. Unit attached to BAFO Headquarters. The post in Berlin had been filled. Not to worry, I was back with the same unit I'd left at the Victoria Hotel Minden, albeit many of the original types had left.

EPILOGUE

While I went on to complete two more years in the RAF, I flew only twice more during that time, a return trip to Croydon in April 1946. From then until my release in May 1948, I kept both feet on the ground because of my work, not from personal choice. I did, however, accumulate a considerable amount of driving, my travels taking me all over the British Zone of Germany, as well as the French and American Zones and through the Russian Zone into the British Sector of Berlin. I visited the bomb-scarred towns of the Ruhr; Kassel, Hanover, Brunswick, Hamburg, Nuremberg, Frankfurt, Munich, Lubeck, Bremen and others.

My activities during those twenty-four months were varied and of extreme interest, and were entirely taken up with Press work: Air Ministry public relations; Press liaison/administration at the Nuremberg trials (a story in itself); attachment to the Public Relations Information Services Centre of the Control Commission and, finally, on the editorial staff of the Foreign Office publication *British Zone Review*.

Thus, leaving the RAF at the age of 28 I had spent one-third of my life in uniform. I had seen much and had made many friends from many countries. I never regretted my act of volunteering for aircrew duties, but I often wonder what course my life and service career might have taken had I not done so. I certainly wouldn't have had the unique experience of being one of a few hundred to witness the verdicts and sentencing of the twenty-one top war criminals at Nuremberg.

Apart from two flights in an RAF Dakota to and from Berlin in 1948, I didn't fly in a military aircraft again until June 1959. By that time I had got back into the realm of aviation as assistant editor of a monthly technical aviation magazine. One or two Air Ministry Press facility trips came my way, many of them including an airlift. I gathered another eighteen hours in eleven types (see Appendix 'B' for breakdown of types), all but one new additions to my list.

However much times have changed its *rôle*, I still have a very soft spot in my heart for the Royal Air Force.

APPENDIX 'A'

*To simplify identification, rank, type of aircraft and unit have
been added against the date when first I flew with each pilot.*

DEDICATED TO:

Allen	Sgt	14.6.40	Blenheim	13 OTU, Bicester
Arbuthnot	G/Capt.	2.10.42	Defiant	13 OTU, Bicester
Arderne	P/O	10.10.40	Blenheim	110 Sqdn, Wattisham
Armstrong	F/Lt	29.5.40	Anson	13 OTU, Bicester
Baker	Sgt	20.5.40	Anson	13 OTU, Bicester
Ballands	F/Lt	8.9.41	Blenheim	107 Sqdn, Luqa, Malta
Barriball	F/Sgt	31.7.43	Ventura	487 Sqdn, Sculthorpe
Beaman	F/Lt	29.5.40	Anson	13 OTU, Bicester
Beazer	F/Sgt	7.8.43	Ventura	487 Sqdn, Sculthorpe
Bennett	F/O	25.6.40	Battle	13 OTU, Bicester
Bennett	P/O	19.10.40	Blenheim	110 Sqdn, Wattisham
Bird	F/Lt	22.10.42	Master	13 OTU, Bicester
Blagden	P/O	16.6.41	Hampden	CGS, Warmwell
Blair	Sgt	25.6.40	Blenheim	13 OTU, Bicester
Bowen	Sgt	7.7.40	Blenheim	13 OTU, Bicester
Boxall	P/O	12.6.41	Hampden	CGS, Warmwell
Brand	F/Lt	4.4.40	Battle	5 B & GS, Jurby, I.o.M.
Brice	F/O	11.9.43	Boston	107 Sqdn, Hartford Bridge
Briggs	F/Lt	1.1.46	Lancaster	231 Sqdn, Full Sutton
Bristow	P/O	28.4.42	Blenheim	13 OTU, Bicester
Brittain	F/Lt	20.1.44	Boston	107 Sqdn, Hartford Bridge
Brooks	F/O	7.5.48	Dakota	TC, from Buckeburg-Berlin
Bundy	P/O	21.5.41	Wellington	101 Sqdn, West Raynham
Cannell	F/Sgt	9.6.41	Hampden	CGS, Warmwell
Cappleman	W/O	8.10.42	Mitchell	13 OTU, Bicester
Castle	S/Ldr	1.8.42	Bisley	13 OTU, Bicester
Caunt	Sgt	26.4.41	Blenheim	101 Sqdn, West Raynham
Ceary	F/O	25.2.45	Dakota	TC, from Northolt-Brussels
Chadwick	Sgt	10.3.40	Battle	5 B & GS, Jurby, I.o.M.
Chattaway	Sgt	25.5.40	Anson	13 OTU, Bicester
Coombes	F/Sgt	24.6.40	Blenheim	13 OTU, Bicester
Court	F/Lt	7.5.43	Blenheim	13 OTU, Bicester
Cree	S/Ldr	4.2.41	Blenheim	101 Sqdn, West Raynham
Day	W/O	1.4.42	Anson	13 OTU, Bicester
De Little	Sgt	27.9.40	Blenheim	110 Sqdn, Wattisham

Dennis	Sgt	23.5.40	Anson	13 OTU, Bicester
Dodwell	Sgt	12.5.41	Wellington	101 Sqdn, West Raynham
Dunkerton	P/O	1.6.41	Wellington	CGS, Warmwell
Dunn	Sgt	12.7.40	Blenheim	13 OTU, Bicester
Elworthy	S/Ldr	29.6.40	Blenheim	13 OTU, Bicester
Evans	F/Lt	11.3.43	Boston	107 Sqdn, Massingham
Fisher	Sgt	4.7.40	Blenheim	13 OTU, Bicester
Forsythe	S/Ldr	1.8.42	Bisley	13 OTU, Bicester
Fowler	F/O	30.11.44	Anson	137 Wing, Vitry, France
Fuller	F/Lt	26.5.42	Blenheim	13 OTU, Bicester
Fuller	F/Lt	11.5.48	Dakota	TC from Berlin-Buckeburg
Gay	Sgt	8.5.42	Bisley	13 OTU, Bicester
Geere	F/Lt	19.9.45	Dakota	1382 TCU, Wymeswold
Gericke	F/Lt	5.12.40	Blenheim	110 Sqdn, Wattisham
Glass	P/O	2.4.40	Battle	5 B & GS, Jurby, I.o.M.
Glen	P/O	6.11.42	Blenheim	13 OTU, Bicester
Graham	S/Ldr	2.2.41	Blenheim	101 Sqdn, West Raynham
Greenhill	F/O	7.8.41	Blenheim	107 Sqdn, Massingham
Griffiths	F/Lt	21.2.45	Dakota	TC from Brussels-Croydon
Grove	F/Sgt	30.6.42	Bisley	13 OTU, Bicester
Hale	P/O	20.6.40	Blenheim	13 OTU, Bicester
Hall	P/O	10.3.40	Battle	5 B & GS, Jurby, I.o.M.
Hallifax	P/O	1.12.42	Blenheim	13 OTU, Bicester
Hampson	F/O	1.8.45	Mitchell	? from Buckeburg-Blackbushe
Hawkins	P/O	5.4.42	Anson	13 OTU, Bicester
Hill	F/Lt	31.1.41	Blenheim	101 Sqdn, West Raynham
Hissey	P/O	18.5.40	Anson	13 OTU, Bicester
Hobday	Sgt	2.5.40	Blenheim	13 OTU, Bicester
Hohnen	P/O	28.6.40	Blenheim	13 OTU, Bicester
Holland	Sgt	25.7.40	Blenheim	13 OTU, Bicester
Houlston	F/Sgt	3.5.40	Blenheim	13 OTU, Squires Gate
Hume-Wright	W/Cdr	20.6.40	Blenheim	13 OTU, Bicester
Hutchinson	Sgt	30.6.40	Blenheim	13 OTU, Bicester
Iredale	S/Ldr	5.10.42	Blenheim	13 OTU, Bicester
Jennings	F/Sgt	2.9.43	Ventura	487 Sqdn, Sculthorpe
Johnson	Sgt	2.6.41	Wellington	C.G.S., Warmwell
Jones	P/O	6.4.41	Blenheim	101 Sqdn, West Raynham
Jury	Capt.	9.2.45	Dakota	T.C. from Vitry-Brussels
Kinder	P/O	16.3.40	Battle	5 B. & G.S., Jurby, I.o.M.
Knowles	S/Ldr	25.5.42	Blenheim	13 OTU, Bicester
Lawrence	P/O	5.1.44	Boston	107 Sqdn, Hartford Bridge
Lindsaye	F/O	2.5.40	Blenheim	13 OTU, Bicester
Lings	F/O	9.8.40	Blenheim	13 OTU, Bicester

Llewendon	F/O	11.12.42	Junkers 88	Special Flight, German a/c
Lynch-Blosse	F/O	6.7.40	Blenheim	13 OTU, Bicester
Lyon	F/Lt	7.10.40	Blenheim	110 Sqdn, Wattisham
Maher	S/Ldr	9.12.42	Blenheim	13 OTU, Bicester
Mansell-Villiers	F/Lt	12.8.43	Ventura	487 Sqdn, Sculthorpe
Matylis	P/O	15.6.41	Defiant	CGS, Warmwell
MacDonald	G/Capt.	30.4.44	Boston	137 Wing, Hartford Bridge
MacDougall	S/Ldr	28.11.40	Blenheim	110 Sqdn, Wattisham
McBride	W/O	24.7.45	Anson	2nd TAF Comm. Sqdn, Brussels
McCarty	1st.Lt	26.1.45	Fortress	USAAF, Lavenham
McColm	F/O	4.5.40	Blenheim	13 OTU, Bicester
Menaul	F/Lt	8.7.40	Blenheim	13 OTU, Bicester
Molyneux	Sgt	16.3.40	Battle	5 B & GS, Jurby, I.o.M.
Morrison	W/O	5.5.42	Tutor	13 OTU, Bicester
Murray	F/Lt	17.6.40	Blenheim	13 OTU, Bicester
Newberry	S/Ldr	17.10.42	Blenheim	13 OTU, Bicester
Newland	P/O	2.6.40	Blenheim	13 OTU, Bicester
North	W/Cdr	19.9.44	Boston	137 Wing, Hartford Bridge
Norton	P/O	24.10.44	Boston	88 Sqdn., Vitry, France
Parry	P/O	30.9.40	Blenheim	110 Sqdn, Wattisham
Pickard	G/Capt.	4.8.43	Ventura	487 Sqdn, Sculthorpe
Pollard	W/Cdr	27.10.42	Blenheim	13 OTU, Bicester
Powell	F/O	26.7.40	Blenheim	13 OTU, Bicester
Ralston	Sgt	30.6.40	Blenheim	13 OTU, Bicester
Rathbone	F/O	21.6.40	Blenheim	13 OTU, Bicester
Reade	F/Lt	2.6.45	Anson	2nd TAF Comm. Sqdn, Brussels
Redmond	Sgt	16.5.41	Wellington	101 Sqdn, West Raynham
Reeve	F/Lt	25.8.42	Blenheim	13 OTU, Bicester
Schonbach	Sgt	10.5.41	Blenheim	101 Sqdn, West Raynham
Searby	P/O	26.5.40	Blenheim	13 OTU, Bicester
Shackleton	P/O	23.10.42	Blenheim	13 OTU, Bicester
Shand	Sgt	27.3.40	Blenheim	5 B & GS, Jurby, I.o.M.
Shaw	F/O	4.3.43	Boston	107 Sqdn, Massingham
Sigurdson	F/O	7.7.40	Blenheim	13 OTU, Bicester
Sillito	F/O	15.8.40	Blenheim	13 OTU, Bicester
Sims	P/O	15.7.42	Blenheim	13 OTU, Bicester
Sinclair	W/Cdr	28.8.40	Blenheim	110 Sqdn, Wattisham
Smyth	F/O	28.3.40	Battle	5 B & GS, Jurby, I.o.M.
Spencer	S/Ldr	3.3.43	Boston	107 Sqdn, Massingham
Stanbury	F/O	4.6.41	Wellington	CGS, Warmwell
Staples	P/O	30.4.42	Blenheim	13 OTU, Bicester

Stone	Sgt	5.12.40	Blenheim	110 Sqdn, Wattisham
Taylor	Sgt	26.3.40	Battle	5 B & GS, Jurby, I.o.M.
Taylor	P/O	19.6.40	Blenheim	13 OTU, Bicester
Thompson	F/Lt	18.5.40	Anson	13 OTU, Bicester
Thompson	S/Ldr	11.9.42	Bisley	114 Sqdn, West Raynham
Tivey	F/O	12.11.44	Mitchell	226 Sqdn, Vitry, France
Todd	P/O	12.5.41	Wellington	101 Sqdn, West Raynham
Trevor-Owen	F/O	25.4.43	Ventura	13 OTU, Bicester
Tully	F/O	13.8.40	Blenheim	13 OTU, Bicester
Van-Dael	F/Lt	6.6.45	Dakota	TC from Croydon-Brussels
Vickers	F/Lt	28.7.44	Boston	88 Sqdn, Hartford Bridge
Vivian	P/O	31.5.42	Tutor	13 OTU, Bicester
Wade	P/O	18.6.40	Blenheim	13 OTU, Bicester
Walker	F/Lt	20.6.4	Mitchell	? Press courier duties
Waples	F/Lt	11.7.41	Blenheim	21 Sqdn, Watton
Webster	W/Cdr	25.7.41	Blenheim	21 Sqdn, Watton
Wheeler	F/Lt	31.7.42	Boston	13 OTU, Bicester
Wilcocks	F/O	31.7.45	Dakota	TC from Northolt-Buckeburg
Williams	P/O	30.5.40	Anson	13 OTU, Bicester
Williams	Sgt	12.7.40	Blenheim	13 OTU, Bicester
Wilson	W/Cdr	5.8.43	Ventura	487 Sqdn, Sculthorpe
Woods	P/O	26.6.42	Blenheim	13 OTU, Bicester
Wright	Sgt	10.12.40	Blenheim	110 Sqdn, Wattisham
Yarrow	P/O	24.9.40	Blenheim	110 Sqdn, Wattisham
Young	S/Ldr	22.9.40	Blenheim	110 Sqdn, Wattisham

NOTE: B & GS = Bombing and Gunnery School
CGS = Central Gunnery School
OTU = Operational Training Unit
TC = Transport Command
TCU = Transport Conversion Unit.

APPENDIX 'B'

Military aircraft flown in to date:

Bristol Blenheim Mks I, IV and V (Bisley).	(476 hours 10 mins.)
Douglas Boston (A-20), Mks III, IIIA and IV.	(105 hours 50 mins.)
Douglas Dakota (DC-3).	(93 hours 5 mins.)
Avro Anson Mks I, X, XII and XIX.	(43 hours 25 mins.)
Lockheed Ventura.	(40 hours 25 mins.)
Armstrong Whitworth Albemarle, Mk I.	(12 hours.)
Fairey Battle.	(10 hours 5 mins.)
Vickers Wellington.	(9 hours 40 mins.)
North American Mitchell (B-25).	(9 hours 20 mins.)
Handley Page Hampden.	(8 hours 20 mins.)

Avro Tutor.

Handley Page Hastings.

Avro Lancaster.

Boulton Paul Defiant.

Vickers Valetta.

Airspeed Oxford.

Bristol Britannia Z53.

Percival Pembroke.

Boeing Flying Fortress Mk VII (B-17) USAAF.

de Havilland Comet 2.

de Havilland Comet 4C.

de Havilland Tiger Moth.

de Havilland Mosquito Mk VI.

de Havilland Canada Beaver (Army Air Corps).

Miles Master Mk II.

Hunting Jet Provost Mk III.

Auster Mk I.

Junkers Ju. 88.

Bristol Beaufighter Mk II.

Bristol Sycamore (helicopter).

Hawker Siddeley Argosy.

Commercial aircraft flown in (since the war):

Douglas DC-3 (Sabena).

Douglas DC-4 (Sabena).

Vickers Viking (BEA and Eagle Airways).

de Havilland Rapide (London Airport).

Airspeed Ambassador (BEA).

Vickers Viscount (BEA, Air France, BUA).

Convair 540 (Demonstration flight).

Sud-Aviation Caravelle (Air France).

de Havilland Dove (Demonstration flight).

Vickers Vanguard (BEA).

de Havilland Comet 4B (BEA).

Hawker Siddeley Trident (Demonstration flight).

Piaggio 166B, Portofino (Demonstration flight).

Breguet 941 STOL (Demonstration flight).

de Havilland Canada DHC-6 Caribou (Demonstration flight).

Lancaster To Berlin

F/Lt Walter Thompson DFC & Bar
As a Pathfinder Walter Thompson led the
bombing raids into Germany. Above all,
he flew to Berlin, in the thick of the 1943-
44 offensive against 'The Big City'.
200 pages, paperback B format illustrated.
ISBN 0907579 37 X. £4.99

Uncommon Valour

A.G. Goulding DFM
A comprehensive view of Bomber
Command's part in the Second World War
and an important re-appraisal of the
importance of Bomber Command in
World War Two.
192 pages, paperback B format illustrated,
ISBN 0 85979 095 9. £4.99

Wing Leader

Air Vice-Marshal 'Johnnie' Johnson
The thrilling story of the top-scoring
Allied fighter pilot of World War Two.
320 pages, paperback B format.
ISBN 0 85979 090 8. £4.99

Night Flyer

S/Ldr Lewis Brandon DSO DFC & Bar
The exciting story of one of the most
successful RAF night fighting
partnerships of WW2.
208 pages, paperback.
ISBN 0 907579 16 7. £3.99

Enemy Coast Ahead

W/Cdr Guy Gibson VC DSO & Bar DFC
& Bar
The autobiography of Guy Gibson VC,
one of the greatest books written about
RAF Bomber Command in WW2.
288 pages, paperback.
ISBN 0 907579 08 6. £3.99

Other Goodall paperbacks from Crécy Publishing Ltd

No Moon Tonight

Don Charlwood
A Bomber Command classic, a book of
deep feelings depicting the human cost of
the Bomber Command air war.
192 pages, paperback.
ISBN 0 907579 06 X. £3.99

A WAAF in Bomber Command

"Pip" Beck
The story of an R/T operator in Bomber
Command who talked down bomber
crews returning from operations, met
them off-duty and, all too often, mourned
their loss.
171 pages, paperback.
ISBN 0 907579 12 4. £3.99

Beyond The Dams To The Tirpitz

Alan Cooper
The is story of 617 squadron – The
Dambusters – and their 95 further
operations after the famous dambuster
raid, including their part in the destruction
of the *Tirpitz*.
198 pages, paperback.
ISBN 0 907579 15 9. £3.99

Wings Over Georgia

S/Ldr Jack Currie DFC
The story of Jack Currie's entry into the
RAF, his early training in the UK, initial
flying training with the US Army Air
Corps and return to England to join
Bomber Command.
154 pages, paperback.
ISBN 0 907579 11 6 £3.99

Lancaster Target

S/Ldr Jack Currie DFC

Described as one of the best three books
about life in Bomber Command,
Lancaster Target is the story of one
crew's fight to fly and survive a full tour
of operations in the night skies of wartime
Europe. *Lancaster Target* featured in the
award-winning BBC documentary 'The
Lancaster Legend'.

200 pages, paperback B format illustrated.
ISBN 0907579 32 9. £4.99

Mosquito Victory

S/Ldr Jack Currie DFC

The compelling, highly readable sequel to
Lancaster Target, graphically describing
the life of an RAF bomber pilot on 'rest',
first instructing trainees on the four-
engined Halifax bomber, then flying
gliders, and lastly posted to the élite
Pathfinder force.

176 pages, paperback B format. ISBN 0
85979 091 6. £3.99